Praise for *Digital Content in*

'Digital content is increasing s fulfil their mission and reach new audi of working and case studies showing good practice, Brooke sets out a comprehensive guide to delivering effective online content. For digital teams working in the sector, it will provide a practical hands-on guide and reassurance that their work really matters.'
**Robert Cawston, Director of Digital and Service Transformation, National Library of Scotland**

'Digital content roles often require a breadth of expertise that any amount of training will struggle to cover. But this book has all the foundations you need – from website usability to social media – all tailored to the museum professional. Georgina Brooke's book is a fount of useful detailed information, supported by a variety of case studies. Read it front to back or dip in when you're facing your next knotty problem. If you work in museum content, you will want this on your shelf.'
**Louise Cohen, Senior Content Strategist, One Further**

'Practical and packed with examples and expertise, this is an essential guide to online engagement for all of us in the cultural sector.'
**Catherine Eagleton, University Librarian and Director of Collections and Museums, University of St Andrews**

'This is the book I wish had existed when I first started messing around with websites and social media for museums. Georgina Brooke has collected together all the collective wisdom and best practice in content strategy, and has broken it down into understandable chunks, inspiring case studies and practical next steps. Put this book into the hands of your boss and colleagues.'
**Adam Koszary, social media and content consultant**

'Digital content remains one of the cultural sector's greatest untapped opportunities. While functionality and design matter, it's often content that makes the difference between a good digital experience and a great one. Georgina charts a clear insightful path through the complexities of digital content, offering guidance that's both strategic and practical. An essential read for anyone working in the cultural sector whose role touches digital in any way, whether or not you consider yourself a "content person".'
**Ash Mann, digital advisor, strategist and facilitator**

'From strategic frameworks and case studies to implementing best practice, this book is an invaluable resource and reference for everyone working in digital in museums.'
**John Stack, Director of Digital Innovation and Technology**

'Georgina Brooke's book is an essential guide for cultural professionals navigating the complexities of digital content and strategy. With clarity and precision, she breaks down content strategy, accessibility, and audience engagement into practical, actionable steps. Drawing from global client work and field research, she helps museums and cultural organizations define how to launch their impactful narratives and mission-driven goals. Whether you're working on a website redesign, social media strategy, or digital content planning, this book offers a clear roadmap to expanding reach and deepening community connection. It's a must-read for anyone in the GLAM sector seeking to grow meaningful digital engagement with clarity, confidence, and purpose.'
**Jennifer Talbott, Deputy Director for Operations and Innovation, Spencer Museum of Art, University of Kansas**

'Most writing on digital practice in museums assumes prior knowledge, instead Brooke's *Digital Content in Museums* assumes prior interest. Interest in actionable insights, demystifying technical terms, explaining digital publishing strategies and understanding how the apps and algorithms work. This is a great toolkit for museum people who want to tell compelling digital stories and reach new audiences.'
**Keir Winesmith, Chief Technology Officer, National Film and Sound Archive of Australia**

'A comprehensive yet digestible examination of a subject that is rightly being recognised as an essential area for further study in our sector. Packed with practical knowledge and excellent case studies, this highly readable guide will inspire digital content professionals and gently enlighten those more senior (or cynical) colleagues on the opportunities and challenges they face.'
**Nik Wyness, Head of Marketing and Engagement, The Tank Museum**

# Digital Content in Museums

## Museum and Gallery Essentials

*Series Editors:*
Maria Blyzinsky, Heritage Consultant and co-Founder of The Exhibitions Team
Rhiannon Goddard, Head of Public Engagement Projects and Business Management, Historic Royal Palaces

Today's museum and cultural heritage professionals are multi-taskers, under pressure to operate efficiently and effectively in the face of many competing demands. There are rarely enough hours in the day to prepare well for critical tasks and meetings. Taking time out to think things through and plan properly can sometimes be seen as a luxury, which can lead to feeling overwhelmed by the tasks ahead. In addition, today's fast-paced world can throw up unforeseen challenges – such as the lockdowns of the COVID-19 pandemic or economic downturns. We may not be able to predict every challenge, but we can develop creative and critical thinking to help with problem-solving.

*Museum and Gallery Essentials* taps into the expertise of established professionals from across the sector. The series provides guidance that supports practitioners managing today's complex situations and challenges while also providing students with the frameworks and knowledge needed at the start of their careers. Each guide is carefully crafted to provide a highly practical road map, helping readers to think effectively, creatively and strategically when solving issues under pressure and with limited resources.

The Editors welcome proposals from cultural heritage professionals across a range of topics, including approaches to decolonisation, tackling the climate emergency, interpretation, collections management and care, registration, learning and outreach, financial management and curatorship. For more information, please contact info@facetpublishing.co.uk.

# Digital Content in Museums

## Delivering Discoverable, Usable and Strategic Content in Museums, Galleries and Heritage Institutions

Georgina Brooke

facet publishing

Published by Facet Publishing
c/o Woburn House, 20–24 Tavistock Square, London WC1H 9HQ
www.facetpublishing.co.uk

Facet Publishing is wholly owned by CILIP: the Library and Information Association.



*British Library Cataloguing in Publication Data*
A catalogue record for this book is available from the British Library.

ISBN 978-1-78330-718-0 (paperback)
ISBN 978-1-78330-719-7 (hardback)
ISBN 978-1-78330-720-3 (PDF)
ISBN 978-1-78330-721-0 (EPUB)

First published 2025

FSC www.fsc.org
MIX
Paper | Supporting responsible forestry
FSC® C013604



Typeset from author's files in 10/13 pt Palatino and OpenSans by Flagholme Publishing Services.
Printed and made in Great Britain by CPI Group (UK) Ltd, Croydon, CR0 4YY.

# Contents

# Figures, Tables and Case Studies

## Figures

## Tables



## Case Studies

# About the Author

Georgina is a Senior Content Strategist at One Further.

She has worked for clients such as The National Archives, Tate, National Museums Scotland and the National Museum Wales. She leads on projects relating to content design, content strategy, search engine optimisation (SEO), digital strategy, website discovery, social media and digital user research.

Previously, Georgina held roles leading digital content teams at National Museums Scotland and Oxford University Museums and Gardens. She began her career working under Sarah Winters (was Richards) during the first iteration of gov.uk as part of the Government Digital Service.

Georgina publishes the fortnightly newsletter *Cultural Content* (https://culturalcontent.substack.com), which has an international readership of around 4,000.

She is Chair of the Museums Computer Group, which hosts and moderates a discussion list of 1,800 GLAM (Galleries, Libraries, Archives and Museums) digital experts and convenes the annual conference MuseTech.

You can find Georgina on LinkedIn at www.linkedin.com/in/georginabrooke and on e-mail at georgina@onefurther.com.

# Acknowledgements

This book sits on the shoulders of many brilliant supporting figures.

In the first instance, thank you to my boss and founder of One Further, Chris Unitt, who's given support by taking the view that 'what's best for Georgina is best for One Further'. Thank you for giving me the freedom to write this and for prodding me to set up *Cultural Content*, the newsletter that became my test bed for writing much of the material that went into this book.

To all the readers of the newsletter – your support, comments and follow-up conversations gave me the impetus to make this book a reality.

Thanks also to my other One Further colleagues and ex-colleagues, particularly Simon Jones and Louise Cohen who have frequently read articles and developed my thinking with their points. I'd also like to specifically mention Ed Bankes who was my 'reader in mind' when I wrote this book and generously read and commented on specific passages.

Thank you to my brilliant case study authors: Danny Birchall, Alicia Eames, Anna Faherty, Kelly Forbes, Stephen Franklin, Joanne Karcheva, Beks Leary, Marie Lemaire, Rachel Mapplebeck, Martin Poulter, Caspian Turner, Chris Unitt and Nik Wyness. It's been an absolute privilege to work with you and a mighty coup to be able to quote your words in this book.

I'd also like to acknowledge Sarah Winters, Adam Koszary, Louise Cohen, Kristina Halvorson and Seb Chan for their provocative work, thinking and writing at formative times in my career. A career in MuseTech would have been much less interesting without you.

Interesting client work has definitely shaped my understanding of the topics written about in the book. Thank you to the Spencer Museum of Art (Elizabeth Kanost, Sara McClure, Jen Talbott and Ryan Waggoner), British Heart Foundation (Jordan Ahmadzadeh), The National Archives (Steven Franklin), Tower Bridge (Drea Lee), Tate (Fionnula Cavanaugh), Art Fund (Mike Keating) and the Museums Association (Sarah Briggs).

Lastly, thank you to my husband, Peter Hill, for inspiring me to find a career that feels meaningful and opening my eyes to how rewarding the process of writing a book can be. Thank you to Peter and my parents for love, support and giving me the confidence to believe I could write a book.

# Introduction

Cultural heritage and internet culture start from quite different places.

Museums and cultural heritage organisations are defined by their physical holdings, built up over decades. Internet and internet culture 'moves fast and breaks things' (Taneja, 2019) – it is irreverent, it can be unsettling and it is forever changing.

But we limit the potential value of museums and heritage institutions if we only think of them in relation to their physical presence. What you see on display is usually a small fraction of the total holdings. What you can read about a museum object on a physical label represents a tiny amount of what is known about it. The objects themselves are often behind glass. We often can't see the maker's mark, the preparatory sketch, the clues to the thinking and identity of the piece – these are only visible to those with the keys to the cabinets.

The internet opens up vast possibilities for museums. We can talk to more people than we can in the physical space, including audiences we would never reach in the physical space. We can give them more information about a wider variety of objects and better access to the curators and conservators who have unique knowledge of the pieces. We can tell stories in three dimensional ways and invite conversation and collaboration more easily than in a physical space. But the reality is that most museums don't understand digital content as well as they might and therefore are not realising its full potential. This book seeks to change that.

The title of this book is *Digital Content in Museums*, but what do we mean by 'digital content'? In theory, digital content can be anything in digital form. Wikipedia defines the term as 'any content that exists in the form of digital data'. In practice, when we talk about 'digital content' in the sector, we're referring to website or social media content. This is what this book looks at.

This book is designed for those working in museums, galleries, libraries and other heritage institutions, but it is also relevant to those working in the performing arts. This book is also for digital content editors, producers and those working in social media. It will be valuable for anyone managing these teams who feels they don't understand digital media enough to make sensible decisions about it. The next generation of museum leaders must understand how to harness digital effectively, as part of their audience development, or be left behind. Unlike with a curatorial career pathway, there's no formally recognised professional qualification in how to be skilled in digital content and marketing. Internet advice abounds, but it changes frequently, can be inaccurate or inappropriate in a heritage context and can assume previous knowledge. Or, these days, AI might have misinterpreted the original context and provided you with a response that is simply wrong.

In writing this book, I've sought to provide a corpus of material that will take the reader from start to finish, covering the tools, techniques and applications to help make the best use of digital content and marketing in a heritage context.

Ultimately, I wrote this book as the book that I would have wanted to read when I was starting out in the sector and at various other points in my career. The intersection of digital roles and the museum sector isn't always easy to navigate or to progress and learn new skills in. I wanted this book to act as a primer for the different facets and skills that make up digital roles in the cultural sector.

Part 1 of this book focuses on the **discoverability** of museum digital content: how institutions can make themselves more visible, particularly to new audiences, in the digital space. In Chapter 1, we look at how this applies to websites, making your website more visible in search engines and how you can measure your progress in this space. In Chapter 2, we look at how museums can become more discoverable in third-party platforms, such as social media platforms.

Part 2 looks at the **usability** of digital spaces and audience needs. This section provides a number of templates for particular page types, designed in a way that meets user needs, including: homepages; exhibition/performance pages; about pages; online collection pages; and accessibility pages. Chapter 3 ends with an explanation of the discipline of 'content design' and how this evolving professional practice can be applied in the cultural sector. In Chapter 4, we look at what applying that content design process might look like for a new site build and examine many of the tools you might need to undertake such a project (including usability surveys, usability testing and navigation testing). Part 2 ends with a case study from Museums Galleries Scotland looking at how inclusion can be baked into a website redesign.

Part 3 focuses on **creative and strategic content** and how heritage institutions can produce content that builds a loyal audience. In Chapter 5, we look at how people read online and how this is different to print. We then apply this to articles and how to write good editorial or blog content online. The chapter also presents two case studies. First, Anna Faherty, a freelance journalist, explains what she has learned about collections-based storytelling while working with the Wellcome Collection. The second case study comes from the perspective of the Wellcome Collection itself and how Anna's storytelling fitted into the institution's wider strategy and editorial output. The chapter ends by taking a step back and thinking about the purpose of long-form editorial content and how different types of content creation affect digital audience development.

Chapter 6 takes on the meaty topic of 'content strategy'. In the sector, we use the term to mean a vast array of different things. The first section of this chapter unpacks the term and makes the case that the most successful cultural sector content strategies are really digital audience development projects. We then look at different tools that can help provide the data you need to begin a digital strategy or audience development project. These include demographic surveys, focus groups, personas and competitor analysis. The final part of Chapter 6 looks at how you can pull all the data and insights from these research tools into an effective strategy.

Chapter 7 considers content strategy in action through two case studies. First, a case study from the Tank Museum looks at the opportunities the creator economy affords the cultural sector. The second case study comes from Opera North and presents their award-winning 'From Couch to Chorus' project. Both these projects successfully engaged a mass audience and community online. They were also highly successful in terms of raising money, which is not always the case with digital content in the sector. The last part of Chapter 7 looks at the principles of effective monetisation of cultural content.

In Chapter 8, I briefly pull everything together and ask 'why does all this matter anyway?'. As professionals working in the cultural sector, we're not generally in it for the salary! Why does our work as digital professionals in the sector matter?

Finally, I include an Appendix about navigating a career in the cultural sector. Whatever point you're at on your journey: good luck!

# Part 1
# Discoverability

Let's think about museum marketing in an analogue world. New audiences might find out about a museum or visitor attraction by:

- walking past the building
- hearing about it on the radio
- watching a television programme
- reading about it in a newspaper
- seeing a poster about it in their town
- hearing about it from a friend or colleague
- reading about it in a book.

Reaching people in these ways is not especially efficient. Many of them require you to already be considered 'noteworthy'. For example, the BBC is unlikely to commission a documentary on your museum if no one there has heard of you.

Now, let's think how someone might hear about you online:

- by Googling things to do in their local area
- by searching for top things to do in a city they're visiting (e.g., on TripAdvisor)
- by seeing a local event you're promoting on Facebook
- by seeing an advert for your exhibition (e.g., on Instagram)
- by watching a video about an item in your collection (e.g., on YouTube or TikTok)
- by Googling a specific question that picks up an online article you've written
- by looking online for a community of people who share a passion for a topic or skill they want to develop.

There are two key differences with how you can reach people online:

1. Reaching people using the techniques in the second list relies much less on your legacy reputation.
2. Being well known is still helpful in terms of online presence, but smaller, more nimble organisations can become much more visible online than they could before by using digital effectively.

Part 1 of this book will look at how museums can bring in new and relevant audiences online. Chapter 1 considers how you can make your website more discoverable via search engines. In Chapter 2, we look at how you can improve your visibility on third-party platforms, such as social media and Wikipedia.

CHAPTER 1

# Making Your Website More Visible in Search

When you create a website, you instantly have access to a globally connected online audience. In theory! Unfortunately, billions and billions of other website owners have also had the same idea.

There are lots of routes people might take to land on your website. For example, they might type the web address directly into their browser or they might click on a link in a social media post or e-mail. However, a significant percentage of website traffic will come from search engines, principally Google.

## How does Google work?

A lot has changed since Google's launch in 1998. When it first launched – and was blithely using six exclamation marks on its homepage (see Figure 1.1 below) – there were 2,410,067 websites on the internet (Internet Live Stats, 2024). Today, there are an estimated 1.13 billion websites on the internet and over 50 billion pages (Forbes, 2024).

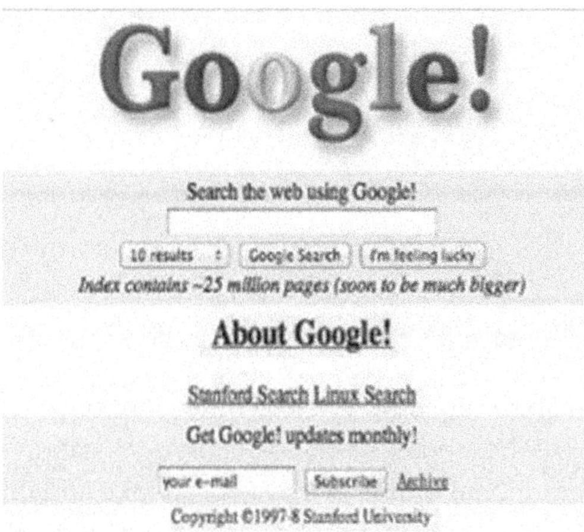


**Figure 1.1** *Google's homepage in 1998*

Google has to index a huge amount of content. To keep up with that content, and with increasingly sophisticated customer demands, it has had to become adept at working out how people want to search, what a user might mean when they enter a given keyword, and how to use a vast raft of metrics to rank and return (in seconds) millions of websites for a given search term.

It is easy to forget that Google is a business and that its primary means of making money is through digital ads. If we enter the search term 'eye test', the first two results in the search engine results page (SERP) have the word 'sponsored' next to their listing (see Figure 1.2 below). This means that Specsavers and Boots have paid to appear above non-paid search results for the phrase 'eye test'. The first non-paid listing, also from Specsavers, references the city I live in – Newcastle upon Tyne. If we think about why someone might be entering the term 'eye test', it's quite likely that that person wants to book an eye test near to where they live or currently are. Google is therefore personalising the results to what it knows about the user and thinks is most relevant.

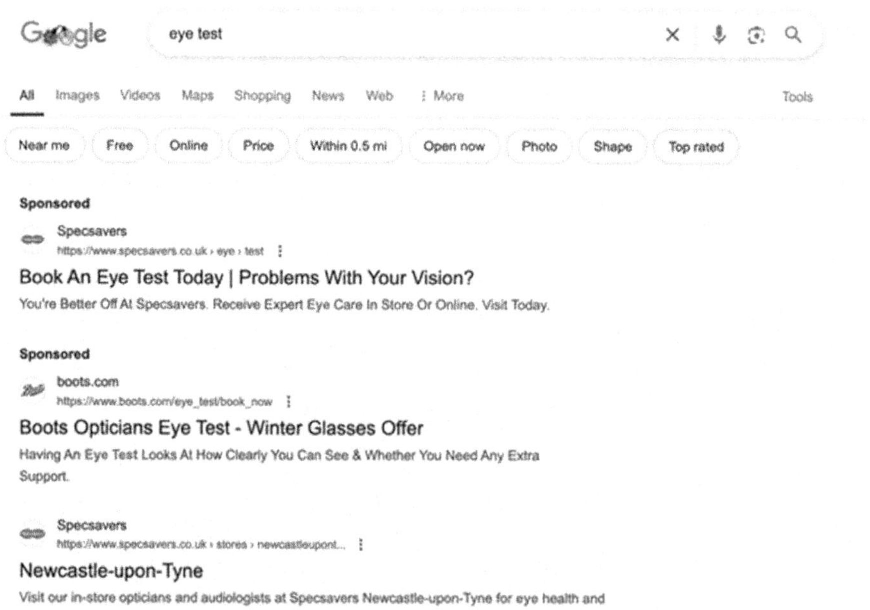


**Figure 1.2** *Search engine results page (SERP) for the query 'eye test'*

When I tried the same search for 'eye test' but on holiday near the Portuguese city of Albufeira, I get different results, based on my location at that time. This includes a few international online eye tests I can take and one local opticians I could visit (see Figure 1.3 opposite). This is just one example of how Google uses what it knows about users to serve them more relevant results.

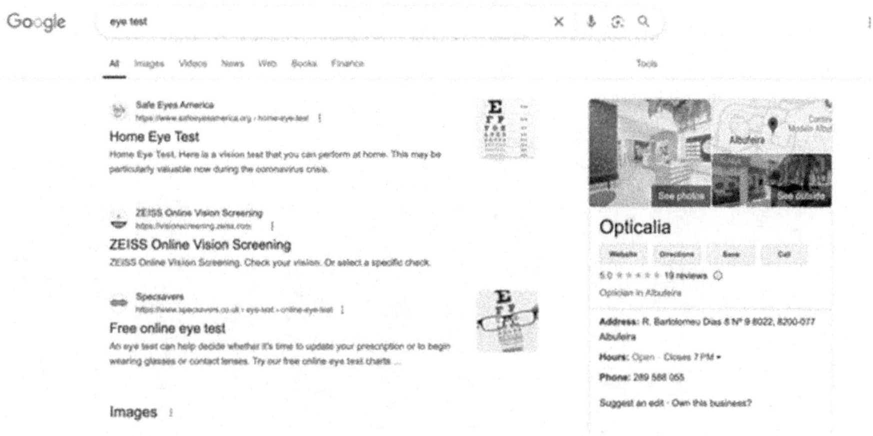


**Figure 1.3** *The same search for 'eye test' but from a different location*

The SERP also tells us that there are 3,490,000,000 results on the internet for the term 'eye test' and that Google has taken 0.36 seconds to rank and score these results. On average in the UK, 27,100 searches are made for the term 'eye test' every month, but the results Google displays will be different depending on what it already knows about you and where you're making the search from (location and device type), among other factors.

## What does all this mean for the sector?

We started this section with the 'nice idea' that when you put content live, you instantly gain a large and engaged online audience. Unfortunately, it isn't that simple. The process of making your content more visible in search engines – known as search engine optimisation (SEO) – has become an industry in its own right and in the sector we're not terribly good at it.

In 2022, the company I work for – One Further – surveyed 169 cultural organisations on their use of digital content as part of the *Cultural Content Report* (One Further, 2022). Figure 1.4 on the next page shows the wide range of content tools used by cultural organisations, for example, content plans and branding guidelines. The main anomaly in the results was around SEO guides: 67% of organisations surveyed did not have one; 14% had one but didn't use it; and just 19% of cultural organisations had an SEO guide and used it. So, while most organisations have a content plan for the content they're creating, very few have a guide for how that content can be discovered through search. This tell us that there is a lot of untapped potential in the sector in terms of better optimising content for search.

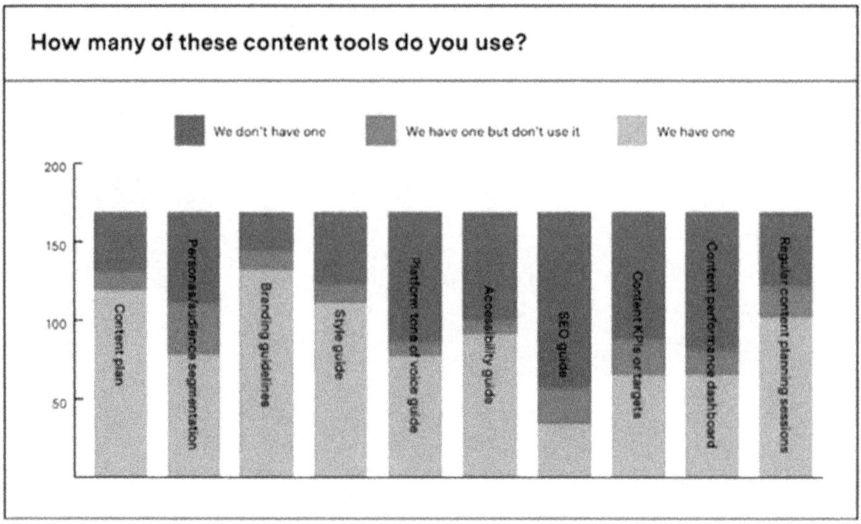


**Figure 1.4** *Cultural Content Report 2022 survey results for the question 'How many of these content tools do you use?'*

The potential value of search to galleries, libraries, archives and museums (GLAM) is significant. A 2023 One Further study found that search was the primary traffic source for online collections, accounting for 75% of traffic (One Further, 2023). However, within that, there was a large degree of variation – from 88% of traffic at the top end, to a minority of sites whose collections were not searchable by Google and, as a result, were invisible to audiences who hadn't already heard of the institution and their online collections.

If you're a web editor or manager, one of the more technical aspects of your role is going to be around understanding SEO and how writing for the web is different from print. One reason the sector might not be geared up for SEO is that, in order to have a well optimised site, you need to draw on a range of different skill sets, not all of which traditionally sit in in-house roles in cultural sector organisations.

How well optimised your site is for search will depend on:

- how well structured your code is
- how quickly your site loads (including on mobile)
- how intuitive your site navigation is
- whether the text editor/what you see is what you get (WYSIWYG) field in your content management system (CMS) and style sheet makes it easy to add subheadings in the form of H1, H2, H3, etc.

Many of the most useful tools and data relating to SEO are not available for free and come at a steep monthly cost, which few cultural organisations feel they can justify. As a result, there is misunderstanding and untapped potential in the sector relating to search visibility. A good SEO strategy will build visibility over time and grow awareness among a more engaged audience.

In this chapter, we'll discuss how to make your content better optimised for search. In later chapters, we'll look in more detail at how search can form part of your overarching strategy, for example, the role of SEO in audience development (Chapter 5) and creating a competitive search content (Chapter 6).

## How we read on the web

Part of the conversation about creating content that's well optimised for search is about understanding how we read on the web. Search engines like Google look at how engaged readers are on your site and they use this as part of their ranking criteria. Before we dive into the technicalities of how search engines rank content, it is therefore worth understanding how humans read content online, so that we can create better content.

Humans process information differently in different scenarios. In the book *Thinking, Fast and Slow* (2011), the behavioural theorist Daniel Kahneman classifies the way humans process information into two systems:

> System 1 operates automatically and quickly, with little or no effort and no sense of voluntary control.
> System 2 allocates attention to the effortful mental activities that demand it, including complex computations.
> The operations of System 2 are often associated with the subjective experience of agency, choice and concentration.
>
> (Kahneman, 2011, 21)

For example, as someone who regularly drives, I instinctively know how to do that, which is system 1. I don't need to think a great deal about it or how to react to changing conditions on the road. If, during the working day, I have to complete a cognitive test or write a paper, I'm more likely to be in a deliberative, effortful and slow mental state, which is system 2.

The way we've been taught to write at school or university assumes a reader has no distractions, a limited amount of text to read and a degree of motivation to read it. It assumes a reader is in system 2 for the duration of the reading task. But when we're reading web content, there is much more information to process with many more distractions and that has implications for how we write for the web. It's rare that readers will read a web page in system 2 as it's not an efficient way to process the colossal amount of information at our disposal on the internet. While we're browsing a website, we may also have notifications pinging from our social media, e-mail and phones. None of this was factored into the writing rules taught to us by the education system.

So, how do people read on the web? The short answer: they don't. The slightly longer answer: they don't, they scan. When you are writing for the web, you are writing for an audience whose attention is not solely focused on you. The job of writing for the web is to reduce the cognitive load of the content. We can do this by making it easy to find specific information and by making that information as clear and easy to understand as possible.

The most substantial body of research into this has been made by the Nielsen Norman Group (NNG) (Nielsen Norman Group, 1997; 2024). They developed eye-tracking as a research method to look at how people get meaning from online content. Their work established the difference between reading (which we actually don't do a whole lot of online) and scanning.

Reading includes looking at most words in chronological order in a section or on an entire page. When scanning, people look at words, headings or sections of pages, often out of order, fixating on only some of the words rather than entire lines of text. However, scanning is not a random sequence of visual fixations. Rather, the method can be extremely targeted and, sometimes in less than a second, a user can complete an initial appraisal of a page – estimating the nature, quality, importance and potential value to them of the information.

NNG's eye-tracking heatmaps show predominant activity along the top left of a web page – essentially from the first page title and the first few sentences under it. Users then generally move vertically down the page but their eye will track horizontally across headings, images and site sections that attract their eye. NNG called this the 'F-shaped pattern', in that a user's eye follows an 'F' shape, browsing horizontally along the top, vertically down the page and then periodically reading left to right across the page when the eye is drawn to subheadings and visual elements. (Incidentally, the same pattern is broadly observed the opposite way round in right-to-left reading languages, such as Arabic.)

The main takeaway of this research is that when someone lands on a page, they will give it a quick assessment to get more context on what information the page contains, whether it provides them with what they were looking for and how reputable the site seems to be. They will not sit and read each word in sequence to get this information. If your content passes that initial test, users will then go through and read the page more methodically, but again fixating on sections that appear most relevant to them.

So, what does this mean for how we create content for the web?

## Use clear and descriptive page titles

If a user reads one thing on the page, it is most likely to be the page title. Don't try to tease the user with mysterious titles. Make it clear and unambiguous what the page is about. Ideally, your site will make clear where in the navigation a certain page exists, for example, through the use of breadcrumbs and/or side bars.

In Figure 1.5, the white bar displays the breadcrumb of a page on the Historic Royal Palaces website. This navigational element shows users where in the site this page on Elizabeth I is located. It's called a breadcrumb because – much like Hansel and Gretel – it allows you to see the path you've followed to arrive at this place and lets you trace your way through the site structure, should you wish to.

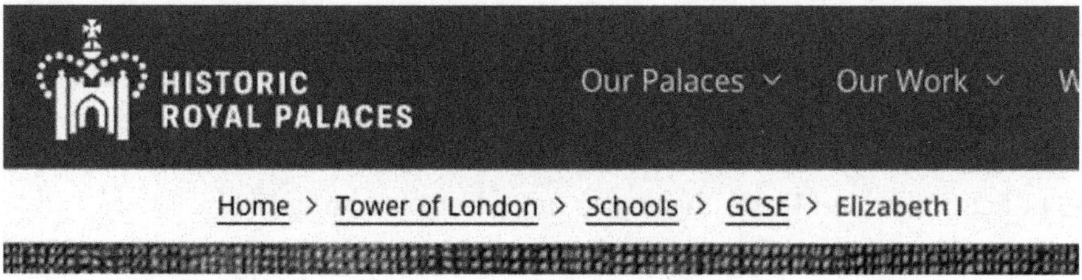


**Figure 1.5** *An example of a breadcrumb on the Historic Royal Palaces website*

Users will typically scan for elements like the title and breadcrumb to get some context as to where on a site a page appears and where in the navigation it exists. Users arriving on a site via a search engine have much less context about the authority and credibility of the content than, for example, a reader reading a book from start to finish. Making clear where a page appears in the overall navigation makes it easier for users to get context on how a page relates to the site as a whole and allows them to make a judgement on whether the site is a credible source of information.

Users want to know where a page sits in your overall site structure. They also want a sense of the content of a page without having to scroll to the bottom. You can include a couple of simple sentences at the top of the page that explain its contents, for example, 'Browse here for more information about making a school trip and our learning resources'. You can also use an anchor link bar, which is a set of quick links that allows users to jump to the subtitles or subsections on the same page that are relevant to them.

## Break up large walls of text

There is nothing more likely to make a user leave a web page and find information elsewhere than long, dense paragraphs of unformatted text. These require us to enter Kahneman's system 2 – and make us want to take a break and have a cup of tea. For simple types of information, large walls of text are unlikely to be the most efficient way to convey information. A user is well aware of this and, if they're finding it too cumbersome to locate the information they want on your site, there's almost always somewhere else on the internet they can get that information more quickly. Note, though, that this doesn't apply to content that users are reading for enjoyment rather than to get information quickly. We'll look more at writing creative content and online storytelling in Part 3.

Ways to break text up and make it more digestible include using:

- headings and sub-headings
- images or multimedia elements – some concepts benefit from a visual explanation, for example, instructions for how to find a park may be easier to understand using a diagram or map rather than described in words
- bullet points and lists – these also help draw attention to key or summary points within a section
- links – these are useful for many reasons, including for SEO, but they also help draw a user's eye to key words and phrases that help make sense of the topics being discussed.

Organisations like NNG and the Government Digital Service (GDS) have looked at how online readers' eyes skip over words in sentences. An 'eye-skip' in this context is known as a 'saccade'. Users are not reading each word in sequence, they're being more strategic than that. By focusing on nouns and some verbs, a reader can get the gist of what a passage of text says without sequentially registering each individual word. That is, they can understand the main point of something, even if they don't know all the details.

This has important implications. For example, passives, particles and negatives are all small, inconsequential looking words that we're likely to gloss over if we're scanning text quickly. This means that someone looking over your text may come away with the opposite of your intended meaning. Some will go back and reread your text to make sense of it, others won't bother and will either carry on with an incomplete understanding or become disenchanted with your text and leave the web page.

By looking in detail at where saccades happen in paragraphs of online text, we can develop granular recommendations about how to write content online that communicates effectively and engages users, even when the content is scanned.

## Search engine optimisation (SEO) checklist

We've looked at how humans digest information online. It is also useful to think about how search engines analyse web pages and what that means for how we create content that is optimised for search.

One of the most common scenarios I faced as a content editor was being sent article copy that I'd then need to edit in a search friendly manner. Articles are the content on your site with the most potential to be effective in search, mainly because they contain the most words. This checklist is designed to be a guide and reference point to use when writing or editing new articles.

Note, these tips do not replace a robust SEO strategy. In fact, the impact of all the items on the checklist may be limited if you have not:

- conducted a technical SEO audit to check your site code is well optimised
- conducted a keyword analysis to determine what the greatest topic opportunities are for your organisation and what the subtopics, keywords and most important questions to answer are within these major topics
- looked at the overall architecture of pages, such as your 'discover' or blog section and your collections section. A lot of organisations by default list all their articles chronologically, which makes it quite easy for articles to become invisible once they fall off the blog homepage.

The following checklist details what you can do to optimise your individual articles for search. (We look in more detail at both overall site keyword strategy and the findability of articles in Part 3.)

### Before writing a new article

*Research your topic*

Before you begin, conduct a thorough search on your chosen topic. Has it already been covered extensively on the internet? If so, how can you make your content distinctive? Consider incorporating original pictures, multimedia elements or unique insights and expertise to set your content apart. In knowledge-based institutions, we have plenty of these resources to call on, but we don't always think about that unique selling point when optimising digital web content.

*Choose evergreen stories that will not date*

Typically, when I audit a blog or editorial section, between one and five articles will be driving the vast majority of the traffic. These posts have all been written in a different style, are typically longer than the other articles and contain a lot of high-ranking keywords. Often, the success of this kind of post is accidental.

There tends to be a longtail of articles that get little to no traffic a few weeks after they are posted, normally when they are no longer visible on the front page or in the blog or editorial section. Articles that describe temporary events and museum happenings can date very quickly and become irrelevant. Below are examples of article titles I've worked with that performed badly:

- Visit XXX Museum this Christmas for a Festive Lighting Display
- Diwali: Festival of Light – XXX Museum and the Community and Schools Project
- Competition time! Name the panda.

Firstly, the titles are too broad and non-specific to rank in search, but why else did these blog posts perform poorly?

1 The first article is written as a press release describing an upcoming event. Three years after the event, the original point of this piece, which was to promote the event, is now redundant.
2 The second article is a case study of a programme led by the Museum's learning team. This kind of project write-up sits much more happily in a Learning > Projects website section where it is more likely to be found by peer professionals than in the overall editorial section, which should focus on generalist readers and engaging new audiences with the most interesting museum stories.
3 The third article describes a competition that has now closed. This would be better formatted as a social media post or e-mail campaign that would be visible for the duration of the piece but not beyond.

The most effective use of blogs for SEO is to write articles about aspects of your permanent offer. That will drive and build the most relevant long-term traffic and will be most likely to convert readers to visitors to a permanent part of your offer.

*Use keyword research*

Keyword research helps define the most popular search queries you want your article to answer. You can then use this information to structure your content.

When you Google a visitor attraction, the results page will typically display a few top URLs and then introduce a 'People also ask' structured content block (see Figure 1.6 below). This is a great (and free!) way of getting an insight into the most popular longtail keyword searches around your search term.

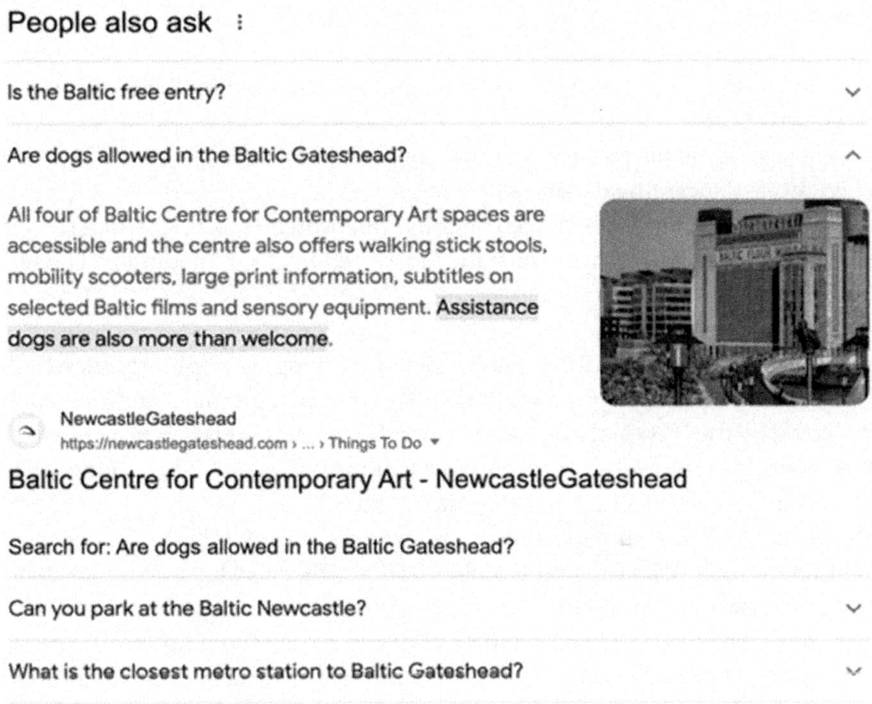


**Figure 1.6** *'People also ask' structured content block in a Google SERP for 'Baltic Gateshead'*

In the example in Figure 1.6, I searched for 'Baltic Gateshead', an arts venue in the North East. The search engine suggested the following search phrases:

- Is the Baltic free entry?
- Are dogs allowed in the Baltic Gateshead?
- Can you park at the Baltic Newcastle?
- What is the closest metro station to Baltic Gateshead?

For some of these questions, Google provided an answer taken from the Baltic's own website. In other cases, Google pulled a suggested answer from somewhere else, for example, the tourism site NewcastleGateshead.com. If I was working for the Baltic, I might suggest that, to get more traffic to their site, they include a paragraph about metro stations in their Plan Your Visit section (and so direct traffic currently going to the council website from Google to their site instead).

This strategy also works for topic related pages, such as collections articles. If I Google 'Flying Scotsman' (Google, 2023), the first entry is the URL for the collection item 'Flying Scotsman' on the National Railway Museum website. Beneath that, Google's 'People also ask' questions are:

- Where is the Flying Scotsman now in 2024? (answered by the Railway Museum's site)
- Where is the Flying Scotsman now? (answered by www.eastlancsrailway.org.uk)
- Why is the Flying Scotsman so famous? (answered by a BBC article)
- Can you ride the Flying Scotsman? (answered by The Caledonian Travel website).

In these examples, we can see that Google is serving us popularly searched for questions relating to items in UK collections. Not all these questions are answered by the National Railway Museum's website and this is not unusual. A 2023 study conducted by One Further (Cultural Content, 2023) found very few instances of collections' online sites returning search traffic from these 'People also ask' questions. This is a missed opportunity for GLAM websites to improve their SEO for selected object pages. By creating website content that answers these frequently searched questions, you make it more likely that your website will be shown in response to those search queries.

Google's 'People also ask' suggestions can also help you plan your editorial content. By Googling your article topic, you can use the suggested questions as headings or talking points within your article. For example, if I Google 'Roman Shoe Facts' the 'People also ask' questions are:

- What kinds of shoes did Romans wear?
- What shoes did they wear in Rome?
- Did Romans wear shoes inside?
- Did Roman soldiers [sic] shoes have spikes?
- What shoes did poor Romans wear?
- What did Roman shoes look like?

This provides an idea of the kinds of questions and topics that a broad audience are interested in and that you could incorporate into your article. If you address these questions in your article, you improve your chances of appearing in relevant searches.

You can also use this technique to create topic clusters related to key 'pillars' or themes your organisation is uniquely positioned to tell. Table 1.1 below provides an example of how you can use multiple themes (in this case inspired by the British Museum's Legion exhibition in 2024) to build a content plan under key pillars. All the queries are based on results from Google's automatically generated 'People also ask' snippets.

**Table 1.1** *Example of using multiple themes, inspired by British Museum's 'Legion' exhibition, to build a content plan under key pillars. The queries are based on results from Google's automatically generated 'People also ask' snippets*

| Romans in Britain | Life in a Roman Legion | The Vindolanda tablets | Women Roman army |
|---|---|---|---|
| How long did Rome occupy Britain? | What was life like in a Roman legion? | What do the Vindolanda tablets tell us? | Were women allowed in the Roman army? |
| Why did the Romans leave Britain in 410? | Could Roman legionaries marry? | Where are the Vindolanda tablets now? | How did the Romans treat women? |
| Who defeated the Romans in England? | What were the living conditions for Roman soldiers? | How old are the Vindolanda tablets? | Could Roman soldiers have wives? |
| Why did Romans abandon Britain? | What was a typical Roman legion? | What were the contents of the Vindolanda tablets? | Did Rome have female warriors? |
| Who ruled England after the Romans left? | What was the most notorious Roman legion? | Why is Vindolanda so well preserved? | What did Romans do with female slaves? |
| What happened to the Romans in Britain? | Were Roman legionaries feared? | Why didn't the Romans take Scotland? | How did Romans view women? |

### *Images*

The best way to tell a story might not be purely with words. When I'm doing user testing of blog sections, I find that participants are drawn to the title, subheadings and pictures. Browsing users are far more likely to scroll through an image gallery and take in a story visually than they are to sit down and read paragraphs of text.

Pictures can be a great way of engaging less motivated readers. They can also be a better way of delivering a story by showing, not telling. Image galleries don't have to replace article text, but a series of images and captions can be an evocative and impactful way of getting your message across and to complement the textual narrative.

### *Optimal article length*

There is a misconception in the sector that short articles are best. However, Google deliberately prioritises 'in-depth' articles and long articles rank highly. I recommend aiming for a word count of at least 1,200 words. This equates to a 7-minute read time or around 16 paragraphs of text.

### *Linking*

Another misconception in the sector is that linking out of your articles is bad because it is better to keep people on your page. From an SEO perspective, this is shooting yourself in the foot. One of the key metrics Google uses as to the trustworthiness of your content is how widely it references other high credibility sites. If Google has a choice between two articles, one that references other websites in its text and one that has no external links at all, the first is more likely to be credible, in the absence of any other metrics. Links are the lifeblood of the internet and are what Google uses to understand the context in which your content is important and to whom it's relevant. Use them.

### *Use proper headings*

We know that people rarely read web text word for word. Most users will land on an article page, give it a quick scan to get a sense of what the page contains and then decide whether the article is interesting and/or will answer the query that they landed on the page to answer. You can give your content the best chance of passing the 'skim-test' by creating subheadings that signpost the main stages of your article and the key topics and keywords covered.

Royal Museums Greenwich has a very successful editorial section on their website called 'Stories'. These articles frequently rank highly in search engines. If you Google the term 'first woman in space', Royal Museums Greenwich is often one of the first listings you'll see (alongside specialist heavyweights like NASA).

Their article 'Who was the First Woman in Space?' (Royal Museums Greenwich, n.d.) is 2,138 words long and the title uses the query the museum is hoping to rank in search results for. The first subheadings read:

- The first female astronauts
- The first British woman in space
- First African American woman in space
- First American woman in space
- The first Indian woman in space
- What year was the first woman in space?

What's interesting here is that if we use a competitive search intelligence tool to find the most widely searched terms around 'first women in space', a lot of them are covered by these subheadings. Royal Museums Greenwich has evidently done their keyword research homework and are using that to guide their article structure.

When you enter free text into a website's CMS you are generally entering text in what is known as a WYSIWYG ('what you see is what you get'). It's a text editing interface that's not dissimilar to the toolbar you find in Word or Google Docs. It provides you with options to format text in a few different ways (e.g., italics, bold) and to create a variety of title styles. These styles might include 'title' and 'subtitle', but should also give you the option of formatting text as 'heading 1', 'heading 2', 'heading 3' and so on (often known as H1, H2 and H3). Instead of using bold text, use H2 and H3 tags for subheadings as this is what Google will use to understand the structure of your article. If you also include important keywords in these headings, Google will be more likely to return your page (or a subheading on your page) in search results for a relevant query.

## The first draft

### *Write a custom meta description for your article*

A meta description allows you to describe your web page to a new user seeing it via search results. Most CMSs will by default include the first lines of text on the page as a meta description, but this isn't necessarily the best way of describing the page to someone who hasn't landed on it yet.

Custom meta descriptions are good for SEO as they mean that more relevant and qualified traffic lands on your page. This means that traffic is likely to spend longer and click on more pages, which sends good signals back to Google. They also allow your pages to stand out in search listings more than sites that haven't done the hard work of writing custom meta descriptions. The Museum of English Rural Life (MERL) has done some fantastic work on creating custom meta descriptions for all their pages, including their blog articles (see Figure 1.7 below).

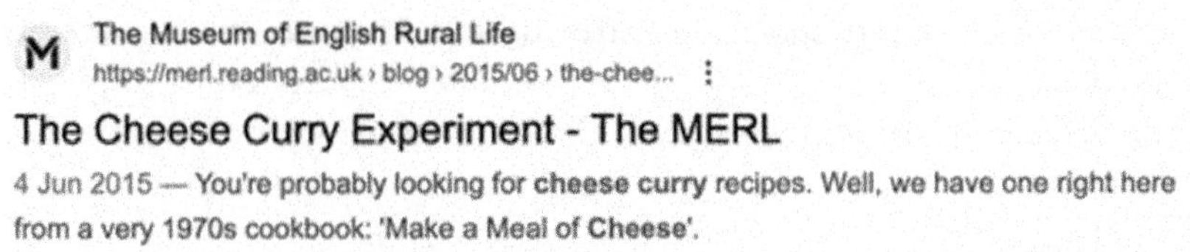


**Figure 1.7** *Example of an effective custom meta description*

*Improve readability*

Once you've written your article, pass it through a tool like the Hemingway App (https://hemingwayapp.com) to grade your copy and give it an estimated reading age. Aim for a readability level of Grade 8 (ages 13–14). This ensures your content remains accessible to a broad audience, including an audience whose first language might not be English.

*Think about onward journeys*

In an age of content overload, it's rare that a reader will reach the end of an online article. But if your hard work has captured a reader's attention so that they read to the end, what do you want them to do next? Where do you want to signpost them to? It might be to thematically related articles, to a donation or membership ask, or to book a visit to see items from the collection described in the post.

*Optimise images*

Ensure that your images are resized correctly. Pages that load faster improve user experience and SEO. There are lots of free browser-based tools that can do this, for example, Photopea, Pixlr and Canva. If you're part of a larger institution you may get access to organisation-wide software, such as the Adobe suite.

## The published article

*Seek backlinks*

A backlink (also known as an inbound link) is a link from another website to a page on your website. In the sector, we tend to ignore them, partly, I suspect, because there's no free tool that allows you to measure how well you're doing in terms of backlinks. (Paid tools do this and show you how you stack up compared to the competition.)

Backlinks also aren't widely understood – why should it matter which and how many websites are linking to your site? Think about it from Google's perspective: if lots of reputable sites are linking to your website about spinning wheels, it's likely that your site is a reputable source on the topic. If someone searches for 'spinning wheels', Google is going to heavily rate the site with the highest number of quality backlinks in the order that it returns search results. Backlinks work like citations in academia: if your web page is widely linked to by authoritative sources, this gives Google a good signal that it's got high credibility and influence in the field.

Another reason we are a little hesitant around backlinks in the sector is that it requires us to get in touch – and ask a favour of – people we don't know. An effective 'backlink strategy' is simply seeing who's writing on similar topics to you online and reaching out and making them aware of the new content you've created. You should outline how your new content is different from what's already online – perhaps it's more authoritative than Wikipedia, shows sides of an object that no one has seen before or contains original research. You then need to ask the site owner if they would consider linking to you on their page. You could offer to build reciprocal links, for example, by linking to their content in your article where it provides additional information or context on the same topic.

We don't tend to think about backlinks as part of SEO when publishing web content, but it's one of the most effective things you can do to make your content more visible – and to make Google more aware of it. It is also good web practice; you're joining up the dots and positioning your content as providing something new in the context of what's already been written elsewhere on the web.

You could also consider collaborating with external experts or organisations on your article, which will make them more likely to link to your article from their own website.

### *Contribute to Wikipedia*

Wikipedia is still a misunderstood and underused resource within the cultural sector. Wikipedia's purpose is 'to create a web-based, free content encyclopaedia of all branches of knowledge, in an atmosphere of mutual respect and cooperation' (Wikipedia, 2024c). The goal of an individual Wikipedia article is 'to create a comprehensive and neutrally written summary of existing mainstream knowledge about a topic'.

Wikipedia doesn't want you to upload marketing material from your museum, since that is not 'neutral'. But it does want to develop the richness and breadth of topics it talks about online. Adding information and images from your collection supports Wikipedia's purpose. It's good for Wikipedia, but it's also good for you. In addition, it's good for those people online who want to know more about the topics you have expertise in.

Once you've published an article on your website, consider if any of the facts or images would add to the information on existing pages on Wikipedia. If so, consider adding these details to the Wikipedia page and citing your new article as a reference. Or, if the topic you're writing about hasn't been covered on Wikipedia, you could consider writing a new Wikipedia article. However, it is often worth doing minor edits to existing Wikipedia articles rather than starting a page from scratch.

Adding more imagery and information to Wikipedia about your collections is a great way to bring in new audiences who are interested in the topics your museum can talk about but might not know that you own the material they are interested in.

For more information, see the case study on Wikipedia in Chapter 2.

### *Image search and multimedia*

Image search is an important area of SEO and it is often forgotten about in the sector. This is a huge shame as GLAM institutions have access to so many unique and brilliant images.

The simplest way to upload images to a website is to upload a string of files straight from your camera. The filenames for these images will typically be a string of numbers, for example, PXL_20241029_11344938. This tells you which device took the photo and the date it was taken. Unfortunately, it doesn't tell you what the picture is of!

For photos to be visible in Google search, you need to manually add keywords to the metadata describing what the photo is of. There are different metadata fields that you can edit on images. The most important to know about are the filename and alt-text.

The filename is what you will use to find this image again in your website media library. But it also helps Google understand what the image shows.

Alt-text is an important field. Not everyone who wants to browse the internet can see. Many blind and partially sighted users use 'screen readers', which read the content of web pages aloud. When a screen reader comes across an image it will 'read aloud' the alt-text. When writing alt-text for your image, think about what someone would need to know to make sense of it in the context of the page. Supercool has provided some great advice for when you're writing alt-text: 'think how you'd briefly describe the image over the phone' (Supercool, 2020).

In conducting search keyword audits for clients, I frequently find that people are searching for visual media, such as timelines, quizzes and family trees, alongside a given historical or collections keyword. These are more time consuming to create, but also have a bigger opportunity for GLAMs. There are hundreds of articles on the internet about any one aspect of your collection, but there will be far fewer visual media. Creating custom visual and interactive media around your collections and the themes you can talk about is a good way of setting yourself apart from the competition and delivering something more unique in the search space (although check in advance that no one has done this for your area already!).

## Additional considerations for SEO across your site

The checklist above is designed to be used in the day to day context of article writing. There are additional considerations to bear in mind for other parts of the website and we'll cover these below.

### E-commerce

E-commerce here means online shops, although similar rules apply if you have a complex online ticketing system with multiple products and offers. The rules that apply to e-commerce pages are similar to site pages as a whole, but there are a few additional considerations.

#### *A clear URL structure*

Have you ever tried to share an item from an online shop, only for it to generate a long URL full of numbers and not many keywords to indicate what it is you're linking to? It might stop you sharing the link as it won't necessarily be clear to the recipient what they're supposed to be linking through to (and it could look like spam).

Google has a similar nervousness. It's much better to have a clear URL structure that provides context as to where a product lives on your site. For example: www.site.com/category/product.

#### *Product descriptions*

It can be tempting, particularly if you have a large number of products to add to the shop, to simply copy and paste the manufacturer's description or to leave little or no description. This is not a good idea from an SEO perspective. Google wants original content and is unlikely to display your online shop over the retailer's website if your site gets less traffic than theirs and is copying their content.

You can get an edge on competitor sites that are stocking the same products by thinking about what you can uniquely contribute to the products. It could be quotes from the author/artist, if you have a relationship with them. Could there be better or more authentic images? Or a description that better chimes with the sensibilities and culture of your specific audience?

## Boost your presence in search engine results pages

### *Google Business Profile*

Your 'Google Business Profile' is the sidebar that appears on the right-hand side of a Google search engine results page (SERP) – see Figure 1.8 below.

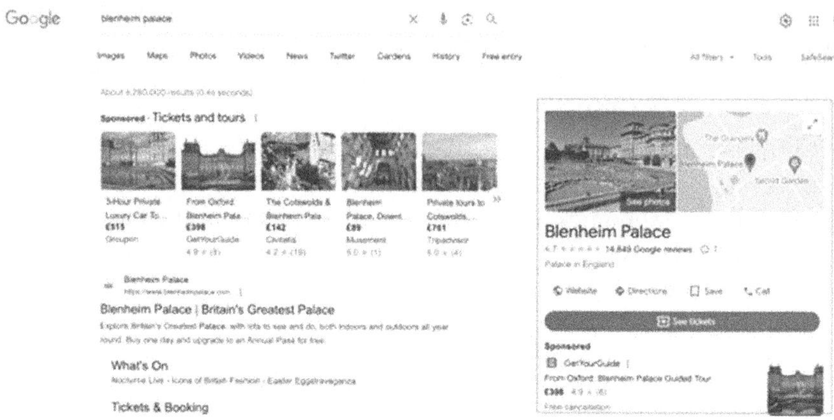


**Figure 1.8** *Google Business Profile listing for Blenheim Palace*

The listing can be easy to overlook when managing your web presence as it's not always clear who's responsible for it. Like SEO as a whole, it doesn't sit neatly in a traditional cultural sector job role.

The simplest and most effective thing you can do for your Google Business Profile listing is to check the information is up to date and attractive (e.g. that good images are pulling through and the location and contact details are correct, etc.). If you are proactive in updating your profile you can make great improvements, but inaccurate information left for a long time can be difficult to unseat. Google won't necessarily remove it just because you – as business owner – have corrected it on the back end.

## SEO audits

If you're interested in SEO, it is worth commissioning a technical SEO audit. This uses a range of industry standard scripted tools to crawl every URL on your site and identify pervasive issues, for example, if meta descriptions aren't being used or if certain pages have a title that is too long for mobile search results. This is a good time saver and gives you a quick list of actionable fixes to boost your SEO.

### *Site loading speed on mobile devices*

One metric that an SEO audit might flag is how fast your site loads, particularly on mobile devices. Globally, over 58% of internet searches happen on mobile devices (Smart Insights, 2024), but cultural sector websites aren't always well optimised for mobile.

The *Discovering Online Collections: Benchmark Report* (One Further, 2023) found that the vast majority of participating organisations' online collection web pages loaded very slowly on mobile. This was principally because there were no mobile fallback images and small screens were having to load the same large images as desktop users.

## Measuring your progress

In order to track how many people are viewing your web content (and how they are using it) you need to understand digital analytics packages. By far the most common analytics package is Google Analytics, which in 2024 moved all of its tracking from 'Universal Analytics' (UA) to Google Analytics 4, commonly known as GA4.

If you're working with digital content and want to know how to use GA4 effectively, Case study 1.1 below by Chris Unitt, Founder of One Further, a consultancy that specialises in analytics support for the cultural sector, provides some valuable insights.

## Case study 1.1: Measuring content with Google Analytics 4 (GA4)

*Chris Unitt, Founder, One Further*

For the uninitiated, in March 2022, Google Analytics announced it would be sunsetting 3 (called Universal Analytics) and moving over to GA4. It's a tool with many improvements, as well as its fair share of quirks.

In this case study, I'm going to talk specifically about measuring content performance. We'll look at what you get from GA4 by default, then we'll see how you might want to improve your reporting and data capture.

**What we mean by 'content performance'?**

If you're spending any sort of time producing content for your website, you'll want to know how well it's working. Let's be more specific. We want to know if a given page (and the contents and functionality featured on that page) – or a group of similar pages – are getting people to do what we want them to do. And that's likely to be different for different types of content.

We also want to know about the conditions that might affect how people interact with our pages. For example, people might be looking at the content on different types of devices or they might have stumbled upon it (perhaps via an advert) or specifically sought it out. This will affect how they approach the website.

So, it stands to reason that we're not going to measure everything in exactly the same way. Of course, there are some metrics that will apply across multiple content types, but to truly understand what's happening you need to go beyond these basics and home in on what truly matters.

**What GA4 gives you out of the box**

By adding Google Analytics tracking code to your website you'll be capturing some useful data, including:

- page views and average engagement time
- traffic sources
- device types.

This is enough to be getting started with.

The report you need to find for this information is called 'Pages and Screens' and you will find it in the left-hand navigation in the 'Reports' section and under the 'Engagement' drop-down menu, see Figure 1.9 below.

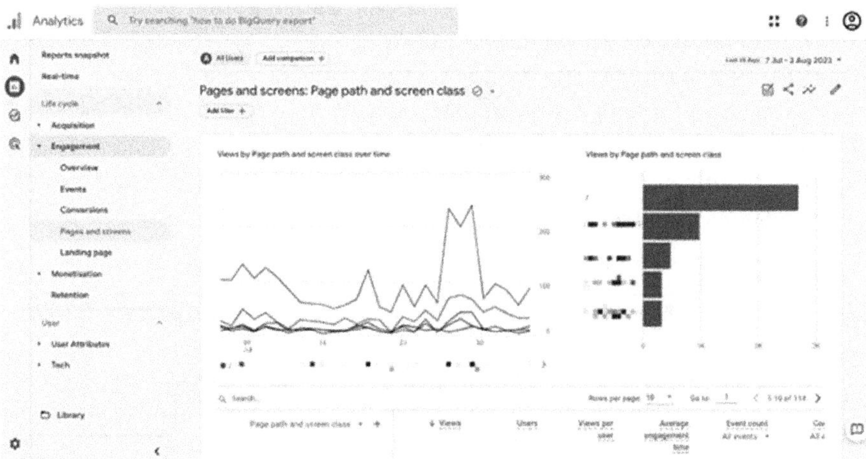


**Figure 1.9** *GA4 navigation to 'Pages and Screens' report*

From here you can do a few things. You can:

- use the search bar to find particular pages
- use the search bar to find all pages containing a common word in the URL (at this point the columns of metrics become more interesting, because you're more likely to be comparing like with like)
- click the blue plus sign at the top of the first table column to add additional columns – try 'Device Category' to see whether people are looking at a particular page on mobile or desktop, or 'Town/City' to see where in the world people are looking at your content.

There's more you can do, but just knowing how often your content is being accessed is a good starting point.

### Improving your content reporting in GA4

Off-the-peg clothes might fit well enough most of the time, but sometimes an adjustment here or there can make all the difference. This is also likely to be the case when it comes to your content reporting.

Let's take a look at customising your reports and how to find them.

#### *Creating custom reports*

The 'Pages and Screens' report is helpful, but if you have areas of the site with lots of similar types of content (e.g. events, exhibitions, articles, online collections, shop products, etc.), you might want to find statistics about those more easily.

The good news is that it's easy to create custom reports in GA4. A good way to get started is to create content reports for particular site sections. To do that, you need to have a suitably high level of access to your GA4 property. Then you need to:

1. Click the 'Edit' button in the top right-hand corner of the 'Pages and Screens' report.
2. In the panel that appears on the right-hand side, add a filter to select the pages you're interested in (e.g., 'Page Path and Screen Name' contains '/events/') – see Figure 1.10 below.
3. Click 'Apply' and check your table is showing the pages you were hoping for.
4. Click 'Save' and select 'Save as a new report'. Give it a name, click 'Save' and you're done.

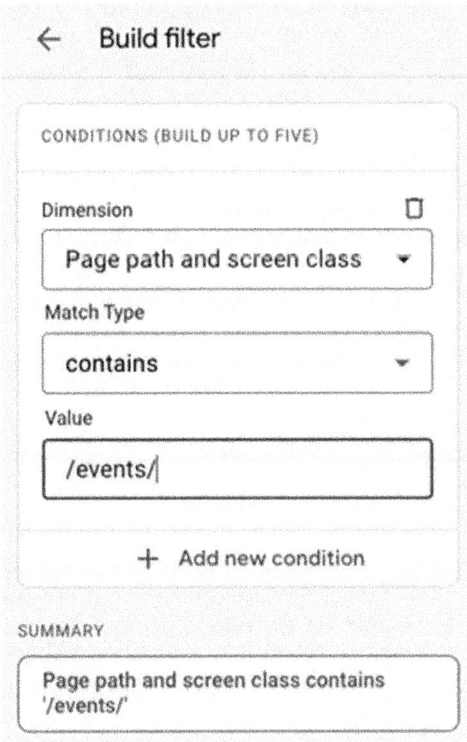


**Figure 1.10** *GA4 custom reports filters*

If you're interested in creating more of these kinds of custom reports, One Further have created a GA4 Reporting Kit (https://coach.onefurther.com/p/google-analytics-4-reporting-kit) aimed at helping arts marketers.

But where can you then find saved GA4 reports?

*Customising GA4's navigation*

Report navigation in GA4 is easily customised. I'm not going to provide the instructions for doing that here as Google has some excellent instructions on how to customise GA4's report navigation (Google, n.d.). However, for a bit of inspiration, we could create a series of reports under 'Content', for example:

- Pages: All
- Pages: Stories
- Pages: What's on
- Pages: Collections
- Pages: Landing pages.

Having everything laid out neatly with recognisable names can make a huge difference to someone's experience of GA4, especially for less frequent users.

**Improving your data capture**

This is where it gets nerdy. To really understand how your content is performing, you need to know more than just how many times it was viewed. To make your reporting easier, you might want to pull together different types of content in different ways. For this, we need to talk about event tracking and custom definitions.

*Content-focused event tracking*

Every page should have a primary purpose. That purpose should inform the design of the page, the content that goes on it and, of course, how we measure its performance.

In some cases, it's pretty obvious what that primary purpose is, for example:

- event or product pages (e.g., events, exhibitions, workshops, shop products, etc.): clicks on 'book now' buttons
- membership/support us pages: clicks to become a member or donate
- online shop product pages: clicks to add products to the basket
- search results pages: clicks on search results
- learning resource pages: downloads of resources.

In some cases, it might be a bit trickier. For example:

- articles: a common instinct is to measure consumption – people reading to the end of the article (or watching to the end of a video) – but you can also measure e-mail sign-ups or clicks on links to related exhibition pages
- collections objects: we might want to find any indication that a person has found something useful (e.g., zooming in on an image, cycling through an image carousel or clicking to download or license an image).

All these are measurable, but you may need to set up some custom tracking using Google Tag Manager in order for GA4 to capture them. The technicalities of that are a bit involved for this book, but it's worth knowing that it's possible and can result in much more tailored reports. A customised reporting dashboard might look like the example in Figure 1.11 below.

| | Page | Page Views ▾ | Member ship CTA | Member ship CTA CVR | Email signup | Email signup CVR |
|---|---|---|---|---|---|---|
| 1. | /resources/ | 9,638 | 21 | 0.22% | 0 | 0% |
| 2. | /resources/ | 4,823 | 365 | 7.57% | 0 | 0% |
| 3. | /resources/ | 4,496 | 3 | 0.07% | 0 | 0% |
| 4. | /resources/ | 3,898 | 51 | 1.31% | 4 | 0.1% |
| 5. | /resources/ | 3,746 | 19 | 0.51% | 0 | 0% |

1 - 50 / 604 ‹ ›

**Figure 1.11** *Example of a customised reporting dashboard in GA4*

The organisation the dashboard in Figure 1.11 is based on wanted to know which of their online resources lead to people investigating membership or signing up to their e-mail list. They set up a custom report for those resources that monitored page views, clicks on the membership call to action (CTA), the conversion rate of clicks on the membership CTA, number of e-mail sign-ups and the conversion rate of the e-mail sign-up CTA.

You can see how a custom report like this can provide much more granular reporting, tailored to your objectives for that page or page type.

*Custom definitions*

Out of the box, Google Analytics will collect the URL and Page Title of your content. That's a good starting point, but when doing reporting there might be other information you'd be interested in looking at, for example, the author, publish date and any categories. We call that sort of information 'metadata' and it is possible to pull it into GA4 so you can use it in your reporting.

Being able to easily group together all content published in a given year – or being able to show an author the statistics for the pieces they've published – can add a valuable extra dimension to your content reporting.

### Conclusion

Google Analytics can be an effective tool for understanding the performance of your website content. The content report that's included by default is fine; it will show you how many people are accessing your content and allow you to dig a little deeper to understand more about how people are doing that. If you want, you can take things further by:

- creating custom reports to make it easier for you and your colleagues to access data about your site and its content
- collecting more tailored data about your content and how people are interacting with your pages.

Hopefully, I've opened your eyes to what's possible and what others in the cultural sector have been doing in this area. Of course, having these data and reports sitting in your Google Analytics account isn't going to do you any good if nobody's looking at it and using it to inform the action you take. Whether you have a team of content producers poring over the latest statistics every Monday morning or you're only able to take a look every few months as part of a planning exercise, a little customisation can go a long way.

## Summary

In Chapter 1, we've looked at how you can use SEO to make your web pages more visible. We've also looked at how you can use GA4 to track changing user behaviour.

There are lots of different ways to measure SEO effectiveness. Some key metrics include:

- volume of traffic from search – has this increased three months after you made changes to improve your SEO effectiveness?
- Google Search Console data – Google Search Console is a free tool that shows which queries are used in Google to land on your website. It's a useful gauge of the most visible keywords on your website; you might be surprised by which queries draw in the most traffic to your site. When reviewing the queries in Google Search Console you should consider whether these are the terms you expected to be most visible. If not, you may wish to create content around such terms and keywords. This means you can review the list of queries after new content has been created to see if they are generating new traffic.

If you have a competitive search tool you can get much more granular insights about your site as a whole in terms of search competitivity and for specific web pages. Here, you can monitor metrics like your domain authority, check the amount of search traffic particular pages are pulling in and monitor the number of backlinks your site has (and the most effective backlinks for you in terms of volume of search traffic).

It's useful to remember that not everyone will find you on your website. The website works best for those who have already heard of you and those who are interested in topics you cover. It's unlikely that your website will be found by those who don't think it's relevant to them. That's where third-party platforms come in. In the next chapter, we'll look at Facebook, X, Instagram, YouTube, TikTok, Threads, Wikipedia and Pinterest in terms of what opportunities they offer the cultural sector.

CHAPTER 2

# Using Third-party Platforms to Make Yourself More Visible Online

Making your website more visible in search is important, but it's only really relevant to those who already have an interest in a subject you have content on. After all, it still relies on someone typing a query into a search engine in the first place.

Third-party platforms allow you to reach people passively. Someone can be scrolling through their social feeds or be on a website for a different task and 'happen' upon your content.

We can distinguish between 'paid' third-party content, which appears in a user's feed in the form of a digital advert and/or sponsored post, and 'organic' content. Organic content is content that has appeared in a user's feed 'naturally' with no paid targeting behind it. That said, there is still a great deal of algorithm-driven decision making into how, when and why organic content will appear in someone's feed.

This chapter looks at the world of third-party platforms, covering both paid digital ads (on Google and social media) and 'organic' social media. It also looks at the world of Wikipedia and what significant third-party websites can do in terms of driving traffic to your website and as another platform for hosting information related to your collections.

## Digital ads

The world of paid digital ads in the sector is generally divided into Google Ads, which is split into 'search ads' (like the sponsored eye test results we saw in Chapter 1) and 'display ads' (the ads that follow you around the internet when you've abandoned a purchase on an e-commerce site). Display ads – as with all the digital ads packages – are configurable and, as an advertiser, you can control how and when these ads appear.

Within the sector, most organisations are eligible for a Google Ad Grant. Google Ad Grant is a scheme that allows cultural not-for-profits to claim up to $10,000 in kind advertising spend per month for free. Why does Google do this? Because it knows that, by default, paid-search listings will be dominated by companies with money and not always companies that are actually very interesting to the majority of searchers. Cultural organisations hold a lot of interest for people, but they aren't always well-represented online in ads.

The Google Ad Grant scheme addresses this disparity. The only catch is that Google doesn't give you $10,000 to spend on ads willy-nilly; you'll only be allowed to publish lots of ads if they are delivering well. It's often easier to outsource digital advertising to a specialist, at least in the first instance, to get you 'up and running'. It's then possible either to take out a third-party retainer with an agency to manage these services or have the account handed over in a 'low maintenance mode', where you can have a high level of free ad spend ticking over with minimal input from yourself (One Further, 2024).

The other major type of paid digital advertising package relevant to the sector is social media advertising. All the major social media platforms have an ads package, including Facebook, Instagram, X, TikTok, LinkedIn and YouTube. All these platforms are free to join and create and consume content on, so the way the companies behind these platforms make money is through their advertising packages. Over the last decade, digital advertising packages have become more sophisticated and the revenues they generate for companies have ballooned.

The promise of digital advertising – both search and social – is that it delivers the right content, to the right person, at the right time. If we think about something like a static billboard – or any of our traditional, non-digital ways of advertising – we have very little steer over who sees it, in what capacity and how relevant it is to them. It's also very difficult to demonstrate return on ad spend (ROAS) for an analogue campaign as we have no metrics to show the numbers who acted on the information they saw in the physical world.

Digital advertising disrupted all this. Unlike with analogue marketing, digital marketing can target your ad at those people to whom it is relevant. Within that, you can create different 'audience groups'; for example, when advertising an upcoming theatrical production of *Emma* at the Theatre Royal Margate, you might create an audience group that includes people within a local radius who have visited the theatre's website in the last six months. You might then create another audience group within a slightly wider geographic radius who are fans of theatre or Jane Austen.

The ways in which you can target people are granular and multi-layered. On Meta Business Suite (the advertising package that powers ads to Facebook and Instagram), you can target people by interest, profession, political inclination, whether they have children and what age they are – the list goes on. You can also target people who have demonstrated interest in your institution, for example, by 're-targeting' those who have landed on your site before.

Digital advertising has benefits in terms of its measurability. When you set an ad up you can measure the size of your target audience and the platform will then advise whether your target is too broad or too specific. Best practice advises that you create a number of different versions of your ad (as well as different audience groups to target that ad at). This means that once your ad begins to run, Meta will evaluate which creative is performing best to which audience. It will then optimise your budget for the goal you've set in place. The platform itself is very adept at running A/B and/or multivariant testing and – through trial and improvement – optimising the best variation for the goal you have set it to achieve.

Ads have different goals. For example, you can create ads that:

- raise awareness on a social media platform
- generate link clicks to your website/sign-up form
- generate an ROAS, i.e. generate sales on your own website/ticketing platform to offset the cost of these ads.

Google Ads are slightly different in that there are two main types of ad – 'search' and 'display'. Display ads work in a similar way to Meta ads: you put together a 'creative' (generally an image cropped to different sizes or a video) and a few lines of text and this ad is then targeted at users at different stages of their internet browsing. Search ads appear when someone enters a relevant search term into Google. 'Sponsored' listings generally appear above 'organic'/non-sponsored listings and this is because companies have paid to boost their rankings.

There isn't a linear relationship between ad spend and high search rankings. Google does not want to be seen as a spam site. It will only rank your site highly if it assesses your content to be relevant to the keywords you want to rank for and if your ad – once live – generates engaged traffic when it lands on your site from the search ad. It can be tricky, particularly with Google Ad Grant, to spend all your available budget as Google will only charge you for ads that are seen. If it thinks your ad is no good in the first place, you won't get charged very much (if at all) and your ad won't be distributed very widely.

It is rare for in-house teams in the cultural sector to manage their own digital advertising. This makes sense to some extent – the advertising platforms are quite complicated, always changing and it takes time to get your head around the jargon and structure of each. However, sector professionals can only benefit from improving their understanding of what digital advertising platforms offer. There is a great swathe of job roles in the sector tasked with growing audiences and increasing revenue and footfall. To try and perform these roles without knowing how digital advertising platforms work is limiting.

Given how frequently the ad platforms update their interfaces, it would be difficult to write a comprehensive book on this subject that didn't quickly become out of date. One Further has an online training platform that provides a 'Facebook Ads for Arts Marketers' online course: https://coach.onefurther.com/p/facebook-ads-arts-marketers, as well as a 'How to Run a Successful Google Ad Grant' online course: https://coach.onefurther.com/p/google-ad-grants-for-arts-organisations. These are updated as and when changes happen on the platforms.

By contrast, sector professionals tend to put a lot more attention on organic social media. This is free and speaks directly to your existing audiences.

## Organic social media

In website terms, your organic traffic is made up of those sessions that have landed on your site 'naturally' (i.e. not via paid or targeted media). Organic social media content is similar: it's the social media content that has no paid spend behind it and is distributed 'naturally' to user's feeds. The process of becoming more visible via organic social media is a much subtler and more unpredictable process than creating paid ads. Unfortunately, there is no checklist to creating organic viral social media content.

Just as you wouldn't go to the cinema just to see the trailers, most social media users say they aren't on social media to look at advertising. The sweet spot between what we as arts marketers want and what social media companies want is organic social content that is immersive, engaging and shareable. This type of content keeps people on the platform longer and generates brand affection, both for the organisation that posted the content (which is good for the organisation in terms of visibility and brand building) and the platform itself (which is good for the companies that run them and their statistics around average monthly users and their attractiveness as an ad platform).

In the next section, we'll look at the different social media platforms, where they came from, who's on them and how their algorithms work. This will help us understand what social media companies care about, which is, broadly speaking, keeping people on the platform longer so that they consume more content, including ads, to generate revenue for the companies.

## Facebook

*Where did this platform come from?*

In 2004, 'TheFacebook' was launched, initially to Harvard students, but rapidly expanding to other universities and, by 2006, to e-mail addresses outside academia.

When it first launched, the site was different to the Facebook we know today:

- Facebook originally had quite random ads, lots of 'meet hot singles' and university-specific ads (like ads for participants in medical trials).
- Facebook launched as a website, not as a mobile app. There was no infinite scroll – you could quite feasibly get to the end of your Facebook notifications and go about your day when there was nothing else to see.
- In 2009, Facebook launched the 'like' button. This was similar to existing sites, such as Reddit's upvote, but it was not as ubiquitous as it is today. (Twitter didn't create a 'like' button until 2015.)
- When you originally created your Facebook profile page, you could enter information about your interests – your favourite films, TV, books, etc., and sometimes follow groups with other people who liked similar things.
- What was super sneaky on Facebook's part (and not well documented) was that, around 2007, Facebook took the words you'd entered as 'things you like' in your bio and subscribed you to follow business pages of companies and brands (that it had gradually been amassing) that corresponded with your interests.

Also in 2007, Facebook began creating its own ad platform. This is where the vast majority of its revenue comes from today and is the key differentiator in profitability between Facebook and X/Twitter. Although X has an ad platform, it is not as lucrative as Facebook's, partly because X users upload much less information about themselves, so it's impossible to do the same level of fine-grained user targeting that's possible on Facebook. Facebook's ad platform allows companies and organisations to target people on Facebook (or Instagram) at a very granular level, including by age, interest and geography.

*What's it doing now?*

There have been lots of news stories over the years about Facebook and countless controversies (most famously the Cambridge Analytica data scandal where millions of Facebook users' data was used – without their consent – to create targeted psychographic political adverts on Facebook to support the 2016 election campaign of Donald Trump (Wikipedia, 2024b)).

Despite this, Facebook still has over three billion monthly active users globally (Statista, 2025), more than any other social media platform. To put that in context, there are only 7.9 billion people in the world and not all of them have regular access to the internet. In the UK, there are 45 million Facebook users and only 67 million people in the country. Facebook is still the only platform where the majority of the UK population have accounts, with the most popular age demographic being 25–34 year olds.

When polled, people tend to say they are on Facebook primarily to keep in touch with friends and family, but also to find out about local events and groups. This makes sense as, of all the platforms, Facebook is the one on which you're most likely to be friends with your parents. Facebook also has tools like 'events' and 'groups' that allow local and special interest networks to organise more easily than on other social platforms.

According to Facebook's 'Most Widely Viewed Content Reports' (Meta, 2024), the posts that did well over the last 2 to 3 years were those that were easy for anyone to engage with and share. A lot of these are quizzes or feature a call to action that only requires users to make a single comment (see Figure 2.1 opposite). Quizzes are one of Facebook's most widely shared content types (although this isn't unique to Facebook). Incidentally, this is how Cambridge Analytica were able to get all their data – through an innocuous-looking 'personality quiz'.

The post in Figure 2.1 isn't cleverly constructed or directly related to the person posting it, but its popularity demonstrates what does well on Facebook: content that's easy to engage with (there is a suggested format for your response) and that tells you something about yourself or is a puzzle/challenge to complete.

Figure 2.2 is a Facebook post I wrote in a cultural sector context that works along similar principles (this was posted the day after Boris Johnson's 'very simple instruction: stay inside' at the start of the UK COVID-19 lockdown).

The key with all social media content is to arrest attention, to make someone stop scrolling. Most people will scan the visual components of your post first, and – if it's interesting – read the text for more context. The visuals are the most important part of your post and the text should build on the interest raised by the visuals.

## Case study 2.1: Video storytelling on social media

*Beks Leary, Senior Content Manager, The National Gallery*

It's easy to fall into the trap of thinking that the video-based social media platforms are TikTok and YouTube. Every platform is after your attention and one of the best ways to get that, and to get users watching ads, is via video. But the lengths and types of video that do

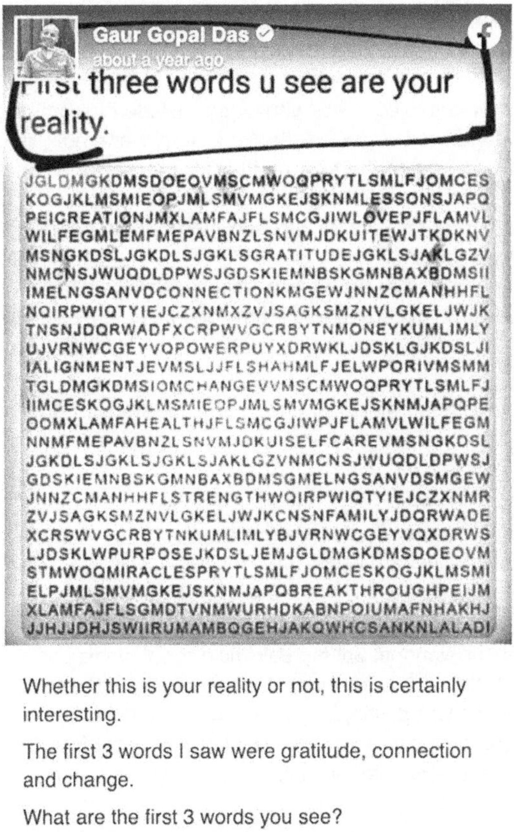


**Figure 2.1** *An example of a popular type of Facebook post (80.6 million content views)*

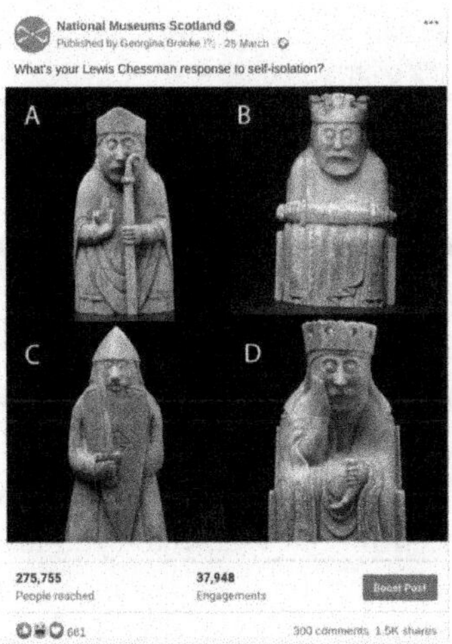


**Figure 2.2** *National Museums Scotland Lewis Chessmen Facebook post*

well differ platform to platform. According to Beks Leary, Senior Content Manager at The National Gallery:

> Facebook video wants to compete with longform video streaming competitors. The video formats compared with YouTube, for example, are more similar than people realise. What's different is where it's optimal for the platform to serve ads within your video, and so – from there – what the optimal length of video is. For YouTube that's upwards of eight minutes, and on Facebook you want to be definitely over one minute, often over three minutes.
>
> I see a lot of people cross-promoting reels on Facebook, but that doesn't really work. Facebook's interested in getting watch time on longer length videos than you typically get from Reels.

I asked Beks about her approach to filming a particular story for distribution on social media: how does she plan footage that can be repurposed in different formats on different channels?

> When we're filming a specific story, we'll typically start with either YouTube or Instagram for our full-length video. If it's YouTube, on average for us that's going to be around 10 minutes. We'll then do around a three-minute cut for Facebook.

Prior to working at The National Gallery, Beks held social media posts at the BBC and the National Theatre. At the BBC, video content was always going to be key, but also the size of the social channels she was posting to gave her an insight into 'the minutiae of how different types of video content perform on a platform-by-platform basis'.

In Beks' view, Facebook is unfairly maligned in the sector:

> There's a perception that it's only older audiences sharing family photos. But the sheer scale of the reach you can achieve with Facebook video means it's not just reaching one demographic. With the exception of the 16–24 year old audience, a well performing Facebook video can reach larger numbers of most age groups, mainly because of the scale that it's distributed at.

## Instagram

*Where did this platform come from?*

Instagram launched in 2010 as a simpler platform to the one we know today. In 2010, there were no Reels or Stories and Instagram's main unique functionality was the ability to quickly add arty filters to square photos. 2010 also saw the beginning of a big growth period in sales of smartphones (Statista, 2023) and it became much easier to take, share and store high quality photos. Instagram was the first major app to offer an easy way to photo edit and make your pictures look cool.

In 2012, Instagram was bought by Meta (the company that owns Facebook). Instagram has since rolled into Meta's highly lucrative ads market and, today, accounts for 42% of Meta's overall ad revenue (Lebow, 2022). It has around two billion monthly active users and is the third most popular social media app after Facebook and YouTube (Search Engine Journal, 2024).

#### *What's it doing now?*

Instagram's algorithm has gone through a lot of changes in the last couple of years. The algorithm favours the newer features, such as Reels and Stories, over feed posts. However, Instagram is also using features like Reels to try and create a TikTok-style discovery experience. Your success with these formats will depend on how well your Reels content performs to a test audience that is not your follower base – if it does well with that test audience, Instagram will distribute your content more widely (but again, not necessarily to your followers or anyone with any prior context on who you are, where you're based and what services you provide).

Most museums will be on Facebook, X and Instagram. Of these, Instagram will typically have the highest organic follower growth and engagement, but it lags behind platforms like TikTok in that regard.

### Twitter/X

#### *Where did this platform come from?*

Twitter launched in 2006, around the time Facebook was expanding out of only providing its service to those at university. The main content that populated the original Twitter feeds were updates ('tweets') from accounts you followed. This was more likely to be authority figures than, for instance, your mum (who's most likely on Facebook). Historically, Twitter has worked well for breaking news, memes and allowing the general public to have a visible dialogue with those in positions of power.

Twitter content was originally predominantly text-based, although today image and video formats are likely to perform better. Initially, posts had to be no more than 140 characters long, but, in 2017, Twitter allowed you to 'thread' multiple tweets together. In 2018, it increased the character count of a single tweet to 280.

There are some great examples of museum-specific Twitter content. Most famously, in 2018, the Museum of English Rural Life (MERL) tweeted a picture of a square-ish looking sheep with the caption 'look at this absolute unit'. The tweet was a huge success, even launching its own range of merchandise. This was one of the first examples of social media content driving global awareness of a local brand and changing visitor demographics in the sector (in this case, ushering in new internet-aware millennials).

In 2020, during the COVID-19 lockdowns, York Museums Trust (YMT) launched a 'Curator Battle'. This was essentially a challenge to find the best object that met a particular theme and included the 'creepiest object', the 'sauciest object', and so on. For each contest, museums across the world would reply on Twitter to YMT's challenge with an object of their own. This created a thread of thematically related objects from collections across the globe. In subsequent analysis of the success of Curator Battle, it was found that the content reached 6.2 million people and generated 1.6 million engagements; plus, one-fifth of the audience engaging with Curator Battle had not engaged with cultural works digitally before (York Museums Trust, n.d.).

In both these cases, we can see how Twitter was successfully used to bring in new audiences at very little cost to the institution (beyond staff time).

### *What's it doing now?*

At the time of writing, X has 586 million monthly active users (about one-fifth of Facebook's figures). It is currently ranked 14th by number of monthly active users after Facebook, Instagram, Snapchat and TikTok (Statista, 2025).

In the UK, 23.3 million people have an X account. Engagement has taken a huge hit since Elon Musk took over in 2022 and the platform has lost around a third of its user base since then (Burn-Murdoch, 2024). In addition, there is an ongoing discussion about the ethics of this platform and its usefulness to cultural organisations. Previous Twitter heavyweights, Monterey Bay Aquarium, talked about their decision to leave the platform:

> When Musk's deal for Twitter closed in late October 2022, we started seeing follower loss and diminishing engagement. Posts that would normally see a thousand likes might get a hundred, and the substance of our replies went from highly engaged and curious to generic or, worse, nothing at all … the Twitter we knew didn't exist anymore. Not to mention the ongoing blue-check verification disaster – suddenly anyone could be Monterey Bay Aquarium and look the part. And as a non-profit, having to shell out $2,000 to $10,000 annually to be a 'Verified Organisation' was a price we weren't ready to pay on a platform that just kept hurting us.
>
> One of the most difficult things to reconcile is that there is no direct replacement for what Twitter used to be in its heyday. There are moments we wish we still had the tool of a tweet to help us reach people, especially the politicians we could @ directly. But having a more diversified social strategy has helped us let go of the past and move on from Twitter.
>
> (Cultural Content, 2024)

The Aquarium has since had viral success on other platforms, including Bluesky and TikTok.

*The Guardian* newspaper in the UK came to a similar conclusion in late 2024:

> We think the benefits of being on X are now outweighed by the negatives and that resources could be better used protecting our journalism elsewhere.
>
> This is something we have been considering for a while given the often disturbing content promoted or found on the platform, including far-right conspiracy theories and racism. The US presidential election campaign served only to underline what we have considered for a long time: that X is a toxic media platform and that its owner, Elon Musk, has been able to use its influence to shape political discourse.
>
> (*The Guardian*, 2024)

Despite organisations moving away from X, there are still some great examples of organisations, like Orkney Library, continuing to get fantastic engagement on the platform.

One of the key characteristics of the platforms we've looked at so far – Facebook, X and Instagram – is that the content you see (certainly in the original iterations of the platforms) is based on those accounts you 'follow'. This is also known as a 'social graph' based platform. YouTube and TikTok are different in this regard as, although they have a 'follow' feature, most people get content on these platforms via the algorithm's recommendations (e.g., the 'For You' page on TikTok or the YouTube homepage). This is a more dynamic discovery mechanism than social graph based platforms as it's not restricted to the people/accounts a user already knows about. It is designed to optimise for attention, not the relevance of the personal connection between you and another account.

In the following section, we'll look at YouTube and TikTok – and also Threads – and what they add to the social media mix.

## YouTube

### *Where did this platform come from?*

In 2005, YouTube looked quite similar to Google (see Figure 2.3 on the next page). It had a large search bar and relied a lot more on the user's input to surface content. Google did in fact buy YouTube in 2006, but has since then been careful to differentiate YouTube as a discovery engine and Google as a search engine.

If we fast forward to the YouTube homepage today, one of the most immediately apparent changes is that it now customises the content it shows you based on what you've watched before and what it knows about you generally (e.g., your location data and whether you're on a mobile or desktop).

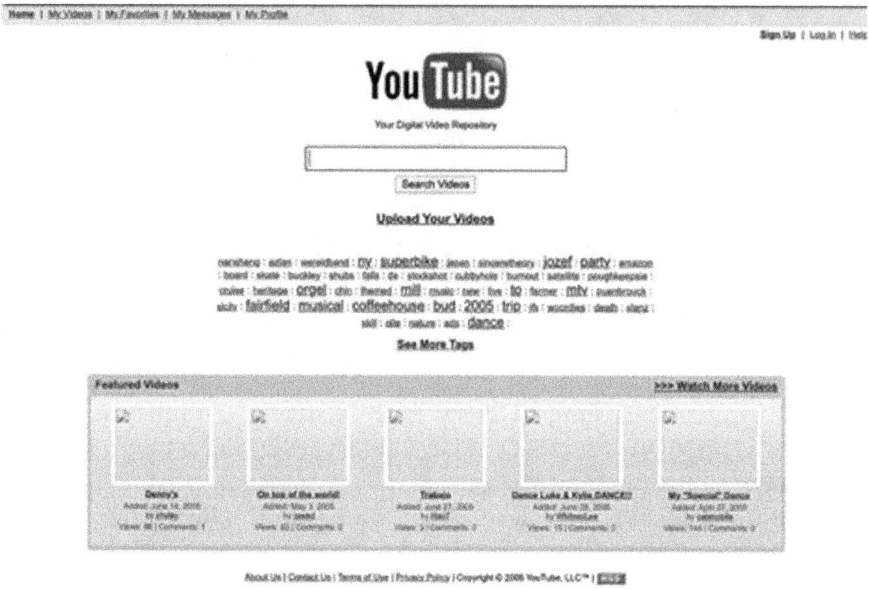


**Figure 2.3** *YouTube's homepage in 2005*

### *Who's on the platform?*

Today, 2.5 billion people in the world use YouTube on a monthly basis, making it the next largest platform after Facebook (which has 3 billion monthly online users). Within the UK, that number shifts to 41 million people (compared to 45 million Facebook users); this is a high penetration considering the population of the UK is 67 million.

One interesting feature of YouTube as a platform for cultural sector organisations is that it has a more balanced gender and age split than Facebook and Instagram typically do. In every cultural sector Facebook and Instagram account I've looked at (with the exception of military and science museums), there is a significant gender bias towards female followers, with a typical age profile of around 35 on Instagram and 40+ on Facebook. YouTube viewer stats always have a more even split of male/female viewers and a much more even breakdown across the age brackets.

For most cultural sector accounts, at least 95% of their YouTube views will come from non-followers. This means that discovery engine platforms like YouTube and TikTok provide a higher likelihood that you'll reach audiences that don't already know about you organically, but have a topical interest in the content you're creating.

*How does the YouTube algorithm work?*

YouTube is a business and one that's been growing and evolving for over 16 years. It's in the business of monetising your attention: the longer you're on YouTube viewing ads, the more money it gets. The algorithm wants to understand what the content is about, so that it can match it with users who have similar interests. So, how does YouTube do it? How does it keep people on the platform wanting more?

To explain this, we're going to go back in time and look at how YouTube has evolved.

*2005–2012: All about the views*

From 2005 to 2012, the YouTube algorithm largely prioritised videos with the most views. This incentivised creators to make videos that looked interesting but didn't necessarily deliver interesting content. This resulted in a lot of clickbait, which in turn frustrated users and lead to them spending less time on the platform. All this, of course, meant less revenue for YouTube.

*2012: Watch time*

Around 2012, YouTube changed its algorithm to prioritise watch time. These changes led creators to focus on content with a higher watch time. From YouTube's perspective, this was better in terms of keeping people on the platform longer, but there was still a problem with retention at the end of a video (i.e., people leaving the platform once they'd finished watching a video).

*2016: Machine learning*

In 2016, YouTube published a paper on how it was using machine learning to update its algorithm. Machine learning and neural networks were fed into the algorithm to create a recommendation engine for subsequent video views.

Today, YouTube recommends videos based on what it thinks a user is interested in, based on their history and similar content. This means that what you see in your 'feed' on the homepage when you're logged in will be different to what other people see.

*What does this mean for your YouTube content creation?*

YouTube ranks factors like the watch time, the percentage of people who see your content and click on it (known as 'impressions click-through-rate' or 'impressions CTR') and the view count of your videos to get a sense of how 'good' your content is for a general audience.

It has to work out what subjects your video covers in order to know who to recommend it to, so make sure you're using well optimised keywords that correspond with terms people are actually searching for. It's also helpful if your description field gives the full context of the video and doesn't just assume users already know what, for example, a particular promotional trailer refers to.

### *YouTube series*

YouTube has seen many creators become hugely successful purely through their skill in creating content 'series' for YouTube. A 'series' is a recurring video type with a custom branded thumbnail and a repeated series title and narrative structure. Amelia Dimoldenberg (creator of 'Chicken Shop Dates') and Now We Feast (creator of 'Hot Ones') are two such examples. In both cases, the name of their YouTube series is as famous, if not more famous, than the name of their channel.

Legacy print publishing houses, including *Vogue*, *Vanity Fair* and *GQ*, have upped their game to keep up, designing unique YouTube series to bolster their presence on the platform. Examples include *Vogue*'s '73 Questions' series with different celebrities, *Vanity Fair*'s 'XYZ Celebrity Takes a Lie Detector Test' and *GQ*'s '10 Things XYZ Celebrity Can't Live Without'.

As we know, YouTube tries to understand what users might want to watch next so that it can recommend other videos and keep people on the platform for longer. Series are gold dust in this regard as they provide YouTube with great criteria for recommending something similar to watch afterwards (i.e., something else in the series).

### *How does YouTube understand what your content is about?*

YouTube has a number of different data sources that you can control:

- title
- description
- tags
- thumbnail.

You need to ensure you are putting the keywords in these fields that you would expect to find in search. If you're not optimising your videos with the right keywords, no one will find you.

Free sources of keyword data are available. For example, YouTube itself provides you with the terms your viewers currently search for and the top performing keywords people have entered to land on your content. However, while both of these let you see what's working best with what you're currently doing, neither gives you data that is granular enough to redevelop your strategy around high volume, low competition terms that correspond with the expertise your institution holds.

There are competitive search intelligence tools, for example SEMRush or Ahrefs, give you this data, but they do come with a price tag.

### *Shorts*

YouTube has a 'short-form' video format called Shorts. These videos are similar to TikTok and Instagram Reels, but with less functionality. Shorts are generally one minute long and typically get less views than the same video posted on Reels and TikTok.

Examples of some of the more effective Shorts content include:

- a high octane emotional moment – for example, the National Theatre are expert at pairing high drama snippets from their shows with famous actors and a relatable quote
- a powerful and condensed one-minute snippet from a full length YouTube video
- more trend-based content – users' browsing behaviour on Shorts is similar to on Reels and TikTok.

### *Thumbnails*

When you go to YouTube.com, you will see a grid of videos. Each of these videos is made up of a static image, title, length, date and a short description and when you hover over a particular video, it begins to autoplay. The name for the static image is a 'thumbnail'. YouTube can create a thumbnail for you by automatically selecting a frame from the video (which you can also pick). However, it is good practice to create a custom thumbnail. The custom image helps capture the content of the video and raise interest in a way that a single frame from a video is unlikely to do.

There is a lot written on the internet about YouTube thumbnails. The most followed YouTuber in the world is Mr Beast. Mr Beast (real name James Stephen Donaldson) has said he spends 'between $5,000 to $10,000 per video on thumbnails to get the image right. Because the thumbnail makes the difference between 50 million views or 200 million' (Assetpreneurs, 2022).

The YouTuber Channel Makers looked at two hundred Mr Beast thumbnails to determine what he's doing that's working so effectively at converting impressions to clicks (YouTube, 2023). He concludes that thumbnail best practice (for Mr Beast at least) amounts to:

- using 0–4 words of text in the thumbnail itself
- using an image that communicates a single idea, which – in tandem with the title – should hint at some kind of tension, jeopardy or surprise, but not quite communicate the outcome behind the premise
- having a recognisable 'face' to your YouTube content
- using services like TubeBuddy (www.tubebuddy.com) to A/B test different thumbnails.

Interestingly, these thumbnail findings overlap with the findings of technologist Trung Phan, who describes how Netflix autopicks thumbnails to generate click-through on their platform. Netflix had found that the 'greatest lever' in converting browsing users to viewers was how compelling the content thumbnails were (Phan, 2021).

Netflix originally used promotional metadata images, frequently repurposed from show posters and billboard signs, but they found that these didn't work well in a streaming context. So, they built an algorithm to score millions of frames within the film or TV series, scoring each frame for things like brightness, nudity potential and composition, and used this to generate their own custom thumbnails for shows. What they found was that expressive traits, main characters and brightness were winning combinations.

It's common for cultural sector videos to use a video still as a thumbnail. This will negatively affect the number of people who click through to a video. Building an arresting thumbnail is an important skill of creating effective YouTube content.

### *YouTube and the cultural sector: addressing the weaknesses*

YouTube is an underused platform in the sector. The platform is great for growing engaged audiences, reaching a diverse global audience and improving the depth of engagement with those audiences. YouTube accounts that are achieving this have two key features:

1 Expert understanding of the subject they're dealing with.
  An understanding of the audience they're talking to.
2 An in-depth understanding of YouTube, its algorithms, discovery mechanisms and best practice.

The cultural sector has an expert understanding of subject matter but is weaker at knowing how to translate that to appropriate online formats for different audiences. The sector needs to understand how to communicate expert knowledge more effectively on YouTube and so capitalise on the potential opportunities the platform offers.

Much more work should also be done in the sector in terms of working out where search opportunities exist (for the topics organisations have expertise in) and using that data to build an effective video strategy. Data is a powerful tool and the sector needs to harness that power.

### TikTok

#### *Where did this platform come from?*

TikTok started in China and the earliest version of the platform was an app called Musical.ly. Musical.ly allowed you to record lip synching videos between 15 seconds and one minute long. (This explains a lot of the early content and head scratching when we first came across it.)

In 2016, the company ByteDance Ltd (also Chinese) created a rival app called 'Douyin' (meaning 'vibrating sound') that did something very similar to Musical.ly but just in China. In 2017, it created an international version of the app called TikTok. Just two months after launching TikTok, ByteDance bought up Musical.ly. The following year, it merged the app with Douyin and Musical.ly ceased to exist.

There have been significant concerns raised about the privacy of TikTok data as it's unclear what ByteDance does with user data and – in particular – if it shares it with the Chinese government. TikTok collects data such as your IP address, mobile carrier, unique device identifiers, keystroke patterns, location data and biometric data, including 'faceprints and voiceprints' (TikTok, 2020). The platform is currently banned in India and on government devices in countries including the UK, US, the European Parliament, Canada, Australia, New Zealand and Norway.

#### *Who's on the platform?*

A lot of people. Despite all the above, and being the newest of the platforms we've talked about so far, in 2024, TikTok had 1 billion monthly active users (roughly double that of X and one-third of Facebook).

The UK has 23 million TikTok users and around one-third of the population has an account. In terms of age demographics, the most popular age segment is 18–24, which is younger than the average age of users on other platforms.

COVID-19 vastly accelerated TikTok's uptake and usage and TikTok was the most downloaded app in 2020, 2021 and 2022 (it came in second to Instagram in 2023).

TikTok is not just influential in terms of number of downloads. The amount of time people are spending on the platform is also very different from what we see on platforms like Facebook and Instagram. Children spend an average of two hours per day on TikTok (Social Shepherd, 2024), which is a much higher level of engagement than the equivalent metric on more established platforms.

### *What's it good for?*

TikTok content benefits from time spent on the platform. It takes a while to get used to but there is lots of learning and cultural sector-appropriate content to explore on there. #ArtTok, #BookTok and #EduTok are some good examples for getting a feel for how to present educational content on the channel.

One myth attached to the platform is that you have to be up on and react to the latest TikTok 'trends'. While certain trends (e.g., sounds and dances) can present a good opportunity for cultural sector organisations to reach a wider audience, if they're done badly they can fall flat.

It's also perfectly practical to plan content in advance with planned calendar tie-ins. This has been the Black Country Living Museum's modus operandi on TikTok; not constantly publishing and reacting to short-term trends, but planning a whole 'season' of content at a time.

There are different approaches to creating cultural sector-appropriate TikTok content. For example:

- having a distinctive 'face' or presenter of your content
- character-led accounts (certain actors at Past Pleasures – www.facebook.com/bringhistorytolife – have become TikTok celebrities this way and crop up across multiple cultural sector accounts)
- high emotion snippets of performances
- tie-ins to key calendar dates
- duplicating video content from Instagram to TikTok (although, note that this is unlikely to work as well as a TikTok-first approach).

If this all still sounds too alien, I'd thoroughly recommend Mary McGillivray's *TikTok Creator Directory* (McGillivray, 2021). This is a directory of young active content creators on the platform eager to work with cultural sector institutions.

## Threads

*Where did it come from?*

As we know, social media companies want the attention of users so they can monetise that attention in the form of ads revenue. Meta is the company that owns Facebook, Instagram and WhatsApp (which I haven't included as a 'social media' example here, although, in terms of usage, it is in second place worldwide, just after Facebook) (Buffer.com, 2024). Meta therefore owns a sizeable chunk of the social media attention market, but that top spot is under threat from 'discovery engine' platforms like YouTube and TikTok. TikTok, in particular, has experienced faster growth than Facebook recently, has much greater depth of engagement (in terms of time spent on the app) and is popular with a young audience (whereas Facebook's popularity is associated with an older demographic). This doesn't look good for Meta's long-term dominance in the market.

Enter Threads. Threads is a direct rival to Twitter/X rather than to TikTok. The launch seems to have been motivated by a land grab for dominance in the social space. The timing of the public release seemed rushed – it went live with no accessibility features or web version and privacy concerns delayed it being released in the EU. The launch appeared to be timed to capitalise on a period of instability at X, rather than around any user need for yet another social platform.

*Who's on the platform?*

Threads quickly acquired 30 million users within 24 hours of launching. This was mainly because it was easy for users to create a Threads account from their Instagram account. Six weeks later and the number of daily active users had dropped by 80% (to 2.3 million).

Since then, the platform has stabilised and commentators (Newton, 2023) point out that for current news stories (like the Israel-Hamas conflict) it is a more reliable source of real-time news than X is. While X has fired almost all of its content moderation team and allowed anyone to pay for verified/authority status (leading to a proliferation of misinformation), Threads has given free verification to journalists. Similarly, while X has hidden link previews, Threads shows the headlines of links.

There's a convincing argument that Threads could own the void left by what Twitter 'used to be', albeit this time owned by Meta and tied into the ad revenue business. Similar arguments have been made about Bluesky, one of the newest social media platforms. Time will tell.

Unusually for a platform, Threads has a male skew (68%). It is most popular with younger audiences aged 18–25.

*What does this mean for your content creation?*

As with other platforms, it's worth being aware that Meta hasn't exactly been transparent about what it's doing with all your data. That grey area is particularly murky when it comes to Threads and delayed the release of the app in the EU (Twitter, 2023a). It's also worth knowing that you can't leave Threads once you've joined, at least not without deleting your Instagram account.

Threads is still evolving and it feels too soon to judge if there are significant opportunities here for cultural organisations. It's possible that Meta will take the platform down if it doesn't prove to be a success.

At the launch of Threads, most cultural organisation content on the platform was puns on the Threads name. London Museum is typical in this regard, they posted on the day of Threads going live in the UK with the caption 'we were due some new threads', with a picture of a vintage pack of bobbins. The post gained 123 likes. A year later (and at the time of writing), this is still the only post the museum has put on the platform (www.threads.net/@wearelondonmuseum).

Some cultural sector accounts have been doing a great trade in creating meme-based content on the platform. The National Gallery pairs relatable captions with works in its collection. Recent examples include: 'Patiently waiting for Aperol Spritz season …' paired with 'Portrait of a Lady' by Caspar Netscher (Threads, 2023); and 'Name a better duo, we'll wait …' with 'The Ambassadors' by Hans Holbein the Younger (Threads, 2023). These associate internet parlance ('we'll wait'), topical references (Aperols) and common relatable situations with great works of art in their collection. It's a simple way of generating empathy and relevancy with their art and uses a format that works well in the interface Threads provides.

Other accounts are taking a more proactive and distinctive stance on the platform and are using it like a less monitored version of X. Channel 4 is a good example: one of their posts reads 'Threads is 60% people asking if Threads is still going, 10% people just having a nice time and 30% social media managers for brands losing their minds while their bosses forget that Threads is a thing.' (Since taken down, a screenshot of the post appears in Cultural Content, 2023.)

For now, it's still unclear where Threads will go. Will Meta try to make it more of a direct rival to TikTok (e.g., by bolstering engagement discovery) or will it try to become like the best bits of 'old Twitter': a platform for the public to talk openly with those in positions of power, barmy memes and up-to-the-minute news?

This uncertainty makes it difficult to know how cultural sector accounts can best make use of Threads. It stands to reason that those that build a following now will have an easier time of things if the platform does become more popular down the line, but there's also the possibility that it never takes off and that investment of resource is wasted.

Case study 2.2 below is from Steven Franklin, former Digital Engagement Officer at The National Archives. You might know Steven from his previous role tweeting from Egham Museum in 2020–1, creating the 'Choose Your Own Adventure' Twitter thread and the Egham Oddity podcast. In January 2022, Steven launched The National Archives on TikTok. Since then, he's grown the channel so that – in just five months – it has accrued 2.5 million views, 350k likes and 35k followers. In the case study, Steven tells us how he achieved this. This is followed by Case study 2.3, where Caspian Turner, Founder of Accessible by Design, discusses accessibility best practice on social media.

## Case study 2.2: Building The National Archives' TikTok to 2.25 million views in five months

*Steven Franklin, then Digital Engagement Officer, The National Archives*

TikTok ... the Home of Gen Z, ring lights, trending sounds and dances and content that often leaves you feeling equally bemused and amused. It's safe to say that, on the surface at least, TikTok looks and feels like the Wild West of the social media landscape. It's the platform that starts blaring out noise as soon as it's opened; the platform that has no sense of interconnected coherency, fuelled by the immediate adrenaline rush of dopamine hits for creators and consumers alike. The platform where there is always an 'in-joke' in the form of a trending sound.

For the newcomer, TikTok can be an overwhelming place to inhabit. However, the platform offers incredibly high returns for relatively little investment and the possibility of doing the impossible – that is, *going viral* – has never been more possible.

It is no surprise then that there has been an explosion of cultural organisations that have jumped onto the TikTok bandwagon. The desire to put content in places our audiences frequent, mixed with a collective desire to remain culturally relevant, has acted as the sector's clarion call. Fortunately, the sector has also witnessed the astronomical success of early adopters such as the Black Country Living Museum and English Heritage, followed by anecdotal accounts of increased visits by younger demographics. The wider sector now had the beginnings of a blueprint for success and a trailblazing path to follow.

In 2022 The National Archives launched on TikTok. By May 2022, we had accrued over 32,000 followers, been watched over 2.5 million times, received close to 350,000 likes and posted over 100 videos. One of these videos – focusing on some rude mediaeval marginalia – has had over 1.3 million views! Our TikTok journey has been quite a ride, but also a lot of fun.

Prior to posting our first video, a lot of time was dedicated to thinking about what content streams we might create. A key part of this was seeing what content other cultural organisations, brand accounts and popular creators were making. Our rationale was simple: if it is working for them, then surely it could work for us.

### Individual creators

A big part of TikTok is its focus on the personality of the presenter. Through a combination of green screen effects, cut away shots and voiceovers, creators can make mini history documentaries. There is an onus on the presenter to be a key driver in the selling of the content through a mixture of humour, authenticity, energy and engaging storytelling. Accounts such as Mary McGillivray (@_theiconoclass) and Alice Loxton (@history_alice) provided a good source of inspiration when it came to balancing humour and digital storytelling. Their success also helped to reinforce the idea that TikTok isn't all about dances and sounds. It is possible to communicate historical ideas on the platform and to use it as a tool for education when the content is framed correctly.

### Brand accounts

Outside of the cultural sector, various brand accounts have risen to TikTok stardom. Duolingo and Ryanair have shown that consistency of content, in terms of theme and visual identity, is important. Ryanair's follower count has now crossed the 1 million mark and much of this has been down to the way they have consistently paired a face filter – where eyes and mouths are transposed onto the fronts of planes – with trending sounds. Their content is irreverent and often leans into the tropes that people criticise them for, such as the lack of legroom or charging for extra baggage.

Ryanair's content has proven popular because it's relatable. It has struck a chord with the public and the conversations they have about the brand. Like all social channels, a good mixture of relatability and irreverence tends to go a long way and, at the very least, raises a small smile.

### Costumed interpretation and character-based content

When it comes to costumed interpretation on TikTok, everyone automatically thinks of the Black Country Living Museum and their cast of Midlands-based characters. Equally, English Heritage have deployed the celebrity of Mrs Crocombe to great effect on TikTok.

Followers of The National Archives account will have seen that we also dipped our toe into the waters of costumed interpretation. The release of the 1921 Census of England and Wales offered us the perfect opportunity to bring some '20s people' to life. If the 1921 Census provided us with the characters, then it was our hope that through the power of social media and storytelling we could bring some of the era of the 1920s to life.

We found a company with experience of producing similar content for other heritage organisations – in this case English Heritage – and worked with them to bring eight different characters (and their occupations) to life. We have produced four to five one-minute videos for each character, all designed to provide a brief glimpse into what their lives would have been like and the issues they would have faced. The videos are deliberately short, in keeping with the transient nature of TikTok.

### You have to find your own way

The rules of engagement on TikTok are in many ways no different to other social platforms. Be consistent; be relatable; be engaging; but, most importantly, be authentic. The challenge with TikTok is that the form of communication is radically different. Rather than relying on the wit of the written word, we now find ourselves needing to factor in the personality of the presenter and other visual storytelling considerations.

Seeing what is working for other organisations is a helpful way into this new world. The safety blanket of tried and tested content formats is reassuring, especially in the early days when issues around production are at the forefront of your mind. But imitation only gets you so far – the iteration of content ideas bears far greater reward.

The key to TikTok does not come through overthinking. The key to TikTok comes from taking the plunge, being brave and making content that best reflects the organisation. Some of it will bomb. Some of it will stick. Some of it will go BIG. But that's the fun and the challenge of it. Make content that is authentic, interesting and quirky. Do this in ways that keep people watching and elicit a response. That's the key to TikTok.

## Case study 2.3: A guide to accessibility best practice on social media

*Caspian Turner, Founder, Accessible by Design*

**It is fine to use emojis** – but don't overuse them. Using repeated emojis, as seen in the Red Flag trend (🚩🚩🚩) (Ritschel, 2021), can be extremely frustrating for screen reader users.

**Don't use ASCII text** as this is not interpreted by most screen readers. A screen reader will read a post as though the text doesn't appear at all, which can lead to confusion, lack of information or misinformation. An example of ASCII text appears in a Domino's Pizza (Twitter, 2023b) tweet. The text reads:

i'm just gonna take ur opinions about pineapple

💭
\(´･_･ \)
(      )
 く く

and put them in the garbage

( ´･_･`)
(\    )\
> > 🗑

The point of a post like this is to create a picture using punctuation. It's funny and an unusual way of telling a text-based story on X. However, understandably, a screen reader has no idea what to make of this.

**Use Pascal Case when writing hashtags**. This is capitalising the first character of each word in the hashtag – for example, #ThisIsPascalCase – and is sometimes incorrectly referred to as 'Camel Case'. Capitalising the first character of each word makes the word more easily recognisable for sighted users, but it also makes it more likely that screen reader software will decipher the different words within the hashtag rather than reading everything as a single indecipherable string of text.

**Add alternative text to your images!** Alt text can be added on every social media platform, but there's a tendency now to also include an image description in the captions, particularly on LinkedIn and Instagram. For more information on this see Supercool (2020).

**Ensure that videos are captioned** as auto-captioning is not always accurate. Be sure to verify the captions are correct as it can result in some unfortunate miscaptions if not. YouTube allows you to edit the auto captions in the video editor. This benefits many people including anyone for whom English is not their first language, people who are d/Deaf or people who don't have their headphones and are on public transport!
**The same writing guidelines apply to social media as to any website copy**. Try to keep sentences concise (usually 15–25 words). Avoid using unnecessarily complex language or unfamiliar terms. Bear in mind that the average national reading level is that expected of a 9-year-old.

Within GLAM institutions, when thinking about how to make our digital content more visible, we tend to focus on our platforms: our website and our social media. But for knowledge-based institutions, Wikipedia represents a huge strategic opportunity. I'm reminded of a quote from Loic Tallon (then Chief Digital Officer at The Met) that appears in *The Digital Future of Museums*:

> We have Henry VIII's armour, which is viewed 180 times a month on our website. But the Wikipedia entry on Henry VIII is viewed 405,000 times a month and The Met's object is part of that article. And while the experience of the armour is very different within the context of a larger Wikipedia article, and as one of 22 images on that page, the access to the artwork in that content is really important. It's doing it in ways, in languages, in context which we cannot replicate internally.
>
> (Winesmith and Anderson, 2020, 116)

I wanted to learn more about how Wikipedia can be used to best effect for GLAM institutions, so I contacted Martin Poulter, who I previously worked alongside when he was Wikimedian-in-Residence at the Bodleian Libraries, University of Oxford. Martin is now a part-time Wikimedian-in-Residence at the Khalili Foundation. In Case study 2.4 below, he talks us through how cultural institutions can use Wikipedia to make their collections more visible.

## Case study 2.4: Seizing the opportunity Wikipedia provides the cultural sector

*Martin Poulter, Wikimedian in Residence, Khalili Foundation*

For many well-known cultural institutions, the most common way the public encounters digital images of their collections is on Wikipedia. This is especially true of the Khalili Collections and the Bodleian Libraries, two institutions that have employed me as a Wikimedian-in-Residence. The largest numbers in each institution's metrics report are the Wikipedia image views: more than 40 million in a year for the Bodleian and 78 million in a year for the Khalili Collections. These are views by human beings, from figures published monthly by the Wikimedia Foundation.

Social media might reach thousands of people in a short time, while a Wikipedia article on a cultural topic might only have a dozen readers per day. Yet the time dimension turns out to be much more important. Social media is ephemeral and even a viral post quickly becomes yesterday's news. Over a decade, and over a large number of different articles, those Wikipedia views accumulate.

The audience we are reaching is not just large but diverse. Images from the Khalili Collections are used across 97 languages and some of the articles I have written have appeared in languages such as Arabic, Persian and Indonesian. I work only in English – Wikipedia's volunteers have done all the translation.

The reason for this immense reach comes down to two lessons. One is that we are putting content (images, captions and catalogue descriptions) where people are looking for them. The other is that we are sharing content in a form that can be reused, inviting a wider community to find uses that we would never think of. Many thousands of cultural collections are represented on the wiki platforms, which are gradually collecting vast numbers of digital media and catalogue data. This is why Wikipedia and its sister sites have a central role to play in the future of resource discovery.

### Putting content where people will see it

In my experience, when most cultural professionals consider Wikipedia, they only consider improving the article about their institution. This is a bad idea for two reasons. Firstly, Wikipedia has conflict of interest rules that strongly discourage editing an article about your employer. Wikipedians are alert for anything that looks like promotion or PR and anyone talking up their institution will be perceived as working against the community rather than with it. You can request changes to an article by posting on its Talk page; it is up to volunteer editors whether to accept that request.

More importantly, the article about your institution is not how you achieve enormous public reach, although it may convert people who have merely heard of your institution to people with a better idea of what it does. What Wikipedia can do is convert the audience that has never heard of you at all into one that has heard of you and has at least some idea of what is in your collection. If you have content about places, people or periods of history, you could be helping to improve Wikipedia's open knowledge about those topics, while getting credit.

There are Wikipedia articles getting huge readerships because anyone curious about the topic is going there, whether for their school homework, background knowledge for their current Netflix show or to settle a pub debate. Table 2.1 on the next page shows ten articles and the number of views they get in a year, all of them include images from the Khalili Collections.

Hundreds of articles have been improved with content from the eight Khalili Collections. These can be quite obscure: for example, a Sultan whose article lacked an image, but for whom the Collections have a pendant decorated with his portrait. The more niche articles might only be getting a few visitors a day, but their views add up, making a 'long tail'. Articles have embedded images, which appear as a thumbnail with caption, linked to a larger image, plus information about the photographed object. The information that goes with the image can include the source institution's logo and web links.

### Quality as well as quantity

One way we have reached a large audience is by getting images or links to the front page of English Wikipedia, which gets nearly five million views per day. On this front page, there are

**Table 2.1** *View count for different Wikipedia pages that include Khalili Collections images*

| Article | Views per year |
|---|---|
| Alexander the Great | 4.6 million |
| Mughal Empire | 2.4 million |
| Kaaba | 2.2 million |
| History of Palestine | 2.2 million |
| Chrysanthemum | 731 thousand |
| Sine and Cosine | 547 thousand |
| Kimono | 418 thousand |
| Mortar and Pestle | 372 thousand |
| Meiji Era | 347 thousand |
| Astrolabe | 328 thousand |

sections for 'Today's featured article', 'Today's featured picture', 'Did you know …' (which displays facts from recently created or improved articles) and 'On this day'. For each of these sections, there is a formal process for choosing what is featured, which normally involves some kind of quality review. These reviews are carried out by volunteers, so patience is required; some reviews can take months.

Whereas getting to the front page of most other sites is about being topical, Wikipedia has a completely different agenda: knowledge shared for its own sake. They are very happy to highlight an interesting fact about a Meiji decorative artist or a 17th-century Persian manuscript if the article is written in the appropriate style and properly sourced.

When articles or digital media are reviewed and showcased in this way, another consequence is that they come to the attention of volunteers who might translate them into other languages. This is one, but not the most valuable, way we reach other language communities.

**Putting content where people can reuse it**

There are 300 language versions of Wikipedia, each maintained by its own volunteer community. This is one key advantage of the platform for reaching a large public audience. However good your online catalogue is, there are billions of people who cannot read it or whose access depends on unreliable machine translation.

Khalili Collections images are used across 97 languages. Sometimes this happens because an English article is translated into another language, along with its embedded images. For the most part, we reach other languages because we have shared a large number of images in a way that makes them findable and reusable.

The digital media repository used by all the versions of Wikipedia and many other educational sites is Wikimedia Commons. It is initially surprising that adding images to Wikipedia requires you to visit a different site, but Wikimedia is a connected ecosystem of sites with different functions. Thankfully, they all accept the same log-in. Wikimedia Commons only accepts 'Free Cultural Works'. This means that non-commercial licences or no-derivatives licences are unacceptable.

The upload form lets you add up to 50 files at once, copying metadata across them if needed. For larger uploads, there are dedicated software tools. From the Khalili Collections, I have bulk-uploaded 1,500 images. From the Bodleian Libraries, I shared 8,000. Other institutions have enabled much larger bulk uploads. Each uploaded image has metadata about the depicted object, including a link to its entry in the source institution's online catalogue. So, by uploading one thousand images, we create one thousand incoming links to the catalogue.

A key to success on Wikimedia Commons is findability. It is not enough to simply upload the files: they have to be described and categorised so that users seeking to illustrate a topic will find them. With over 100 million files, many of them shared from cultural collections, the category structure is a bit chaotic but very fine grained. If you want 'Egrets in art of Japan', 'Dragon-shaped door handles' or '17th-century paintings of standing women at full length', there are categories for each. Gradually, over many months, the Commons volunteers and I have added Khalili images to these and nearly 1,500 other categories.

A delightful surprise of working on this platform is that volunteers on Arabic Wikipedia, Persian Wikipedia and Indonesian Wikipedia have nominated some of my uploaded images for review, badged them as Featured Pictures and included them as Featured Picture of the Day on the front pages of their respective sites. This reflects the technical and aesthetic quality of the images and their usefulness for illustrating educational materials. It also helps that I have shared metadata about the artworks in a form that those other languages can make use of.

## Sharing data across languages

The Wikimedia communities do not just aim to make popular websites; part of their mission is 'knowledge as a service'. An example of this is the way that Wikimedia Commons supplies digital media to many different sites. The best example is Wikidata, a store of billions of facts in a form. These include the properties of an artwork: its date of creation, place of origin, material and what it depicts.

Wikidata stores facts in a language-independent way and converts them to specific languages on-the-fly. For instance, an image in Wikimedia Commons can be set up to draw its metadata from Wikidata, presenting the information in the user's language. For the Khalili Collections bulk upload, I first represented the artworks on Wikidata, then told Wikimedia Commons which objects are depicted in each image. A reader of Arabic or of Japanese, even though they cannot read the narrative description, can get an idea of what each artwork is and where it came from.

Wikidata freely shares its data and gives multiple ways to view it, including interactive visualisations like maps and timelines. New interfaces appear all the time, including chatbot or voice interfaces. Wikidata's openness, and the ease of creating datasets or code, make it an ideal basis for the next generation of innovative interfaces, whatever those turn out to be and whether they come from the corporate world, academia or hobbyists.

## The long term

It will not be good news if the future of cultural resource discovery is a platform controlled by a mega-corporation; they have no incentive to link to GLAM institutions, pushing traffic away from their own site. Publicly funded projects can create impressive aggregators, but they are usually focused on one country or continent, not truly international or intercultural. Wikipedia and the other Wikimedia sites are truly a commons, combining the virtues of open access, open participation and broad scope. Their downside is that they are messy and incomplete and permanently under construction.

Institutions can completely ignore the Wikimedia platforms, just as they could in principle ignore the web or social media, but the key disadvantage is the same: you will be spoken about, but won't be part of the conversation. Institutions should at least take an interest in how their collections are represented in this dataset. If you have self-portraits by women, or paintings of horses, or portraits of people playing musical instruments, can they be found using the tools that people are building around Wikidata?

Wikipedia is a long-term project. It is sustained not by sponsors or public funding but by the goodwill of its readers. If you create an article that is not in the correct house style or backed up with the right kind of citations, you should expect that it will eventually be cut down, rewritten or even deleted. On the other hand, if you write in the style and quality the Wikipedia community wants, they will value it, showcase it and protect it from vandals. I can point to text on Wikipedia that I wrote 15 years ago and will still likely be there decades from now.

I have a sense that this is a huge missed opportunity for the sector as a whole: a chance to get image views, public awareness and continuing kudos for the institution. Why would we not make sure our collections and curatorial expertise gets the greatest lasting benefit for its public profile?

# Part 2
# Usability

In Part 1, we looked at the discoverability of digital content – that is, how to get more people to see your content online.

Part 2 looks at how to improve the experience those users have when they get there.

In Chapter 3 we explore what web visitors need from different kinds of web pages and extrapolate from there how to design and create content that matches their expectations. We look at the homepage, the About page, exhibition pages and collections pages. There are case studies from Manchester Collective on how to design a performance page and from accessibility consultant Caspian Turner on best practice for your accessibility web page. Finally, we have a case study from Rachel Mapplebeck and her experience growing online giving for cultural organisations, she takes us through how to create an effective online donation ask.

In Chapter 4 we move on to thinking about a website transformation process from start to finish. We look at some of the research techniques you will want to be aware of, such as content auditing, usability testing, surveys and navigation testing. We examine how to engage stakeholders in a process of transformation like this. We end this section with a case study from Museums Galleries Scotland taking you through their website transformation process and how they embedded inclusion at every stage.

CHAPTER 3

# What Users Need From Different Parts of Your Website

What do users need when they're on different parts of your website? It's difficult to know unless you've tested it out. I've conducted a lot of testing with users, across a range of page types, and it's clear that there's often a difference between:

- what users want to know and hear about, and
- what GLAMs want to communicate to users.

In this chapter, we'll look at common page types for the cultural sector and outline the most common user needs. We'll then consider what this means in terms of translating those user insights into how you design the pages.

## About pages

It is a truth universally acknowledged that, if you want to delay a website launch, simply start a conversation about what should be on the new 'About Us' page. About pages are hard because, like homepages, everyone has an opinion on them. Added to that, you have the problem that some cultural institutions (particularly museums) are not very good at defining what they are as institutions. It took the International Council of Museums (ICOM) two years and four rounds of consultations to come up with a definition of 'a museum' (ICOM, 2022).

One of the easiest mistakes to make with an About page (and with web content more generally) is to write about what you think your head of department will sign off most easily, not what your user wants to read. This tends to result in About pages leading with internally facing mission and vision statements and not what a user landing on this page might want to know.

## Why do users visit your About page?

In general, when people arrive on your About page, they want to know:

- what you are (think animal/mineral/vegetable or look at the first sentence of your Wikipedia entry and try and improve on that)
- where you are
- a few key details on your historical significance (with a hyperlink to a fuller page on history)
- why you exist (what you do and why)
- what's it to them/why should they care/why do you exist in terms of serving your public?
- links to staff pages and policy and strategy pages.

Sector professionals visiting an About page may want more specialist information. For example:

- the strategic plan and/or annual review
- links to staff pages
- contact details
- the history of the institution.

Generally, sector professionals are a fraction of your total audience and tend to be over-catered for as their needs are more intuitive to other museum staff. The pages they want usually sit most happily as child pages that live underneath or are linked to on the About page.

## How to build an About page that meets user needs

The way you design the information on your About page will be different for different kinds of institutions. The main art is getting across WHAT you are and WHY you do what you do in a way that doesn't bat people over the head with internal facing comms priorities. Most visitors will want to know that you're an art gallery before the fact that you're aiming to be climate-neutral in five years.

ACMI (www.acmi.net.au/about), Wellcome (https://wellcomecollection.org/about-us) and the Sir John Soane's Museum (www.soane.org/about) all do a good job on their About page, explaining what they are and why that matters to their visitors (not to their board). At the time of writing, the first line of text on ACMI's About page reads: 'ACMI is your museum of screen sculpture. Navigate the universe of film, TV, videogames and art with us.' The second line then states:

> Located in the heart of Melbourne's Fed Square, ACMI (formerly Australian Centre for the Moving Image) celebrates the wonder and power of the world's most democratic artform – fostering the next generation of makers, players and watchers. ACMI's vibrant calendar of exhibitions, screenings, commissions, festivals, and industry and education programs explore the stories, technologies and artists that create our shared screen culture.
>
> (ACMI, www.acmi.net.au/about)

The following stands out about this text:

- it uses the second person – this is 'your' museum (90% of museum About pages tell visitors all about their own priorities but do little to address the visitors themselves)
- it clearly describes WHAT the museum is (and where it is based) and blends that neatly with WHY it exists.

Below are more examples of why and how these institutions' About pages work so well:

> The Soane Museum is the extraordinary house of Sir John Soane, one of the greatest English architects, who built and lived in it two centuries ago.
>
> The Museum has been kept as it was at the time of his death in 1837. It displays his collection of antiquities, furniture, sculptures, architectural models, paintings – including work by Hogarth, Turner and Canaletto – and over 30,000 architectural drawings. It's a vast, extraordinary collection, full of curiosities and surprises.
>
> Today, the Museum continues to offer free access to visitors, just as Soane intended. We host thought provoking exhibitions, run inspiring events, and maintain a rich research library.
>
> (Sir John Soane's Museum, www.soane.org/about)

> Wellcome Collection is a free museum and library that aims to challenge how we all think and feel about health.
>
> Through exhibitions, collections, live programming, digital, broadcast and publishing, we create opportunities for people to think deeply about the connections between science, medicine, life and art.
>
> We are part of Wellcome, which supports science to solve the urgent health challenges facing everyone. Wellcome supports discovery research into life, health and wellbeing and is taking on three worldwide health challenges: mental health, infectious disease and climate.
>
> (Wellcome, https://wellcomecollection.org/about-us)

The About pages in the above three examples all:

- understand the primary assignment by telling users, in simple language, who they (the institution) are
- convey why they exist, including the history but also today's purpose, and do so in an interesting way
- reference what they offer visitors/people (and don't just repeat internal mission statements).

The examples also demonstrate how About pages don't need to be long or comprehensive. If necessary, an About page can link to more detailed pages about mission/vision, policies and contact details, etc.

By contrast, here are a couple of examples that could do better:

> At The Museum of Modern Art and MoMA PS1, we celebrate openness, tolerance, and generosity. We aim to be inclusive places – both onsite and online – where diverse cultural, artistic, social and political positions are welcome. We're committed to sharing the most thought-provoking modern and contemporary art, and hope you will join us in exploring the art, ideas and issues of our time.
>
> (MoMA, www.moma.org/about)

> The Hammer Museum at UCLA believes in the promise of art and ideas to illuminate our lives and build a more just world.
>
> The Museum champions the art and artists who challenge us to see the world in a new light, to experience the unexpected, to ignite our imaginations, and inspire change.
>
> [...]
>
> The Hammer understands that art not only has the power to transport us through aesthetic experience but can also provide significant insight into some of the most pressing cultural, political, and social questions of our time.
>
> (The Hammer Museum at UCLA, https://hammer.ucla.edu/about-us)

Both of the examples above lead with what the organisation 'believes' – its positioning, mission and vision. They are not directly answering the primary user need, which is to know what the institution is and how a visitor can meaningfully interact with it. I feel welcomed by, and interested in, the first set of examples, and I feel like the museum wishes to show it has committed to being welcoming in the second. There's a difference.

About pages don't need to be the headache they can often become. The key is to see things through the eyes of your website visitors. A number of About pages are very short in terms of their actual text. For example, ACMI's body copy text is presented in full above, the rest of the page then links to child pages addressing areas such as policies and mission/vision.

If you're struggling to get collective sign-off on About page messaging, there are ways to test the different options. Software, such as Lyssna or Useberry, allows you to run controlled studies in minutes. They also have a testing panel that you can tap into, which typically works out at about $1 per response. So, for $60–$100, you can get a robust number of bias-free responses to different versions of an About page. This allows you to A/B test important messaging, for example, by uploading two different screenshots of the About page with different messaging and asking respondents for their preference. Alternatively, or in addition, you could ask participants to select adjectives they might associate with the page. You could then input adjectival options like 'corporate', 'accessible', 'welcoming', 'boring' and 'formal' and see how the different options come out.

About pages are likely to be the destination of those who are curious about your institution. They can be pivotal pages in improving understanding and developing empathy with audiences. However, this will only happen if you provide the information your audience wants and don't bombard them with irrelevant information.

## Homepage

### Why do users visit your homepage?

Based on running lots of user testing sessions (and having spent a fair amount of time analysing user journeys in Google Analytics), there are – broadly – three main types of users who might be on your homepage:

1. Users who know the organisation and what they want – these people make a beeline for the menu.
2. Users who know the organisation but don't have a firm goal in mind. It may be they've found the information they came to the website for and are now browsing (or are a bit lost).
3. Users who don't know very much about the organisation and (for whatever reason) want to find out more.

In general, people who have a very specific goal in mind (user 1 above) will use Google search and or the navigation/site search to find what they're looking for. Museum homepages are too different to be effectively used as a navigational tool. The purpose of the homepage is to meet more browsable/inspirational needs (users 2 and 3 above). It's those needs that we're going to look at next.

## How to build a homepage that meets user needs

A homepage is **not**:

- a dumping group for content that won't fit nicely elsewhere
- somewhere to highlight internal initiatives, strategic documents or business plans that are important to you and your staff, but are not the reason the general public lands on your website
- a good place for internal acronyms and jargon.

So, what is a homepage? A cultural organisation's homepage is like a storefront window display. The job of a window display is to showcase the most attractive and emblematic products in a welcoming, arresting and stimulating way, while conveying a good sense of the overall tone and 'vibe' of the store itself.

In this analogy, website content is your 'product' and your homepage should showcase the most attractive web content in a way that encourages visitors to explore more. When I'm designing content for a new website launch, I create the homepage last – just as you wouldn't design your window display until you've worked out what products you're stocking or write an Executive Summary of a report before you've written the report itself.

A homepage should draw from the most engaging content across your site and cherry pick content that provides entry-point answers to common questions, for example: who are you?; what do you do?; and what's it to me?

## What should a user see 'above the fold' when they first land on your homepage?

Within web design, the phrases 'above the fold' and 'below the fold' are used to describe content that is visible without having to scroll (above the fold) and content that is only visible with one or more scrolls (below the fold).

'Above the fold' content is what a user sees first when they land on your homepage and it should inspire them to scroll further down the page. Such content might include:

- an eye-catching video of your site and/or grounds (note, all videos should have a mobile fallback option that is a still image as video can incur high data charges and make a web page laggy on mobile)
- an instantly recognisable, but beautiful, shot of your entrance or interior
- a shot of audiences in your space enjoying themselves, as long as it's clear to an outsider where they are (note, if you're serious about diversifying audiences, avoid showing pictures of visitors within a

narrow demographic as this can implicitly 'other' less traditional audiences)
- text that focuses on providing a 'welcome' rather than your name – users will understand who you are from your logo in the top left of the page
- details of your current main show/exhibition (particularly for organisations who don't have a 'permanent' reason to visit, e.g., a gallery that is entirely filled with temporary exhibitions or a performing arts venue)
- a link to opening hours, or – better yet – a statement like 'We're open today. **More hours** »' (where 'More hours' reveals a full list of hours)
- a button link to 'plan your visit' – the visit page will likely be the most viewed page on your website, so a big, bright call to action button for users helps signpost the most common user journey from the homepage
- a statement that you're a free to enter institution (if applicable).

The imagery and video you use 'above the fold' should be updated from time to time and be seasonal (particularly if it includes outside/exterior shots).

### What should a user see 'below the fold' when they first land on your homepage?

Below the fold, your homepage content should contain:

- a punchy sentence explaining who you are
- new things to see/do (typically exhibitions and events)
- browsable content (storytelling and/or 'behind the scenes')
- other reasons to visit (things to eat, things to buy, things for children/babies)
- a potential conversion, e.g. a donation, membership or newsletter sign-up
- a testimonial from a member or visitor – this is a way of surfacing human stories and how audiences have connected with your collections or shows.

We'll look at these in more detail below.

#### *Who are you?*

This should be a one sentence summary of who you are and why people should care. For example, ACMI's homepage describes itself as 'your museum of screen culture'.

This summary is often missed on cultural sector homepages. Although you know what your organisation is (and why it's important and why visitors enjoy it), this is not common knowledge. If someone lands on your website homepage for the first time thinking 'who are these guys?', is there anything there to tell them?

It's more difficult to do this on a museum group homepage, but the same logic broadly applies: what are your individual museums and what do they collectively contribute to?

Conversations about 'who we are' can be difficult for any one person to write and can easily hold up a web project. If I'm designing content for someone else, I generally start with copy that's already been approved elsewhere, for example, a modified version of a Facebook or Instagram bio or a nicely positioned contextual sentence in a membership brochure.

### *Reasons to visit now*

This section should present the new and time-limited reasons to visit, typically current exhibitions and upcoming events. All events and exhibitions should display a date range indicating how long they're on for. I'd also add any 5-star (★★★★★) reviews here. In our A/B testing of different show copy for cultural organisations' social media ads, 5-star reviews always perform better than anything else.

### *Browsable content (storytelling and/or 'behind the scenes')*

All cultural organisations are creating some kind of digital content, for example, a blog, podcast or video series. If a user who's broadly interested in your organisation hasn't been grabbed by any of the visit-related information, this content provides more of a behind-the-scenes view of what goes on at the organisation and what's special about it.

The content here should also be refreshed regularly. This could happen dynamically if you're pulling through the most recent article or podcast feed. If you have to update this section manually, it's important to factor those updates into your editorial plan, along with social media and e-mail/newsletter updates.

### *Other reasons to visit (things to eat, things to buy, things for children/babies)*

For many cultural venues, the 'other reasons to visit' will be as important to your visitors as your collection and mission-driven programming. A glance at TripAdvisor tells you enough: people visit museums as social spaces. The cake, toilets, shop and any facilities for children and babies are as much a part of the experience as the pedagogical content.

### *Potential conversions (e.g. a donation, membership or newsletter sign-up)*

As the last module on the page, add a cause-led donation or membership ask. This should include a message about *why* you do what you do, where the money goes and how it helps advance your cause. By emphasising the broader mission around what you do, you give audiences an emotionally rich understanding of why you exist and the social value you create.

It's worth linking to a donation page here, but only if your donation payment page works well! You can quite easily kill all the goodwill you created around your mission if your donation form has lots of usability barriers.

I advise steering away from using a donation or membership ask if the 'other reasons to visit' you've already included on the page are heavily commercial (e.g. mainly advertising money you can spend at the venue in the shop/café, as opposed to free facilities). Having two content modules at the bottom of the page focused on ways visitors can spend money might put audiences off, so be aware of the balance.

If you wanted a different 'conversion' at the end of the page that requires no spend, you could make this last module a newsletter sign-up. In this instance, be clear about what the user will get from signing up (updates on events, notifications of sales in the shop, etc.).

Your donation/membership ask can be the place where you include testimonials, quotes and pictures from other visitors, members and donors. This is a good way of reframing the homepage narrative to include user stories and voices and not just your organisation's messaging. It also helps new users see how they can become more involved with your organisation and the benefits of community that come with that.

## Summary

The tone of your homepage is important. People who land there don't want a Wikipedia entry. It's easy to write copy that makes sense for a staff audience (as we hear staff feedback all the time), but it's more difficult to write for a visitor. Writing for visitors requires us to think about what they need to know, and will be excited by, at every point. Ultimately, the homepage is for your visitors – potential ones and existing ones. Going the extra mile to establish how best to serve user needs is the work of creating good website content.

Figure 3.1 below provides a template for your homepage if you're a free to enter museum or cultural organisation with a mix of a permanent collection and temporary programmes.

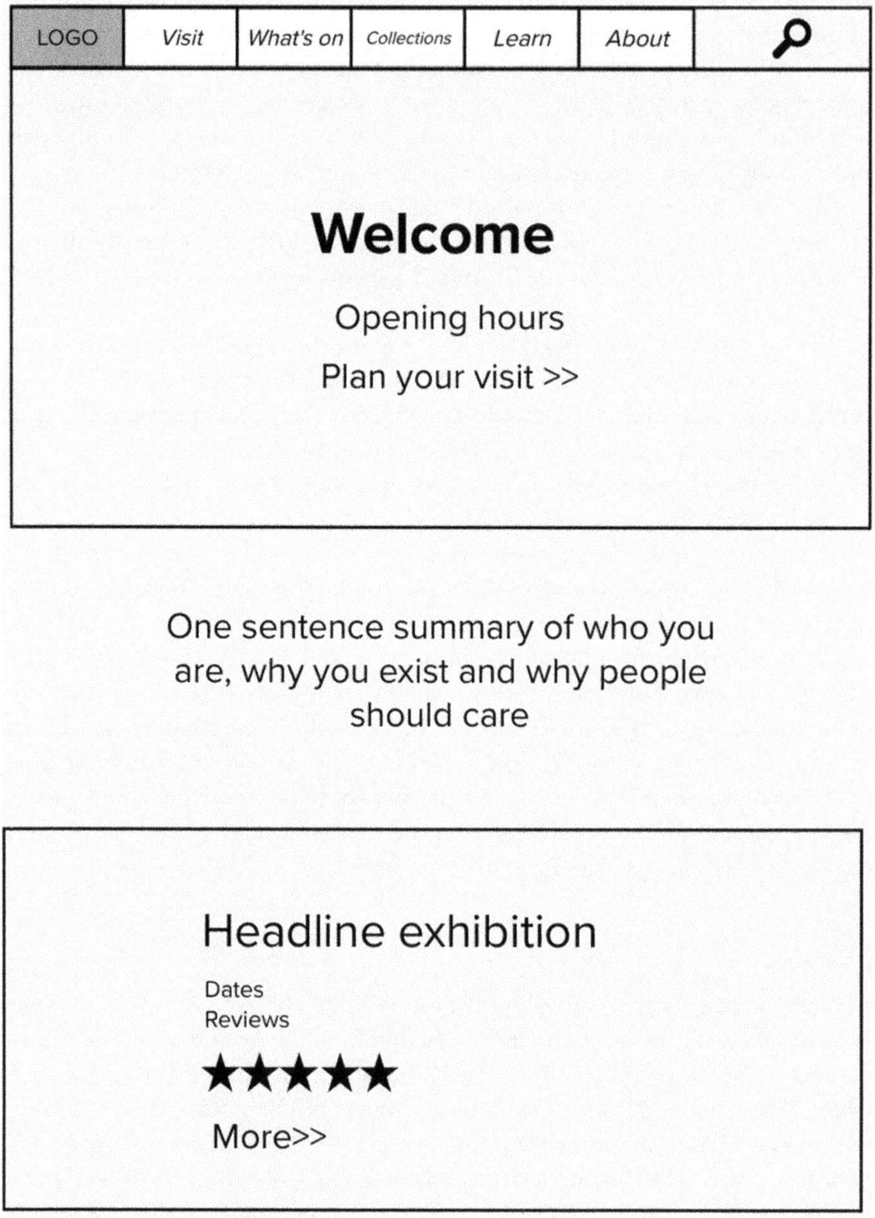


**Figure 3.1** *Homepage template*

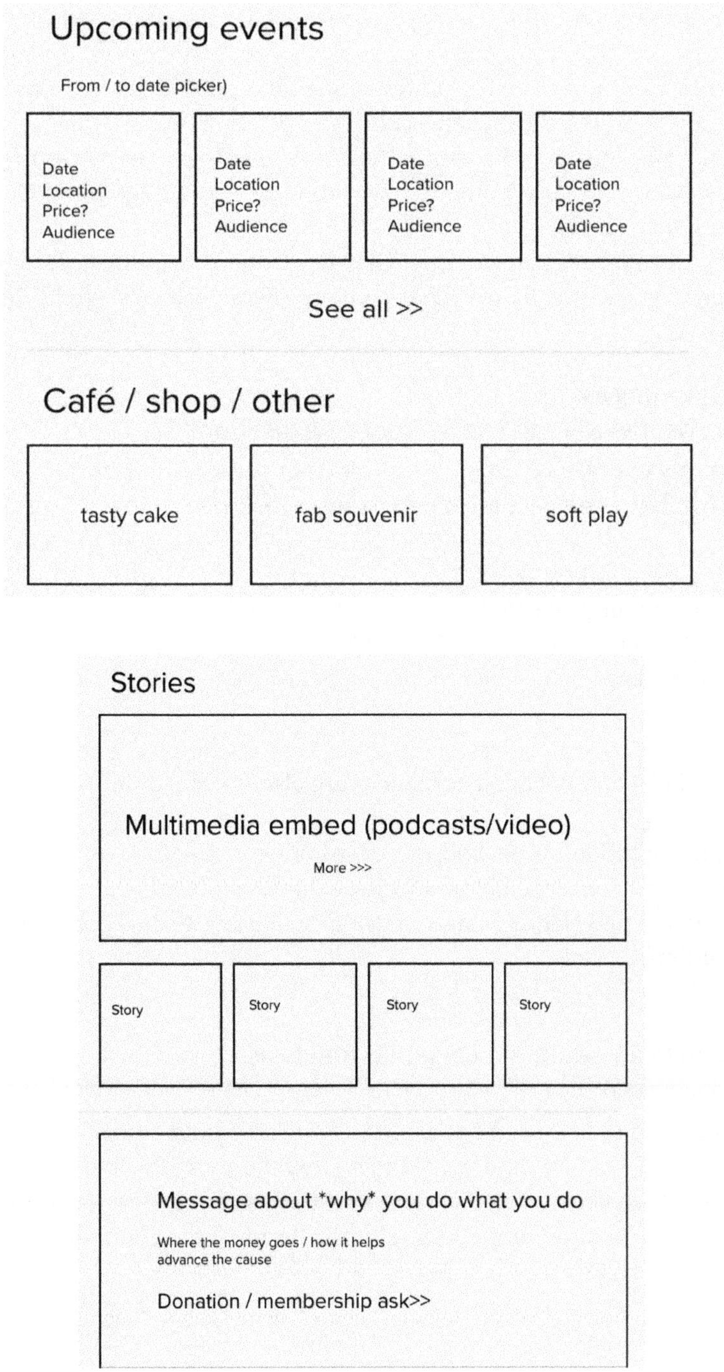


**Figure 3.1** (continued)

Example of museums following this model (or near enough) include:

- Whitney Museum of Art (Structure: Headline exhibition > reasons to visit now > browsable content) (Whitney, 2022)
- Ashmolean Museum (Structure: Welcome/opening hours > 'who we are' > reasons to visit now > other reasons to visit > browsable content) (Ashmolean, 2022)
- Hepworth Wakefield (Structure: Opening hours > headline exhibition > reasons to visit now > browsable content) (Hepworth Wakefield, 2022).

## Exhibition pages

### What do people want to know about an exhibition?

Based on my experience testing these kinds of pages with users (and looking at patterns in usage data), most people want to know:

- when the exhibition is
- what it's about (briefly)
- whether it has a cost
- what they'll see
- reviews.

More specialist and engaged audiences are also interested in:

- related exhibition events and/or publications
- links to collections online for specific exhibition objects
- a link to the newsletter to sign up for e-mail updates on upcoming exhibitions.

### How to build an exhibition page that meets user needs

#### *Above the fold content*

In the previous section on homepages, we talked about 'above the fold' and 'below the fold'. As a reminder, the purpose of the above the fold page content is to encourage users to scroll on and find out more.

On an exhibition page, you should aim to have the following elements visible above the fold:

- a striking image
- the title of the exhibition
- date and location

- whether the exhibition is free, or – if paid – what the cost is. If the cost is included in your general admission fee, state this. If it's free, make that really clear. Otherwise, users tend to assume exhibitions are paid and so may be unnecessarily put off
- if your exhibition is ticketed, a big, bold call to action to book a ticket
- ideally, have a subheading or the first line of body copy text visible – the aim of this is to create a byline that arouses interest and gives users a little more context on the exhibition's unique selling points and core themes.

### *Opening paragraph*

This should be a high level paragraph containing core keywords and answering potential search queries a user might enter into Google to land on the exhibition page. It should explain the remit of the exhibition; what visitors will see/learn; and the significance of the pieces displayed in terms of broad social and human themes.

Ideally, the first line of this module should also be visible 'above the fold', peeking through into the design above. This allows users to start engaging with the keywords and thematic information about the exhibition even before they've scrolled down.

The full module here should form 1–2 short paragraphs written for a non-specialist audience. Using bold text for keywords can help users' eyes skip to the most important or pertinent details in paragraphs.

### *Images*

During user testing, it quickly becomes clear that website browsers are drawn to images, headings and formatted text. This makes sense. Unlike with print media, you can't read the internet cover to cover, so the ways we make sense of what's on a page have evolved, allowing us to get an overall sense of what a page contains and whether it's relevant to our search intent. For something like an art exhibition, images are key to users' perceptions of how attractive and relevant the physical show is. We frequently see users make qualitative judgements of the exhibition based more on the images than the text content.

This module should give users a good visual overview of what they'll get in the exhibition. Captions should be used to explain what the image shows. If it's an image of an object in the museum collection, a hyperlink to the object record allows more engaged users to follow up with more detail. All images should have good alt-text to provide an equivalent experience for people using screen readers.

### *Reviews*

As with homepages, you can't beat a 5-star review for rousing interest and creating engagement. We find this time and time again when A/B testing exhibition copy in digital ads.

### *Exhibition detail*

This should provide more detailed information than the opening paragraph and be pitched to a general public audience. In this section, you can introduce new concepts, provided you explain or tie them back to the overarching themes and their relevance to a lay audience.

Bolded out keywords help users' eyes fixate on elements of the text that are particularly important and give them a quick sense of the content of the paragraph.

This is a good place to include links to other pages on your website and external websites (e.g. third-party reviews of the show), which will also improve the SEO of your exhibitions page. It's also a good place to add a link to a gallery map or, for example, a large-text version of the exhibition text.

A lot of museums put a large amount of lender and funder information and links in the same weight as the exhibition description. User testing has shown that this can confuse users. The Jewish Museum (New York) (https://thejewishmuseum.org/exhibitions/new-york-1962-1964) takes an elegant approach, including the lender/funder information but in smaller text, clearly delineating it from the exhibition description.

### *Plan your visit and access*

It is useful to point users to the 'Plan your visit' page, so that they have the links right at hand if they want to go ahead and see this exhibition.

The exhibition page should also contain a link to your access page and/or a description of any specific access provisions in place for your exhibition. It's helpful to provide the contact details of a specific member of staff that users can contact for additional information.

### *Additional multimedia*

Most museums create some exhibition specific content, for example, a video 'trailer' or a curator blog. This content should be positioned low down on the page so that you're not cannibalising screen real estate from more transaction/core information-oriented visitor content. At this point on the page, it provides extra rich and contextual information for users who have a bit longer to browse.

### *Potential additional content*

Other additional content you might want to feature on your exhibition page includes:

- any related exhibition events – these should have a date and title visible and be ordered by date (and it's helpful if on a scroll you can reveal prices/whether it is free and any specific audience labels, e.g., family friendly)
- any additional reviews (although, depending on the number of reviews you have, this might not be necessary)
- any additional online content you might have (e.g., virtual galleries or a pre-filtered link to all of the online collection).

### *Final calls to action*

Lastly, add a call to action right at the bottom of your exhibition page. Firstly, this should be to your newsletter sign up (highlighting in the body text that the newsletter will give you updates about upcoming exhibitions). Next, add a link to either your ticketing page or to your 'Plan your visit' page. On a long page, it's good to have a number of different calls to action, particularly for a free, unticketed exhibition. For a ticketed exhibition, you should include several links to ticketing throughout the page.

## Summary

Figure 3.2 that follows, provides a useful template for your exhibition page. Depending on the size of your digital estate, there may be lots of other things you could include (e.g., shop products and membership upsells).

Examples of cultural sector websites that have adopted a similar template:

- Jewish Museum (thejewishmuseum.org, 2022): an image carousel you instantly want to play with; lender/funder copy clearly separated from the main exhibition information; well formatted headline press quotes and a more detailed body of quotes further down the page; a punchy opening sentence; and formatted keywords in body copy to make the text easy to scan.

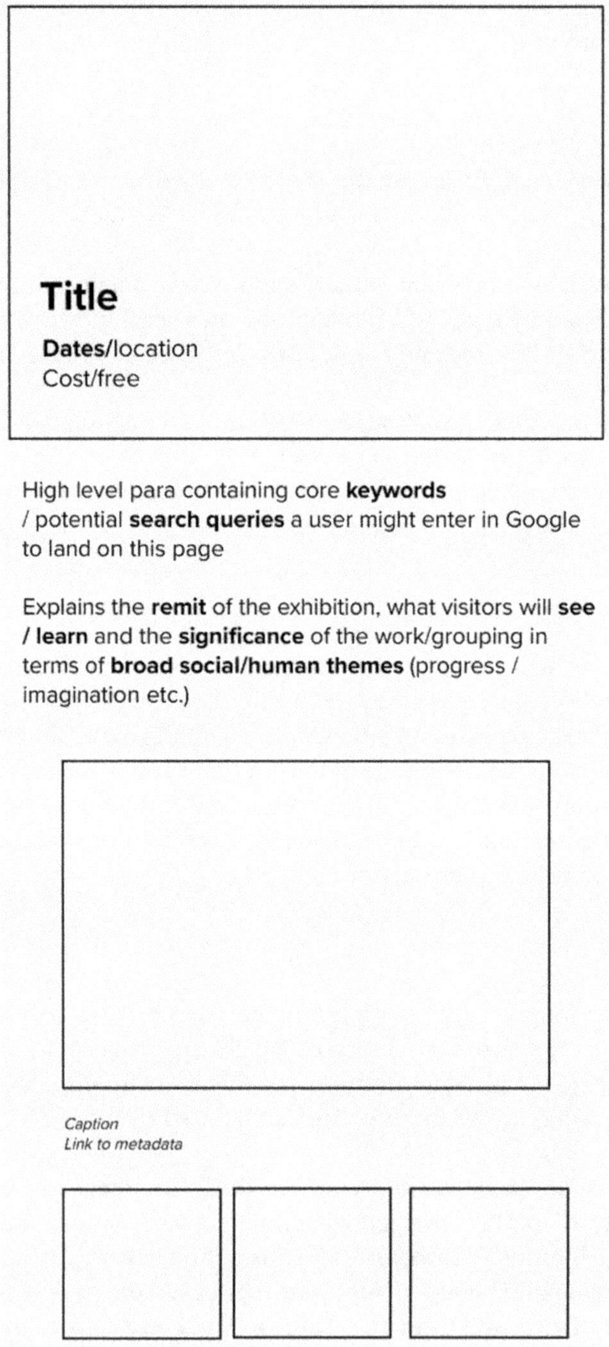


**Figure 3.2** *Exhibition page template*

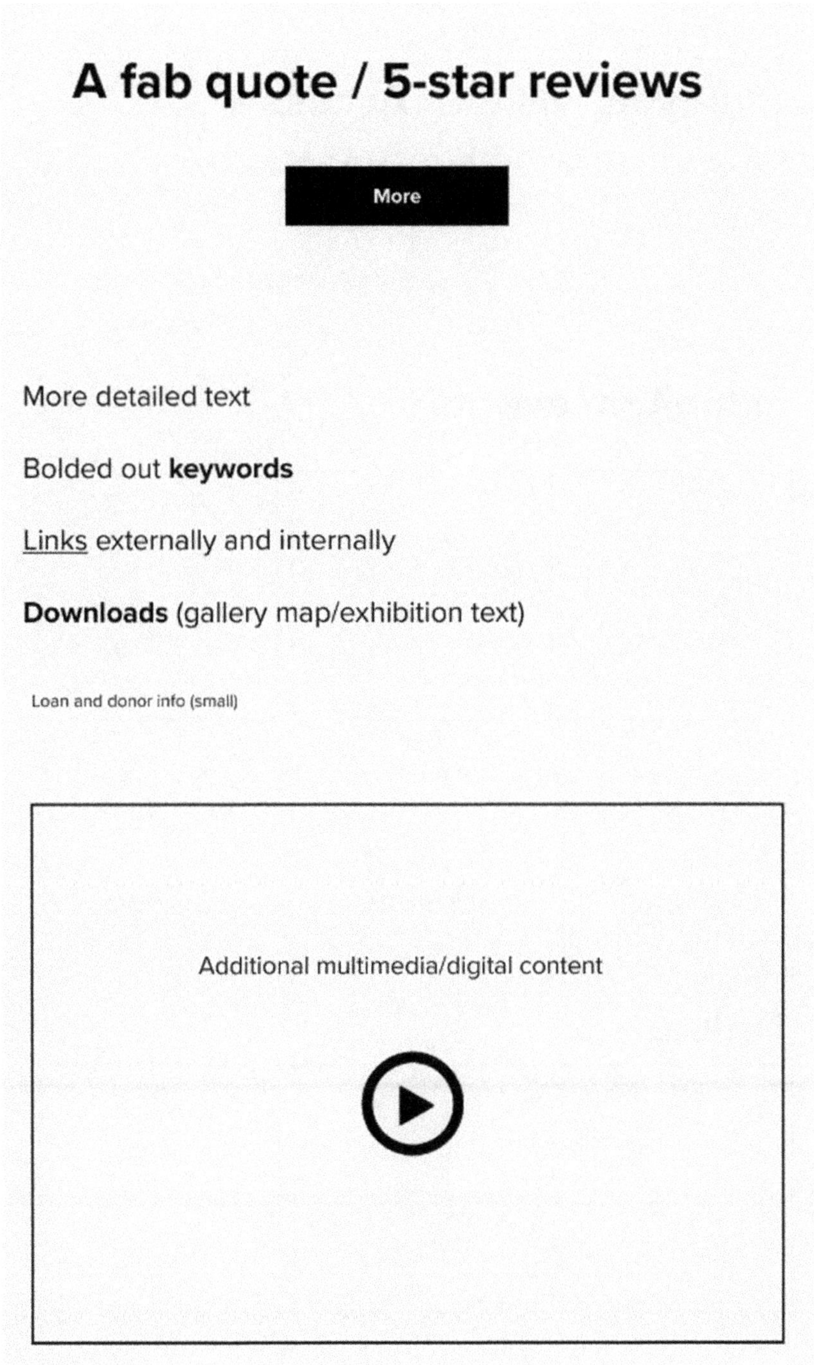


**Figure 3.2** (continued)

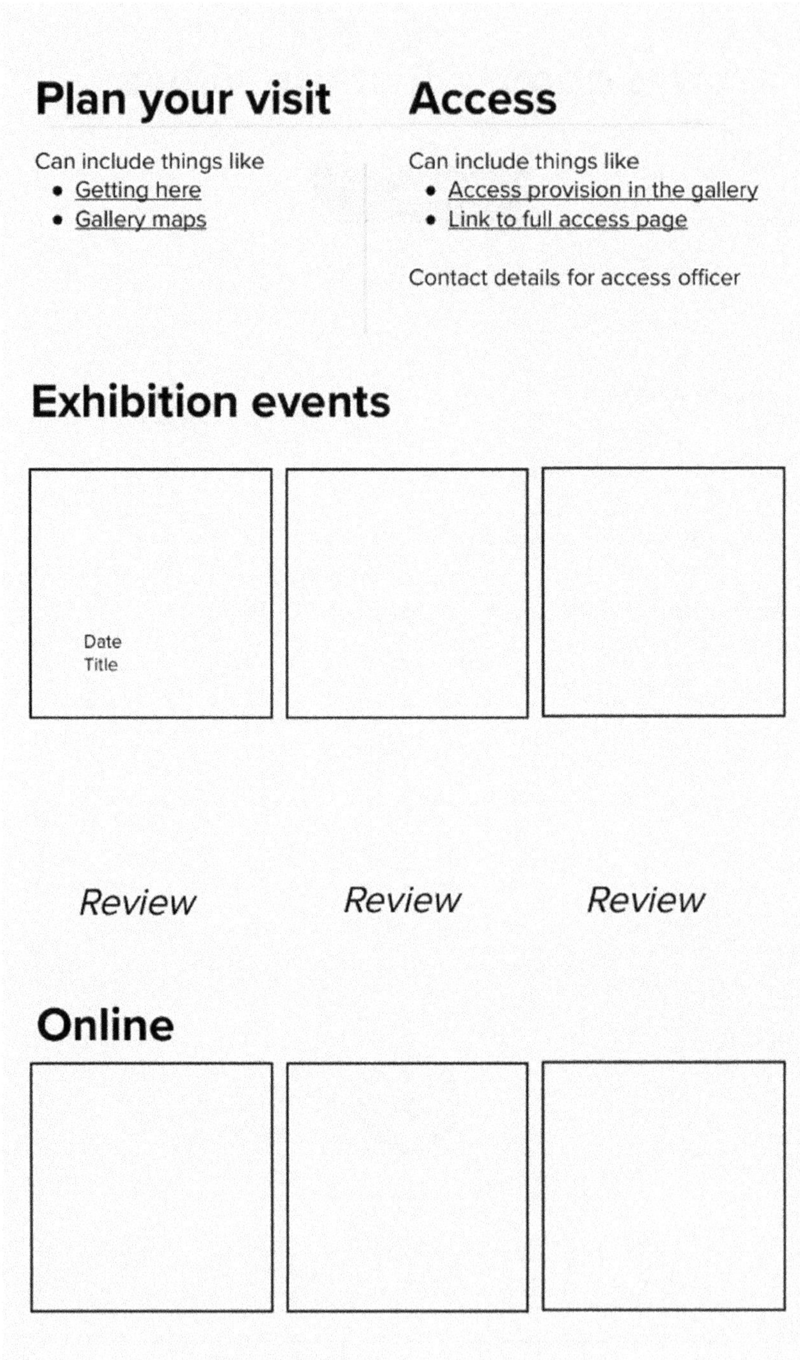


**Figure 3.2** (continued)

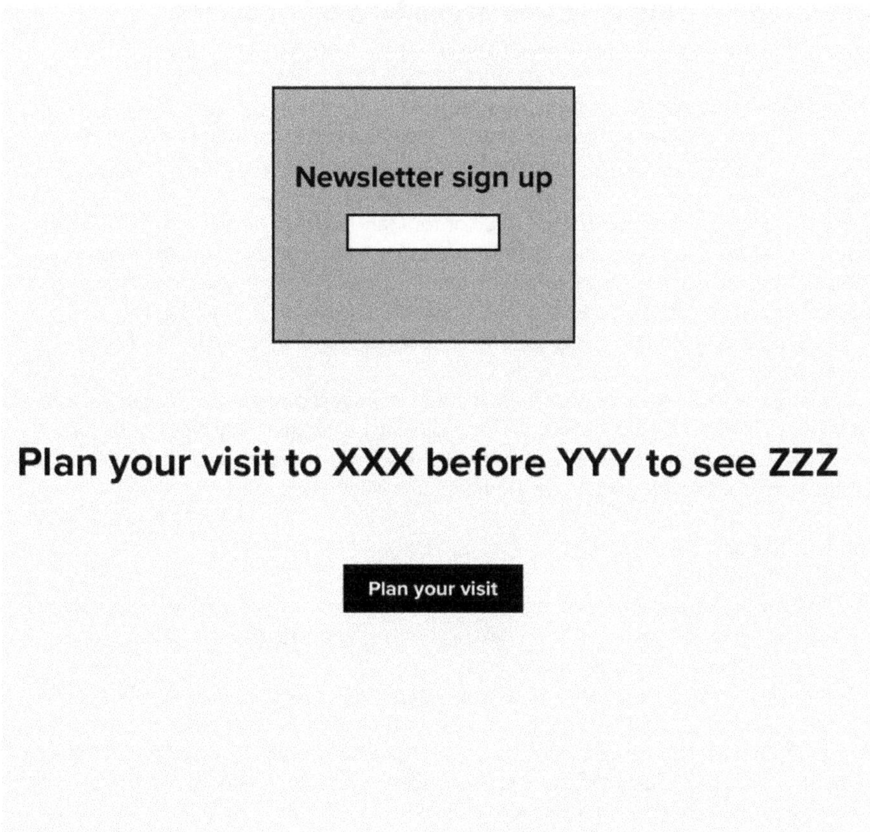


**Figure 3.2** (continued)

- Met Museum (metmuseum.org, 2021): it's easy to hold the Met up as a good example, but the one element of its interface I particularly like is the use of anchor links at the top of a long page to quickly ping users down to the relevant part of the interface.
- Fruitmarket (Fruitmarket.co.uk, 2022): this gallery does a good job on its exhibition page of leading with rich multimedia from the show and it has also included an audio version of the exhibition text. This is followed by behind-the-scenes storytelling; interviews with the artist; and a biography of the artist. The page ends with related shop products.

Next, Joanne Karcheva from Manchester Collective shares her experience of building effective pages for performances. After that Caspian Turner will take us through some tips for creating an accessibility page. Lastly, consultant Rachel Mapplebeck looks at online giving pages.

## Case study 3.1: Building web pages for performances

*Joanne Karcheva, Brand and Communications Director, Manchester Collective*

### Performance web pages: strategy and tactics

What should the ideal web page for a performance contain? In the arts, we have a job of balancing creativity and inspiration with practical considerations that put our audiences' needs first.

As the Brand and Communications Director for Manchester Collective – an innovative touring company and shape-shifting music ensemble – my primary goal is to help people find and connect with our artistic work. We play in spaces ranging from concert halls to warehouses and nightclubs to festivals. The Collective is known for breaking with convention, both on and off stage, and this mindset has to be reflected in our digital presence.

Here's what I have learnt about creating audience-focused performance web pages and the strategic considerations behind them, which can be applied to all types of cultural experiences. The first part is more of a sense-check to your overall approach, while the second part looks at the constituent elements of a killer web page.

### The foundation

*Who is your audience?*

We can think of our audience existing as a series of concentric circles. In the centre, we have our existing audience, beyond that we have a community of interested audiences, and beyond that we have our potential audience.

Before we commit to any text, imagery or web page features, we must establish a crystal-clear understanding within the *whole organisation* of who we serve and how that can vary from project to project. Otherwise, we risk ending up in a loop of conflicting demands that result in a confusing and overwhelming user experience.

Here are some additional questions to consider:

- **Who comes to our shows and, more importantly, why?** Surveys or informal chats with previous attendees can elicit a lot of this information and a good audience segmentation framework will help organise those people into meaningful groups that facilitate decision-making at all levels.
- **Who is following our artistic work and why?** Our audience doesn't just consist of the people who attend our performances. Our *community* also includes people who encounter our work online, as well as our sector peers and existing/potential collaborators – be that artists, venues, funders or local businesses. They all have distinct needs, but at this point it's very important to prioritise and set realistic goals about which audience segments we are seeking to engage with a particular web page.
- **Who isn't engaging with our work just yet but could be, and why?** At any point in time, our potential audience far exceeds our existing one. Each performance that we present opens doorways to new audiences, but there may be a host of interrelated factors that prevents them from attending – from the obvious (not knowing about it or having no one to go with) to barriers that are harder to define (e.g., unfamiliarity with the cultural context). We must constantly act to understand and address these.

*Who is visiting your website and how are they getting there?*

The first question is harder to answer (a temporary pop-up survey may be of help here), but we can look for clues in the actions people take when on our website, as well as basic information such as their location and age, both found in Google Analytics.

How someone gets to our site can help us glean invaluable information about the overall visitor journey. Make sure to review what percentage of traffic comes from the following sources and which leads to higher engagement and, ultimately, action: organic versus paid search; organic versus paid social; direct; e-mail; and referral. In general, paid traffic tends to be less knowledgeable about who you are and what you are offering than all the other types.

*What are they looking for and what drives them to engage?*
Figure 3.3 below visualises where the focus of our work – as digital professionals working in the cultural sector – sits. It's in the intersection of our organisation's world and our audience's world.

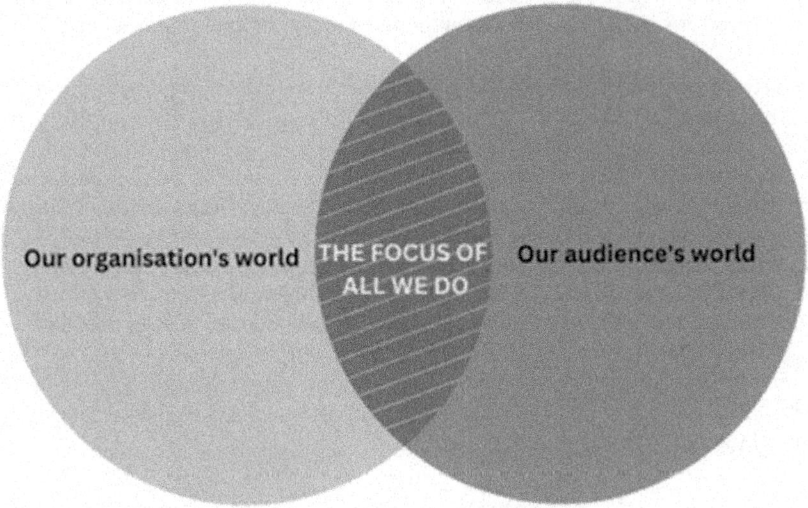


**Figure 3.3** *The focus of all we do*

People can end up on your performance web page out of curiosity, with minimal knowledge or a clear idea of what they want to find or do while there. Or they can land there with intention.

Consider the following things before refining your page:

- What are the key things they need to know to stay and engage further – does it intrigue, inspire and capture interest?
- Why should they care? How does what is immediately in front of them relate to their world and does it 'speak their language'?
- Does what they see on the page meet the primary reason for which they ended up on your website in the first place? If not, has it given them a new one?

### The landing page

Armed with all this knowledge, we can then move onto the constituent elements of a web page. There is no one formula to create the perfect page as it's all about choosing the mix of elements most appropriate to your audience and brand. We can broadly group them into three categories – inspiration, information and action – and pick from the menu of options below to create a unique and engaging user experience.

*Inspiration*

In the arts and cultural sector, our job is to inspire people. We should never forget this and, regardless of whether we operate in the commercial or not-for-profit sector, we must always lead with that motivation. Yes, we must meet our sales and audience figure targets or otherwise our business model will crumble, but, ultimately, we don't exist to grow the shares of stakeholders. More often than not, we start with the practical over the inspirational, but I urge you to consider how your page is genuinely reflecting the cultural experience you are inviting people into, rather than merely informing them about it.

- **Visuals** – consider the impact of the lead image or video banner that invites the visitor into the production's world. It should intrigue and encourage them to explore further. If your lead visuals focus on people, even if they are famous and your audience is likely to consist of those who already know them, ensure there is something else to go on – a hint of a story, an atmosphere or a mood. We are in the business of world-building here.
- **Text** – evocative titles and taglines that conjure up images and feelings and hint at the atmosphere of the event. The same point as above applies to 'names' – don't rely on them to do the work for you. A quote may be of help here too.
- **Experience snapshot** – most important of all: how can you show (rather than tell) people what they are about to experience? Trailers, performance snapshots – or, if you are presenting new work, embedded video/audio players linking to similar work by the same artist – are our best bet at capturing the audience's imagination and reducing insecurity about what it is all about.

*Information*

Start with all the key 'W' questions from the visitor's point of view:

- what – event title, tagline, tags (e.g., performance type, genre, family friendly)
- when – date(s), start time, end time, duration
- where – venue, city, country if relevant
- who – presenting company, key artist(s)
- why – the overall impression created by the page and relating to the visitor's 'why' (e.g., to experience, to socialise, to escape from the everyday)
- (for) whom – not as obvious, but very important: can your intended audience member see themselves reflected in all of the above and what's to follow?

Figure 3.4 opposite shows how these questions are answered by different elements of the page design.

You also need to signpost the 'hows':

- how much – ticket prices, concessions, discounts, booking fees, additional extras (e.g., food and drink, parking)

- how to book – booking link(s) clearly signposted throughout
- how to access – getting to the venue, accessibility (motor, visual, auditory, cognitive) of the production and the venue
- how do I know it's good? – testimonials from press, audience, peers.

It is also important to elaborate on the 'whats':

- what can I expect – show synopsis, content and themes, the nature of the experience, artistic elements, evocative language bringing out the mood and feel
- what is unique about it – spotlight on specific elements, creative team, behind-the-scenes insights
- what else might be relevant – venue layout (e.g., seated, standing, in-the-round, etc.), age suitability, content warnings, detailed programme notes.

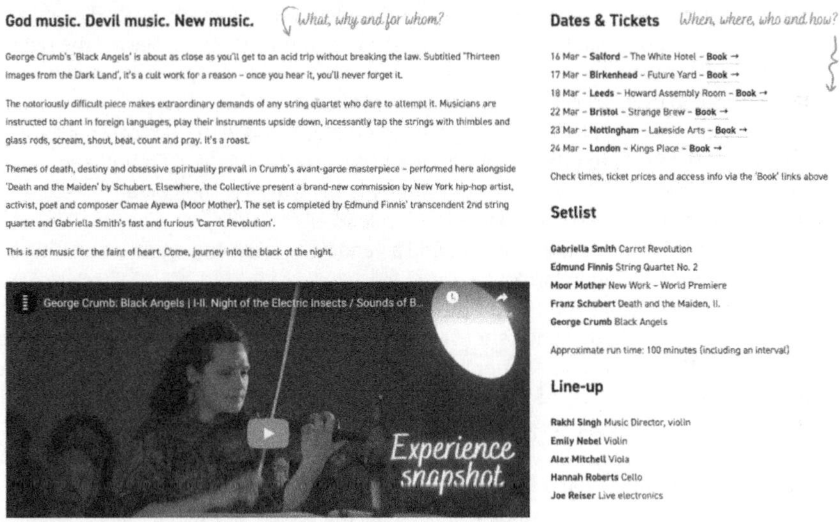


**Figure 3.4** *Answering the user needs for a performance page*

*Action*

Make sure these calls to action appear in the appropriate places and moments in the visitor journey, so as not to overwhelm:

- Book – link to box office, ideally signposted both at the top and middle of the page
- Watch/Listen/Read – embedded or linked audio, video, visuals or text that bring the experience to life in the mind of the viewer
- Ask a Question – opportunity to get in touch with the organisers directly and ask specific questions; this could be a pop-up or an e-mail address
- Subscribe – option to sign up to the general mailing list or a specific one for relevant announcements regarding this production (e.g., tickets on sale notice)
- Browse Further – view other similar productions, find out more about the presenting company/artist.

**Final words**

No matter how much thought is put into the web page experience (and how many back and forths with colleagues), we all have our blind spots. At the end of the day, we are on the inside and, try as we may, we cannot really imagine what it all looks like to someone seeing it for the first time. So, reach out to friends and peers who are one step removed and ask them for critical feedback. Can people understand what you are inviting them into? If not, why not and what can you tweak to get one step closer? Keep experimenting.

## Case study 3.2: Tips for your accessibility page

*Caspian Turner, Founder, Accessible by Design*

**Why do you need an accessibility page?**

In order to welcome everyone, it's crucial to include a dedicated accessibility landing page on your website, combining all the access information about your venue. Having the right information presented in a way that everyone can consume gives people the confidence they need to attend events, knowing their needs will be met.

This case study is written for people working at organisations with physical spaces. It includes some guidelines to ensure your accessibility page can be easily found and contains the content needed and expected when planning a visit. The guidance here is based on feedback from focus groups, user interviews and usability studies that I've held. Most participants said that if they couldn't find a venue's accessibility information, they would simply give up trying to book.

Your accessibility page can link out to other sections of your website. It doesn't need to be unwieldy, but it should be comprehensive. It's also crucial to make sure that people can find the page. Website journeys are not linear; while you may hope users follow a specific journey through your website, each person may start from a different page. Having the accessibility information available in the footer caters to every user journey.

**What content should the page include?**

An accessibility page should be a landing page for all the access information about your venue and events. It should include all the 'evergreen' accessibility information about your venue or organisation, that is, the information that doesn't become outdated over time.

When thinking about what we should include in an accessibility page, we need to think about user needs. What are the types of questions that visitors need to ask before deciding to book a ticket or attend a gallery? These questions could include things like:

- Are there quiet times?
- Is there accessible parking?
- Are there seats at a general admission gig if I need to sit down part way through?
- Is there a lowered bar where a wheelchair user can order a drink?
- Are there changing places? (www.changing-places.org)
- Can audiences leave a performance part way through?
- Are there seats in exhibitions that can be used?
- Are there ways to avoid queues for anyone who is unable to stand for long periods of time?
- Does the production include any loud noises or flashing lights? What time in the production does this occur?

- Is there an interval, if so, when is it and how long is it?
- Will I be able to read the captions?

Some information may be more relevant to a specific event or a particular user journey. Be sure to also make access information available during the booking process – providing users the information they need, at the time they need it.

**Seven tips to create a comprehensive accessibility page**

*1. Include a link to your accessibility page in the footer*

Don't make people hunt for accessibility information. Most people expect to find an accessibility page link wherever they land on your website.

Some organisations choose to include all access information under 'Your visit'. Others use legal sounding or policy-like naming conventions, such as 'Diversity, inclusion and access policy'. I'd recommend using the link text 'Accessibility', 'Access' or 'Access information'.

In most of the usability testing I've facilitated, screen reader users in particular will perform a 'look up' or scroll through links and first search the letter 'A' within links (freedomscientific.com, n.d.). The expectation is that your accessibility page will appear on every page and the link will start with the word 'Access'.

*2. Tell people how they can get in touch with you*

In 2023, I held focus groups with 45 people who had a diverse range of access needs when booking for and attending events. One of the key frustrations was not being able to speak to a person. Sometimes a page on a website will never be the reassurance needed to attend an in-person event, particularly if you've never been to a venue before and you have specific questions.

Make it easy to get in touch and provide a variety of ways to do so. Giving multiple routes to get in touch ensures that you're not excluding people. For example, offer the ability to get in touch by phone, by e-mail and by live chat or through services such as SignLive (https://signlive.co.uk), a service that offers British Sign Language interpretation on demand.

Edinburgh International Festival (EIF) does this very well on their access page (www.eif.co.uk/access). There is a clear route to get in touch via multiple channels and, in addition, EIF includes a sign interpreted video about accessibility.

*3. Be specific and descriptive and avoid ambiguity*

When planning the content for your access page, include everything that is accessible, but also include anything that you know to be inaccessible. For example, if you know that part of the building is not accessible by lift, tell people! It's far more frustrating to turn up only to find this out when you get there.

You may write 'there is step-free access to all levels'. However, there are many different needs for step-free access and indicating that there is step-free access doesn't provide enough detail to know whether – for example – a lift can fit a power chair, a scooter or mobility aids.

A good example is the British Museum's accessibility page (www.britishmuseum.org/visit/accessibility-museum). I like this because it uses clear headings and each heading can be expanded to find further details. The British Museum is also very clear about which galleries have no lift or level access. While this isn't great in itself, it's good to be clear and transparent about this so that visitors know in advance of attending.

*4. Include information in a variety of formats*
Including photos and audio described videos can be particularly helpful for audiences planning a visit. The more information you provide, the easier it will be for your audiences to make an informed decision about whether their needs will be met. This is helpful for everyone.

*5. Direct the page to your audience and visitors using the second person ('you')*
When writing your access page, address your readers using the second person. For example, 'You can get in touch with our access team by phone, e-mail, in person or by live chat'.

Avoid using first ('I') or third person ('he', 'she', 'they') as this can create a distancing effect between your organisation and your visitors. We're all people speaking to one another, talking about the physical spaces that people will visit. Try not to hide behind the guise of a corporation.

*6. Provide details about accessible services and events*
It's likely that your organisation organises accessible events such as sign language interpreted performances, captioned, audio description, touch tours, or relaxed performances. Be sure to include a description of what each of these types of events involve. Don't expect all audiences to recognise symbols or abbreviations related to these services.

Include a list of upcoming access events and accessible performances on your access page. I'd recommend linking to another page that aggregates all access performances or – better still – allowing users to filter access performances directly on your 'what's on' page.

*7. Website accessibility statement*
If you are a public sector body, you need to have a web accessibility page. If you're not, it's still considered best practice to include one. A website accessibility statement tells visitors how accessible your website is. It should state anything that you know to be inaccessible and what your plans are to resolve this.

The website accessibility statement is a legal document and so needs to contain specific information, including some specific statements about your level of compliance. You'll need to have undertaken a web accessibility audit before you create this page. Gov.uk has some really useful advice, including a sample accessibility statement (Gov.uk, 2019).

I'd recommend starting with the sample accessibility statement and developing your own statement from this template. Once you have written your statement, be sure to include a link to this within your accessibility page.

**In conclusion**
The main thing to consider here is that your audiences know best. If you are unsure about any of the information you're including in your accessibility page, check if the content meets user needs through surveys, inclusive usability studies or user interviews. But do make sure you compensate your audience for their time and expertise.

**Further reading**
Last year VocalEyes, Stagetext, Autism in Museums and the Centre for Accessible Environments published the Heritage Access Report 2022 (VocalEyes, 2022). This involved auditing over 2,000 websites and assessing the access information included. VocalEyes also

produced a benchmarking report that details a score for each of the UK museums and heritage sites covered by the project.

There are also a whole host of resources available on the Unlimited website, including the 'Demystifying Access' report (Unlimited, 2018).

And last but not least, 'Access Starts Online' from Attitude is Everything (Attitude is Everything, 2016) is a great read.

## Collections pages

In this section, I'm doing something slightly different to the previous sections. Instead of looking at one page in isolation, we'll look at a journey of pages around 'exploring the collections'.

### What does 'Explore the Collections' mean?

Let's think about 'Collections Search' first of all. On a Collections Search page, you arrive on the page and see a large search bar. This works fine for specialists who already have a reasonable sense of what collection you hold, but it can be a bit baffling to be faced with a search bar if you don't have that knowledge. What if you're not after something specific, but want to browse, immerse yourself and find out more? That's what a good 'Explore the Collections' section does.

Designing content to stimulate curiosity or encourage exploration is trickier than designing for a specific search enquiry. In the next sections, we'll go through a few examples of cultural websites that have done this well in the context of their collections.

### V&A: Explore as a gateway into collections

In 2021, the V&A layered the more immersive 'Explore the Collections' feature on top of their existing 'Search the Collections'. In speaking about the change, Kati Price, Head of Digital Media at the V&A, said, 'We hope it's a bit of a rabbit hole to get lost in the collection because there are so many wonderful stories that can be told' (The Art Newspaper, 2021).

The user pathway through their website is visually represented in Figure 3.5 on the next page.

1 Collections page: this presents users with a search bar, but also a series of themes to browse and click through to.
2 Collections theme landing page: this presents information about the galleries associated with that theme, the individual objects and related blogs and multimedia.

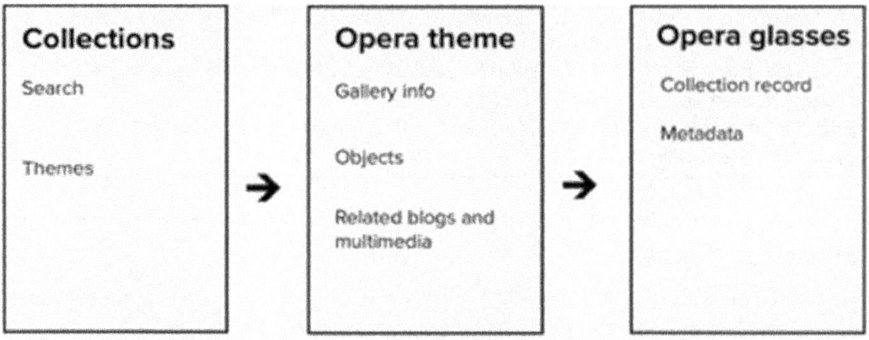


**Figure 3.5** *Diagram of the user journey from 'Explore the collections' landing page to an object detail page on the V&A's website*

3 Individual collections records: this includes collections record metadata and links to related objects.

The journey above is an enhanced version of the typical 'Search the Collections' user journey, which follows these steps:

1 Collections search bar: presents users with a search bar.
2 Individual collections records.

The key differences with the V&A's 'Explore the Collection' compared to a typical search are:

- it adds a series of themes beneath the search bar on the collections search page
- it builds new collection theme pages that aggregate gallery information, objects records in that theme, and related articles and multimedia.

These differences are important because they turn a collections search away from being a tool for the initiated/specialists into a tool for serendipitous discovery and a gateway to countless immersive rabbit holes.

### The British Museum: Explore as a way of promoting the in-person visit

Compared to the V&A Museum, the British Museum has a slightly different starting point to meet a similar user journey.

In this example, you start by choosing a particular Museum gallery page from a list (www.britishmuseum.org/collection/galleries). Each gallery page is incredibly rich, providing users with a map, virtual tour, facts about the gallery, highlight objects, a timeline, videos, blog posts and a link through to collections online. The user pathway is visually represented in Figure 3.6 below.

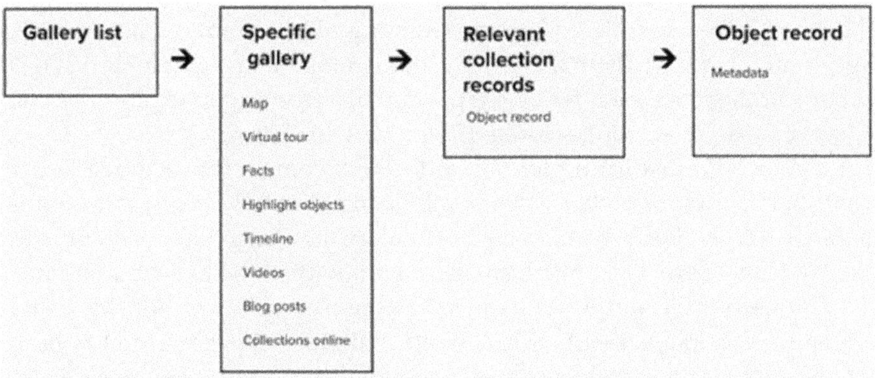


**Figure 3.6** *Visual representation of the user journey via gallery listing through to object record on the British Museum's website*

The journey follows these stages:

1 Gallery list: this presents users with a list of galleries they can visit.
2 Specific gallery page (e.g., 'Sutton Hoo and Europe'): this page includes a gallery map, sometimes a virtual tour, highlight objects in that gallery, a timeline of history covered by the gallery, links to related videos, blogs and a link to all related objects in collections online.
3 Related collections results page (e.g., full collections search pre-filtered by Place: Sutton Hoo and Culture/Period/Dynasty: Anglo-Saxon): this includes collections record metadata and links to related objects.
4 Individual object record (e.g., 'belt buckle').

Nesting browsable content under your gallery structure is a neat way of organising your 'rabbit holes' of discovery through the physical site. It's neat because the number of galleries is more finite than the number of themes (therefore making it less work), but also because while people are exploring online they come to tacitly link their discoveries with specific rooms and galleries on site.

Note, I'm under no illusions about how much time, resource and expertise it takes to create either of these examples of 'Explore the Collections'. The V&A and the British Museum both describe their staff headcount as between 501–1,000 on LinkedIn (V&A Museum via LinkedIn, 2024; British Museum via LinkedIn, 2024). The resources that organisations of this size can deploy are, of course, far larger than for most cultural organisations.

### The Peace Museum: Simple (but effective) collections exploration

The Peace Museum (www.peacemuseum.org.uk) in Bradford lists just six paid staff on its website (Peace Museum, n.d.). During the COVID-19 lockdown, they created a really simple but effective way to explore the 100 objects they digitised while closed (Peace Museum, 2024).

It can be a bit dispiriting to look at the web content that a much larger institution can put together. What's refreshing about the Peace Museum is that they haven't been afraid to create 'Explore the Collections' content with just 100 items. Sure, it's a much smaller quantity than the tens of thousands to millions of objects the national museums can digitise, but, by being strategic and curated about which objects to digitise, this museum has been able to present their collections in a coherent narrative. They designed a simple set of pages that effectively guide users through what collections they hold (and, by extension, what they stand for and the themes that guide their collections policy).

The user journey through to collections records on the museum's website looks like this:

1. Our Collections listing page: this lists a number of collections themes.
2. Collections theme page (e.g., 'Protest materials').
3. Pre-filtered link list of all items in the collection tagged 'Protest materials'.
4. Object record (e.g., 'Jobs Not Trident placard').

It's essentially very similar to the V&A and the British Museum examples, just on a smaller scale. However, with that smaller scale, they've got a high level of focus, choosing representative objects from across the collection and concentrating on the messages and themes they want to communicate with this selection.

## 'Support us' pages

I have seen a lot of bad 'Support us' pages on cultural sector websites. So, why are we not good at asking for money online? And how do you do it well? In Case study 3.3 opposite, Rachel Mapplebeck answers exactly that, using a case study from her recent work with fundraising strategist Nicole Newman for digital-first art education charity, Art UK.

## Case study 3.3: Creating an effective online donation ask: how Art UK grew its online giving

*Rachel Mapplebeck, cultural consultant*

Cultural organisations in the UK are facing a fatal funding gap right now. Public funding is shrinking, while corporate support is hard to secure and can carry reputational risks. But our arts organisations are loved and enjoyed by millions, and many have grown significant audiences online. Can they now mobilise these digital audiences to regularly donate?

### ArtUK.org – growing online giving

Art UK gives everyone free digital access to the UK national collection of art in public museums and other institutions. Rich in content, artuk.org has hundreds of thousands of artworks and thousands of stories to explore. The platform has an impressive audience of 5.4 million users a year.

However, it receives no regular public funding and so the charity is looking to improve its financial resilience and sustainability by diversifying income sources and increasing low level giving.

Although it has tested membership schemes in the past and has an existing pool of around 2,500 warm low level donors, it hadn't yet significantly penetrated and converted a meaningful proportion of its users into regular givers. The conversion to donating was 0.02% of Art UK's web visits annually – a very low proportion considering the number of repeat visits and the demographic of its audiences.

This untapped potential of low level regular givers from Art UK's large and growing audience is seen as a sustainable source of income for its future.

### Online fundraising and memberships – the external context

Art UK is operating on a model closest to the 'Contributions' subscriptions model, i.e. 'help keep us free by donating', similar to *The Guardian* newspaper or Wikipedia. However, there was previously no consistent and compelling supporter ask for audiences to give. There were also no monetisation opportunities being exploited, for example offering premium content for a fee or selling audience data.

For charities, the motivation to join or donate is cause-driven. Donors and members want to know that the organisations they support are making a difference, and the subject and the community they represent is of interest to them.

Research highlights several 'catalysts' for successful donor and membership recruitment and retention and the importance of a real understanding of audiences, as well as best practice examples of online donating. These include:

- a compelling mission and values
- targeted, highly personalised communications
- donor-focused user journeys and a stewardship strategy that deepens engagement with the organisation.

Best practice examples of online donor user journeys we looked at included the following:

- Sadler's Wells, whose 'lean' approach to donor-focused journeys on mobile devices is paying off. It uses simple language and structure on its Support Us page, with clear options in terms of the level of gift to choose from. Only essential content is included with the ask. Then there is a one-step process for payment that is easy, frictionless and designed to be mobile-first.

- Leeds Heritage Theatres' site has outperformed others for donations, especially on mobile, which accounts for 60% of transactions. Their approach uses impact-focused content, supported by strong images and graphics. They have clear and repeated calls to action throughout their donations-focused content pages. It's not one ask but many, which are all tailored to specific initiatives and themes.

**Case for support template – 7 things to always include**

Creating a compelling ask for why people should donate to your cultural organisation is incredibly important. On your site, honing this copy to the succinct essential elements creates the template for a donate page hub, which other content and communications channels can draw from and point to.

Here's what you should always include:

1. **Your headline and standfirst – who you are.** Don't forget the obvious! Spend time whittling down this headline ask and the standfirst description of your organisation to as few words as possible.
2. **What you do and why.** Explain the important work you do and the reason why you need to do it.
3. **The problem you're solving and the impact you're making.** What's the issue you're addressing out there in the (cultural) world? What difference are you making?
4. **Your current work and emotional cause.** This is the chance to talk about what you're working on right now. It can offer a tangible, memorable example that has the ability to emotionally connect with potential donors.
5. **Why you need support.** This could be the place to say how much it costs to run your organisation or deliver your work. Show the value for money you provide and why every donation makes a difference.
6. **The jeopardy.** What would happen if you didn't exist?
7. **The ask – call to action (CTA).** And finally your ask – and thanks – for considering donating to your organisation.

Accompany this copy with a donation form with a fully-tested, frictionless online giving journey, prioritising regular (rather than one-off) giving by direct debit. The Donate page and other channels and related content can be enlivened through the selection of well chosen images and pull quotes.

**What we did at Art UK**

Art UK's case for support is on its Donate page (see Figure 3.7 opposite).

**What are the results?**

For Art UK, making these changes to its online giving is already making a difference. After just a few weeks, daily average donations were hitting £366 per day, getting closer to reaching their £400 target.

Average donation levels are up, with a significant proportion of donations being made from our suggested regular giving amounts, showing that those price points are working well. Social media and e-newsletter content have a positive effect on Art UK donation levels, channels that were not previously utilised for regular giving messaging. Plus, an expanded range of payment methods is encouraging donations, while the new, easier journey for claiming Gift Aid has also seen an increase in take-up.

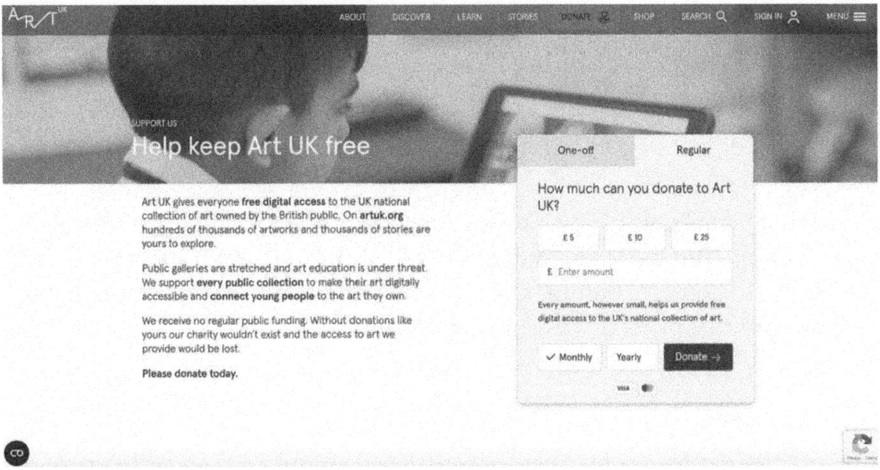


**Figure 3.7** Art UK's 'Donate' page

## Content design

In Part 2, we've looked at different types of pages and examples of what users tend to want from those pages. Understanding user needs helps to prioritise the order of information on a page and inform the design and format of that information. We have also started to look at how this process might apply to a longer user journey, spanning more than one page. In following this process, we've been using the techniques of 'content design'.

### What is content design?

In the last couple of years, I've heard more and more people in the cultural sector talking about content design, but it's not always widely understood. Content design is using user insights to prioritise and determine the order, priority and design of content on a given page.

Some readers in the UK might remember DirectGov (now replaced by Gov.uk, www.gov.uk). It was where we went to access government services like booking a driving test and paying your income tax. It was incredibly difficult to use! DirectGov was made up of an estimated 3,500 separate UK government websites that had all grown independently (Winters, 2016). In each case, departments had made different decisions about the structure, design and remit of how they would present their information. This made it difficult for users to learn how to efficiently use these sites. Without a firm governance structure, a similar situation can arise with GLAM websites, leaving them in a complete mess.

The key difference between the approach DirectGov took and the solution Gov.uk came up with was that the latter used content design.

## Why is content design useful?

### *User testing and data*

The digital team behind Gov.uk were the Government Digital Service (GDS). They weren't the first to conduct user testing and data analysis before building web content, but the scale, methodology and professionalism they built around this process was very significant.

### *Sign-off by web professionals*

Before GDS, government departments individually created and approved their content. The civil servants who were signing off web content decisions had no background in user-centred design, usability best practice or writing for the web.

The person heading up content at GDS at the time was Sarah Richards (now Winters). When she coined the term 'content designers', she was advocating for the validity of her team and their process as a professional discipline. For the first time, there was a word for this emerging discipline of translating user research into web page design that met best practice and delivered against user needs. The content designers were responsible for ensuring vision and consistency across government websites and in leading and evolving the discipline of content design.

This team was responsible for signing off content. Subject matter experts in government departments could fact check the content, but they were no longer responsible for signing it off. This is a key distinction that still seems to be a knotty point of contention on almost every web content project I work on, in or outside the cultural sector.

### *Content isn't just words on a page*

By calling her team content 'designers' rather than 'editors', Sarah was encouraging the team to think of the job of creating web page content as different from purely a 'writing' role.

We've all been taught to write documents and essays. However, the internet is not like print media: you can't start at the beginning and read it linearly until you reach the end. There are more than 50 billion pages on the internet (Siteefy, 2024) and, as consumers of information, we have evolved habits to determine whether the page we've landed on will answer our intent and whether we trust it. Web users are interested to find out the context of the information they're reading. Does it seem to be from a credible source? Where does it sit in the site's overall structure? What is the site presenting on the page about the query I was hoping to answer? Therefore, the way we design web pages shouldn't mimic print media.

A well designed web page will think about the most immediate way to present information on a page. This will involve text, but also visual listing modules, subheadings and calls to action. The art of designing a web page is choosing modules that will convey the weight and importance of different kinds of informational elements.

## What's different about content design when applied in the cultural sector?

There are key differences between the practice of content design as it was originally intended (i.e., for use in a government website context) and its use in the cultural sector.

### *Browsing*

In general, users are on Gov.uk to fulfil a task. This is also the case with some of the user journeys on cultural websites, for example, if someone wants to find out your opening hours or whether you have level access. However, one key difference is that people will come to cultural websites for less defined user journeys. Maybe they've clicked on a blog post that they've seen tweeted and thought it might be interesting. Maybe they're interested in spinning wheels and landed on your site from Pinterest after looking for a specific design style. Maybe they were looking at exhibition tickets and have clicked through to find out about membership benefits (including free tickets).

Content design, as it was originally conceived, didn't have a great toolkit for editorial content or for commercial upsells (like membership). It assumed users had a defined task in mind and aimed to serve them that as efficiently as possible. This works in some contexts, but very few people wake up in the morning and think, 'I simply must donate to XXX/read the latest blog post by XXX'. For these more browser-orientated tasks, we have to use our judgement about where it is appropriate or helpful to add in contextual links to content that users might find relevant, inspiring or interesting.

### *Images*

In general, government departments do not have a host of unique images they can use to illustrate their pages. In the cultural sector, we're generally very lucky to have hundreds – if not hundreds of thousands – of images that are unique to us. This affords us greater flexibility and variety in how we build and design pages. It also forces us to ask more questions about the optimal relationship between image and text.

Images can be a more direct way to meet a user's needs on a page. For instance, a map is much easier to understand than a series of verbal directions. However, we must also be careful about what images implicitly convey. For example, let's imagine that in the membership section of the website all the images show members who are white and of retirement age. This is likely to convey to users browsing the page that there is a member 'type' and, if they don't identify with that type, they may feel alienated from becoming a member – and potentially from the organisation as a whole.

In Chapter 3, we looked at how to build individual pages that meet the needs of users. We explored the discipline of content design and how that professional practice informs this. In the next chapter we look at what this process looks like when you're dealing not just with a single page but with the whole website.

CHAPTER 4

# Re-envisaging Your Content from the Ground Up

In this chapter, we look at the process of re-envisaging content across a whole website or a whole site section. You might be building a new website and want to refresh the content at the same time; or perhaps you're embarking on a project to rework a particular section of your website.

When people think about content they tend to think 'what am I going to write?' and 'where am I going to put it?'. Just as important to the long-term success of those pages is the question of governance. Keep these questions in mind:

- Who manages the pages and keeps the content up to date?
- What processes do the pages need to go through before changes are put live?

Throughout this chapter we'll look at both these questions. We'll look at how to use user research to create effective pages and how to get buy-in from your organisation. The short-term end goal is to publish great pages. The long-term end goal is to have tools, processes and organisation-wide understanding to keep them that way. This doesn't mean that changes can't ever be made after going live. What it does mean is that, going forward, you're able to create new pages in a structured way that conforms to the rest of the site.

## Content audits

### What's the point of a content audit?

The first thing I like to do right at the beginning of a content project is a 'content audit'. A content audit lays out all the pages on your site section by section and against a series of metrics.

The point of a content audit is to give you a blueprint of the site as a whole, including its structure and the patterns of user behaviour in different site sections. Done well, the audit should be able to raise 'red flags'. It can identify sections that have lots of pages that no one is looking at, as well as sections that are getting lots of traffic but don't contain enough content or onward links to develop that user journey.

## Seeing the wood for the trees

My approach to content audits differs from some of the published guidance in the sector (e.g., La Pope, 2024). The published guidance tends to recommend including numerous fields in the audit document (in some cases amounting to 20 to 30 separate fields). If you take that approach, you can end up with a cumbersome document. Most of the time, at least part of the content audit will need to be updated manually, which creates an increasingly large overhead the more fields you add. Having more fields doesn't help you see the wood for the trees by flagging which pages are performing well or poorly relative to their position in the information architecture (IA).

Inevitably, as you get further into the content design process you'll need to do more section-specific audits. For example, the metrics you use to investigate the performance of an editorial section will be very different to a donate pathway.

This initial content audit should just give you an index of pages, performance and owners. Further down the line, you can do deep dives into search engine optimisation (SEO), reading scores and whether your images have metadata, but to do this for every page of the site at this stage isn't helpful.

## Manual versus scripted content auditing

How you do a content audit depends on the size of your website. You can do an audit manually, row by row, entering the fields for each page. Or you can create a scripted content audit (you may need some developer assistance for this option). A scripted content audit allows you to export the fields you need from other data sources and dynamically produce the content audit with the requisite fields.

The dynamic method sounds far more pleasant, partly because it avoids you getting into the nitty-gritty of the content and the patterns of behaviour between different site sections. However, getting your hands dirty and doing a manual content audit is the best way to get to know the shape of your content and to build up a picture of where to concentrate your energy, even if the process is slow and mechanical. All the frustration you feel at ploughing through low performing pages is useful when it comes to culling content that isn't working and seeing where better content is needed.

For some sites, a purely manual approach is unrealistic. Kristina Halvorson and Melissa Rach state that 'if you have less than 5,000 pages/pieces of content, you should probably look at all of it' (Halvorson and Rach, 2012, 59). This isn't a realistic approach for most GLAM organisations so we're not going to cover it here. If you do decide to go down this route, *Content Strategy for the Web* (Halvorson and Rach, 2012, 59 onwards) has some useful pointers.

## Content audit fields: what to include

As described above, my initial content audit is high level. This helps me understand the current site architecture and isolate where patterns of audience behaviour are doing particularly good or strange things. Here are the fields I tend to include:

### *Page identifiers*

- ID of the page, structured as 1.1, 1.1.1: This helps visualise the different site sections and their relationship to one another. Each top-level navigation item will have a new number.
  In a typical museum site structure, Plan Your Visit and What's On would have an ID of 1 and 2 as both are commonly top-line navigation items. A child page of Plan Your Visit, such as Location, would be 1.1. A child page of Location would be 1.1.1.
- URL – the unique identifier.

### *Performance metrics*

- Page views of each page in a 12-month window: No quantitative metric is going to tell you the full story of a page, but it's useful to flag pages (or entire site sections) that are getting very little traffic, as this indicates where content could be more effective – it's a 'red flag' that wants more investigation, which is all you're trying to establish with the initial content audit.
- An engagement metric: These days I tend to opt for the GA4 metrics 'average engaged time' or 'average engagement rate'. It's worth bearing in mind that average engagement will tend to be lower on a landing page than on a detail page. The purpose of a landing page is to convert users to a detail page, so 'time on page' should be small if signposting is clear and direct. So, not all 'low' engaged time metrics are necessarily a red flag.

*Workflow/governance metrics*

- Last updated: This can be useful – in conjunction with other metrics – as another potential red flag. If pageviews are low and the page was last updated years ago, this might warrant further investigation and potentially make a case for deleting or re-envisaging the content.
- Page/information owner: It's useful to get a sense of who created the page content initially and who's maintaining it now. Which department's expertise does it draw on? This can help you map the follow-up chats you'll want to do based on the findings of the audit.

You can read more about how to get the most from your metrics in Case study 1.1 in Chapter 1.

*Notes*

A notes column allows you to start annotating thoughts/observations from your analysis. You can qualify these thoughts when you look at the web page in more detail and in your follow-up chats with information owners.

*Other areas to consider*

As you get further into the web transformation process, you might use your initial content audit to also map the following:

- Status: reviewed/no change required/change required/move to unpublish.
- SEO metrics (e.g., meta description, word counts for article pages, keywords for the page).
- User stories and user needs for a given page.
- Template type: depending on roles and responsibilities, it might be important for you to have a technical handle on how pages/components are moving and where gaps need to be filled.
- Some site tools, such as Siteimprove, allow you to export metrics like the accessibility of a given page, the reading age and SEO 'score'. These are useful metrics for more focused studies down the line but I wouldn't include them in the initial content audit.

## How to initiate conversations with information owners

Web transformation is not all about quantifiable data. Making effective change to your content and your organisation is both an art and a science.

The data can get you so far, but the 'art' is understanding how to interpret the human element: your users, your content editors and your stakeholders. This next part of the process requires working with other members of your organisation.

In this section, we'll look at a subtype of stakeholders: information owners, also known as subject matter experts (SMEs). In a museum or memory-based organisation, these will often be the curators. But across the institution, it will also likely include, for example, visitor experience, learning teams, membership leads, commercial teams and so on. These are all people you need to work with to use their knowledge to inform the content.

These can also be the people that you need or want to wrest control of web content from, particularly if they have produced content that doesn't deliver against user needs (and may be protective of it) or they want to create new content that doesn't conform to best practice or the overall shape and tone of the new site. For your initial meeting with the information owners, my two recommendations are to start with the data and to use that meeting to understand where they are coming from.

Coming to meetings with information owners armed with a content audit gives you the benefit of objective data to talk through any red flags the audit has thrown up. For example, if you're meeting with the learning team and have found that a particular section of the learning part of the website is performing poorly, the data is a useful way of framing that conversation. The audit data allows you to build more context around the authorship, original rationale, current purpose and viability of sections. Often there is some low-hanging fruit to be discovered, in terms of removing out-of-date pages and pages that no longer have a purpose or answer a user need.

The meeting is also a good opportunity to ask information owners:

- how happy they are with their section of the website
- any ambitions they have for the new website
- their understanding of who the audience is and any research they have on that
- what KPIs might be appropriate
- how content planning, creation, review and evaluation happens in their department – and whether this has changed within the time they've been at the organisation
- how workflow/governance works in their section (e.g., can they publish to live?).

From here, you can get a feel for how the subject matter experts see the role of the digital team. Are your team seen as a department that can solve their technical issues (like IT support) or do they think of you as experts who can help them to realise their public engagement ambitions online?

A web project can be a good opportunity to reposition how the digital team is seen within the wider organisation. Done well, a project can move digital from being seen as a reactive team that fixes other people's problems to one that can proactively provide solutions and sets its own priorities for the wider organisation's benefit. How departments see you will help inform the process and internal comms documents you shape for the project as a whole.

Below is an example agenda for an initial meeting with information owners/SMEs at the start of a web content project.

## Example agenda

### *Introductions*

*Particularly important if you don't know each other well, or haven't worked together before.*

Introduce the web project and the extent to which digital is leading the project and how much and what type of input is needed from information owners. An outline of timelines and when information owner participation is anticipated is useful.

This is also a good opportunity to find out more about them and their department. Who is responsible for what? How long have the team been in post and how involved have they been with the website historically?

### *Understanding the background of the web content*

- How involved have they/their team been with creating and evaluating web content, both now and in the past?
- How happy are they with the content there to date?
- Do they have any particular ambitions for the new website?

### *Understanding workflow/governance*

- What permissions do their team have (e.g., can they publish to live?).
- How does content planning, creation, review and evaluation happen in their department? Has this changed within the time they've been at the organisation?

*Looking at the content audit*

By looking at the content audit together, you can ask specific questions about high and low performing pages:

- What's this page/section (indicate the low performing page/section)? Do you know much about it and who created it? As far as you're aware, is it still needed?
- Do you know much about this section (e.g., a section with lots of content updated years ago)?

*User research*

- Is there any demographic data that already exists about who does and doesn't engage with this part of the museum, either in person or online?
- Is there any research around those audiences, for example their motivations?

*Evaluating success*

What KPIs might be appropriate for this new site section?

*Staff availability*

Are there any months/long periods of unavailability in their team in the next six months (or whatever the duration of the project is)?

## User research

User research is a powerful way of gaining more qualitative data on how well your website is currently performing and for whom. There are a number of different user research techniques that can be useful at the start of a web discovery project.

Online surveys can be useful to get an understanding of who's using the site and how satisfied different kinds of users are with different parts of it. Surveys can provide a lot of data in a short amount of time. The easier you make the survey to complete, the more data points you are likely to get. You can also conduct interviews and usability tests with different kinds of audiences. These more focused studies give you a forensic sense of what is causing barriers in different areas.

## Surveys

It is useful for content editors and managers in GLAM institutions to know about two different kinds of surveys: (1) usability surveys and (2) demographic surveys. We'll talk about demographic surveys more in Chapter 6.

Usability surveys are helpful for getting more data points about how people are experiencing different parts of your website and how satisfaction differs depending on what they are trying to achieve (and what site sections they are accessing).

At One Further, the consultancy I work for, we typically run three types of survey:

1 user intent
2 content engagement
3 exit surveys.

These surveys tend to be very quick to answer, containing just two to three questions and a maximum of one text field. This means we can collect a lot of data across the site very quickly.

**User intent surveys** ask users if they found what they were looking for and, if not, what they were looking for. **Exit surveys** are similar, but they are coded to fire when a user is about to leave the website. As you can tell which page a user was on when they answered a survey, you can identify quite quickly where there are most usability barriers across the site.

**Content engagement surveys** are typically coded to appear only on a certain type of page, for example, articles, collections pages or learning resources – any page with a decent amount of written text on it. These tend to ask respondents to rate the page out of five and give a reason for why they gave the score they did. Data from this kind of survey can help you assess the quality range of these types of pages and how well they are received by readers.

### *Best practice for usability surveys*

An effective (and non-intrusive) web survey is a bit more technically difficult to set up. But it's worth putting the time in (or commissioning someone to help you) to get it right. When set up correctly, web surveys can fire on very specific conditions. For example:

You can programme a survey to only load after a number of seconds, so that a user has had time to browse the site before they answer questions about it.

You can programme a survey to load when a user is about to leave (useful for exit surveys).

You can make sure that no one user sees the same survey twice, or doesn't see the survey if they have already dismissed it on a previous visit.

You can set it to load only on certain pages (this can be useful if – for example – you want to find out more information about what users think about specific areas of the website; like articles, or learning content).

## Usability testing

Usability testing assesses how usable your website (or web app) is in the eyes of its users and your audiences.

Usability testing involves:

- recruiting testers that correspond to your target audience (Jakob Nielsen recommends around five (Nielsen, 2000))
- defining a 'test script' that asks users to find info, or fulfil tasks, using your website
- recording whether a test subject has been able to complete the task
- reviewing which aspects of your website were easier and harder for most users to complete.

### *Why is usability testing helpful?*

Digital content is a topic where lots of stakeholders will have opinions about what 'works'. Usability testing cuts through those individual opinions by providing hard data on what the majority of actual users think. It gives you evidence of what users find (and don't find) when confronted with your content 'in the wild' and without the context of being on the staff.

### *Gaining qualitative feedback*

Usability testing is also a good way to get more qualitative feedback from users. For example, about:

- what they like and dislike
- how cultural content intersects with their life (or doesn't!)
- what they think certain navigation terms or buttons mean
- anything that's off-putting or 'othering' about the design, terminology or imagery on the site currently.

### *Writing a test script*

It's helpful, right at the outset, to have a clear sense of what you're testing and why. You might have a hunch that part of your website isn't serving users as well as it might; or you might want to test multiple parts of your website at the same time. This is often done as part of the research for a new website (as part of what's called the 'discovery' phase). In this case, testing can provide prioritised data points on what to change on the new website.

Usability testing can be large or small scale. You can test small tweaks to a single page right up to testing the whole website. You can test with just one group of five testers or multiple different test groups.

Regardless of the size of the study, you will need to write a test script. This is typically a set of 10 to 15 'tasks' for the participants to complete. A purist approach to usability testing would use tasks that have a pass/fail component; for example, 'see if you can find out how to book a ticket for two adults and one three-year-old using the website'. You can also ask more qualitative questions; for example, how interesting they find certain articles, their first impressions of the homepage, and so on.

### *Recruitment*

When you're deciding who to use for testing, it's good to define upfront who your target and actual audiences are.

You might first recruit 'warm' users – those who already know of your organisation. You can do this by putting a pop-up survey on your website. The survey can also screen your respondents, so that you can recruit a mix of genders and ages, for example.

As well as testing with 'warm' users, it can be useful to test with 'cold' audiences – people who haven't necessarily come to your website before but who you hope might be a potential audience in the future.

If you're hoping to target specific types of users, you might want to use a recruitment tool. For example, if you want to test your learning section with primary and secondary school UK teachers from different types of schools in different parts of the country and of different ages and genders, it's going to be much easier to get those participants relatively quickly using a recruitment tool. The other benefit of using a third-party recruitment tool is that these audiences have no pre-existing connection to you.

The main downside with using a recruitment tool is that you have to pay for it and it's not cheap. However, you should be paying your participants for their time anyway and these recruitment tools generally include the participant reward/incentive within the fee they quote you for recruiting the participants.

Participants for user studies can also be recruited via museum social media, e-mail newsletters and web surveys. These people can complement participants recruited via a recruitment tool as they are likely to be more familiar with the organisation than the population at large. Familiarity with an organisation can be quite a significant variable in how participants perceive it and how easy they find the content to understand.

It's worth remembering that getting people to talk to you for an hour during the working day isn't the easiest. However you choose to recruit audiences, you're likely to over-index on people who have free time/flexibility and are able to talk to you during a typical working day.

By comparing the tests of 'warm' and 'cold' users you can see:

- if your site is biased in favour of those who are already familiar with what you have to offer
- if any aspects are confusing or 'othering' to a non-traditional/cold audience
- what elements draw users in and whether this is different for warm and cold users.

A purist approach to usability testing would run separate tests for most audience variables. For example, you might recruit: (i) one cohort of five users for familiar 'warm' audiences; (ii) another group for non-familiar, 'cold' users; (iii) a third for those with low digital literacy; and (iv) another for mobile testers. In reality, most cultural sector budgets don't allow for more than four sets of tests for any particular project or web application. You will therefore need to think carefully about which variables are the most important for you to test.

### *Facilitation*

There are lots of different ways of facilitating usability testing. We'll be covering remote and in-person testing below.

#### Remote

My preference is to conduct tests remotely over video, saving travel time and costs. Testing remotely means you can speak to audiences across the country (or even the world) and you're less likely to introduce bias in favour of those who live locally. If you want your digital channels to reach a broad audience, testing with a broad audience makes sense.

Most types of digital user research work better remotely. With usability testing, you can see what they're looking at and their expression at the same time. It also feels more informal than if they're in a strange environment on a device they don't usually use, being watched. Watching people access content on their own devices throws up lots of unexpected results even before they get to the web page (the Wild West of Bing and Edge internet browsers should not be underestimated!).

For remote sessions, your recruitment process might look a bit like this:

1 Create a privacy policy for the study, outlining what data you'll be storing, how it will be used and for how long (in the UK this keeps you legally compliant with the Privacy and Electronic Communications Regulations (PECR)).
2 Create an overview of the study for potential participants outlining: (i) what the study is about; (ii) what their participation will involve; (iii) more details on the reward/incentive; and (iv) the time window for the study.
3 Create a screener survey to find out more about potential participants, for example, their age, gender and familiarity with you as an organisation.
4 Acquire a list of willing participants (e.g., from a recruitment agency or pop-up survey).
5 Review that participant list and select testers with a mix of demographics.
6 Find a mutually convenient time to conduct the survey (some tools, like Calendly, allow participants to book directly into your calendar based on where you have free slots).

During the session itself, you'll want to start with some 'ice breaker' questions. These questions help you get a sense of who this person is and how culture intersects with their daily life.

After the ice breaker questions, you'll want to ask the participant to share their screens. From there, you can ask them to bring up the organisation's website and begin running through a script of pre-set questions. It's important to let testers know this is very much a test of the website and not of them. It's useful to ask them to 'think aloud' as they are searching, as this gives you a better sense of what's giving them pause for thought.

#### In person

In-person testing may be a better option if you're testing:

- augmented reality (AR) or virtual reality (VR)
- in-gallery digital (digital technology and platforms that enhance or complement the user/visitor experience)

- content that isn't easily shareable (e.g., because it's not yet live to the public).

With in-person testing, you'll need to hire or book a dedicated room to hold the sessions, as well as reimburse travel costs (up to a fixed pre-agreed limit).

### *Note taking and analysis*

It is possible to record an in-person usability session, but it's more difficult to get a view of the tester's expression and the content they're viewing at the same time. This is something video conferencing technology does very easily.

Work out at the start of the process if you want to use recorded clips in your findings. If you are using recordings, you'll need to be explicit about that in the privacy policy. You'll also need to reiterate it at the start of the study when you ask for the testers' permission to record.

One of the simplest ways of documenting the outcomes of usability testing is in a scoreboard. A traffic light system helps distinguish between 1 (pass), 2 (pass with difficulties) and 3 (fail). A scoreboard like this gives you a sense of where the priority usability barriers are on your site.

The full report can explain what lies behind the scores. For example:

- what problems testers were encountering
- what testers were expecting to see
- whether there were significant differences between testers' responses; e.g., were more tech-savvy users more comfortable with certain user interface (UI) elements compared to others? Were more familiar audiences better able to navigate the site?
- what might have helped or removed the barrier in each case?

I tend to run the recordings from tests through an automated transcription process. This is really useful for evidencing why certain tasks were problematic for users. It means that if you remember a helpful quote, you can search for that particular keyword in the text and play that section back.

As you conduct and analyse your surveys and usability testing, you will start learning more about your users' experience of your website. To help capture these observations, I tend to format the insights in the form of a user story. User stories are the building blocks for how you should structure your new web pages: they're your nuggets of how what you offer intersects with your audience's interests.

A user story is essentially a tripartite sentence in the form of:

- as a …
- I want …
- so that …

For example: 'As a busy mum, I want to find out what's on nearby me in the next week, so that I can plan how I'm going to entertain my children this half term.'

As you develop your content, it can be useful to add user stories identified from the user research to the relevant pages in your content audit and/or navigation specification (more on this later). This means that when you come to write the page, you have a set of user needs to write to.

## Navigation and information architecture testing

When you reach this point in your project, you're ready to start thinking about your new navigation structure. So far, we've investigated what online visitors might want from different parts of your website. We're now going to look at organising that content in a logical fashion so that those visitors can more easily find what they're looking for.

But first, two definitions that will help:

1. **Website navigation**: The top line of navigation on your site. This might be a series of buttons with no interactivity but it might also include a dropdown and/or other clickable elements. We're not talking here about in-page navigation, footers and other navigational elements on the site.
2. **Information architecture (IA)**: The overarching structure of your site. Unlike the website navigation, this has no public 'face', it's simply your working copy of the overall site structure. Some sites have URL hierarchy built into their pathways, so the information architecture is present in the page address itself (e.g., www.tate.org.uk/art/teaching-resource). With other sites, everything exists on the primary level and so this hierarchy isn't visible (e.g., www.ashmolean.org/learning-resources). In either case, you're going to want to have a sense of what content sits where and how a user will navigate through the site to access deeper level pages and fulfil core transactions.

In the sector, we are a little change-averse. If you're going to make a change, you typically want to have some evidence for why you're making that change. This is one of the things I really like about digital, this evidence is quite easy to come by. There are different ways of doing gathering this evidence, including:

- tree testing
- navigation design testing
- card sorting (open/closed).

### Tree testing

Why is this method called 'tree testing'? Think about your website structure as a series of branching pathways. You might have eight items on the primary level – these are your eight branches coming out of the root. Your first branch might then have a further ten branches coming out of it, each of which subdivides further, resulting in a 'node' – a final 'destination' at the end of a user journey.

Tree testing allows you to test how logical your subdivisions are; do users intuitively place content where you have it? As humans, we become very comfortable with what's habitual, so if we're used to finding content in a certain place on a website it can blind us to the fact that a new user might not intuitively look for it here.

How does it work? To conduct a tree test you will need:

- a sitemap
- a task list
- a tool to conduct the test.

#### *Your sitemap*

You'll need to upload a sitemap, in spreadsheet form, to the tool you're using. I tend to do this manually, by replicating the visible navigation structures from the homepage. You can do it dynamically by using an actual sitemap. However, typically your actual sitemap will be large and contain areas of the site that you're not trying to test (as well as lots of orphan pages that users can only generally get to in quite specific circumstances, e.g., if they've completed a form). It's not always helpful to provide all these options as some of them would not be part of a browsing user's actual choice at any point.

You may also want to test a variant to determine how well your current sitemap performs against a new navigation. To do this you'll need to identify where you think there are problems with your current navigation and supply potential solutions to those problems that you can test.

In creating a new navigation, I tend to be guided by what pages are most viewed generally and what people are clicking on most and least from the current navigation. It's useful not just to look at the most popular page views as these will include a lot of pages that are only accessed from search and that don't need to appear (or even shouldn't appear) in the main navigation. Also, monitoring clicks on your existing navigation helps you cull items that aren't being clicked on, so reducing cognitive dissonance for existing users.

Try not to change too many variables within one test or you won't be able to identify why one variant performed better than another.

### *Creating a task list*

As well as the sitemap, you'll need to upload a series of tasks into your tree testing tool. For each task, you'll need to tell the tool where the right destination for the answer is. It makes sense to design tasks where the answer is different between the two variants so that you can compare the success rate between the two.

Example tasks might include:

1. Where would you expect to find out about booking a virtual school visit to one of the museum sites?
2. You've heard that the museum has preserved a lot of audio recordings from dockworkers. Where would you expect to find these?
3. Imagine you have a child who's interested in dinosaurs. Where would you look for something that might interest them on a visit?

Try not to lead users with the term you're putting in the question. In the second example above, if the page they're looking for is called 'oral histories', you should come up with a synonym in the task question (e.g., 'audio recordings' is used in the example above) so that you are not 'leading the witness'. You want participants to use their intuition around the logical structure of your categories and not simply look for identical keywords.

### *Choosing a tool*

Both software packages that I've used for tree testing – Useberry and Treejack by Optimal Workshop – work very similarly. Useberry is a little cheaper (at the time of writing) and has the option to recruit users to your study (but you pay extra to use Useberry's recruitment tool – around $1 a user). Having the option for in-tool recruitment is useful, particularly if you want to test the navigation structure with the general public and those who are unfamiliar with you as an organisation.

### *Analysing the data*

When the data comes in, compare the success rate of tasks. In particular, look at how variant A compares to variant B for the same task. This will help you isolate the more and less intuitive elements of your content structures.

Tools like Useberry or Treejack allow you to distinguish between:

- direct success – where users go directly to the right page
- indirect success – where users initially go down a wrong path, go back on themselves, and then find the correct path.

A high indirect success rate may indicate that there are problems with the labelling of higher level/parent pages. The destination itself may be clearly labelled, but perhaps the parent pages are unhelpfully labelled, meaning users are not going down the right pathway initially.

## Navigation design testing

This is useful for testing where people gravitate to in your navigation as it appears in the visual design.

For this test, you'll need:

- a screenshot of two different versions of a navigation design you want to test; e.g., you could A/B test an old or new navigation, or two new ones
- a single question (per test) that you want users to answer
- a tool that allows you to export a heatmap of clicks
- a recruitment tool.

### *When to use it*

In March 2022, Tate's main navigation bar had a big blue circular button saying, 'Become a member' (Webarchive, 2022). Today (in 2024), this button has changed to a much smaller teal rectangle that also says 'Become a member'.

It would be impossible to test the difference between these two using tree testing, as both 'Become a member' buttons exists in the same part of the IA. However, you might want to test the difference between these two designs, in terms of how prominent the signposting is to an online visitor, before making the change. This is where navigation design testing comes in.

### *A tool*

I've used Useberry and Lyssna for navigation design testing. Useberry has a monthly/annual cost attached to it and then additional costs for recruitment. Lyssna allows you to do single tests and just pay for recruitment, making it a good option for one-off/ad hoc testing.

Both allow you to pick a recruitment panel by locality, level of education, household income and so on, or allow you to source your own recruitment. This can be useful for testing with a broad general public audience who don't know a great deal about your organisation, but for whom you would hope your site is intuitive.

You can also use these tools to test how different designs might make a user feel and what impression the designs give of the organisation (not possible using tree testing). To do this, you might ask them to rank a series of adjectives against the navigation design, including terms like 'boring', 'traditional', 'fun', 'welcoming' or 'interesting'.

### *Some final thoughts on navigation design*

Most museums I've come across have a navigation that broadly follows this template:

> Visit | What's on | Collections | Discover | Learn | (Shop)
> (Header links: About us | Support us | Venue hire)

I don't think it's necessarily a bad thing to have a menu structure that is similar to other organisations, so long as you're not replicating mistakes used elsewhere. For example, always opt for 'Support us' rather than 'Support'. In testing, we almost always find that participants think of 'Support' as support you can give them (as in IT support for navigating their website), not support they can give you. 'Support us' helps make this clear.

If you're a performing arts organisation, your 'What's on' page is likely to be the most clicked-on part of your site, so make this easily visible and clickable even on mobile (e.g., don't make users have to go to the burger menu to find it).

Don't forget that a navigation design change may have more profound implications on mobile than on desktop, and this is probably where the majority of your sessions are coming from.

## Card sorting

Card sorting is another method for testing the structure of the pages on your website. It works by laying out all the page names as 'cards' and asking users to group them into logical categories.

There are two types of card sorting: open and closed. Open is where you allow users to supply category labels for the groupings they've created. Closed is where you ask participants to sort content under pre-defined category headings.

Card sorting is less useful for testing or fixing the overarching structure of your website. It's more likely to give you a sense of general impressions and patterns rather than firm statistical analysis of a better performing IA. However, open card sorting does offer something different in that you allow users to supply category names (in a way that's impossible in tree testing). It's therefore a useful technique where the findability of lots of similar pages is key, for example:

- articles in an editorial section
- collections records in a collection online portal
- shop products on an e-commerce site
- pages in an intranet.

In this case, what you're asking users to do is supply filters or ways of sorting similar items into category terms that come to mind for them. Used this way, card sorting is a useful technique for getting ideas on what kinds of category terminology come to mind intuitively for your users (as opposed to just replicating internal categorisation, which might not match the words people use to describe or group these things in the real world).

I wouldn't run a card sorting test with more than 50 items as this can be overwhelming. You can run card sorting remotely or in-person. I tend to prefer remote as you can get much larger datasets and individuals are less swayed by the thoughts of more extroverted participants.

## Writing web content

This section describes the tools and processes you can put in place to keep content consistent as it is being developed. I'll talk about three things I've used that have proved helpful:

1. a digital style guide
2. a content manual for planning page content
3. digital knowledge staff training sessions.

## Digital style guide

The purpose of a style guide is to maintain editorial consistency when writing text. I compile a style guide from the following main sources:

1. You may already have a **style guide** that's used for print content. This is a good starting point for finding organisational-specific conventions around things like capitalisation. But it shouldn't be adopted wholesale – some things that work fine for print (e.g., the use of italics and ampersands) are not good practice on the web.
2. The last word in credible research into best practices for writing for the web is from the **Nielsen Norman Group**. If you read just one of their publications, I'd recommend *How People Read the Web* (Nielsen Norman Group, 1997). This takes you through the data and findings from which we derive writing for the web best practices around formatting and chunking text so that it can be more easily read online.
3. **The Government Digital Service's A–Z Style Guide** (Gov.uk, 2024) has absorbed a lot of this research. Some of their style guide is specific to government departments (e.g., their advice on how to write about 'A levels', but others – like 'abbreviations' – are useful guidelines, based on digital best practice, for your own style guides). Under 'W', there is a great section on 'words to avoid'. This includes entries like: 'deliver: use "make", "create", "provide" or a more specific term (pizzas, post and services are delivered – not abstract concepts like improvements)', 'foster (unless it's children): use "encourage" or "help"'.
4. I've also tended to add in organisation-specific **tone of voice guidelines** so that the digital style guide feels particular to the organisation and informed by agreed communications priorities.

These four inputs should help guide you in creating your own A to Z style guide, helping content editors create consistent web pages that conform to best practice for writing for the web.

## Content manuals – how to get sign-off for your web content

To make effective change and to get people on your side, you need to explain your thinking. To get buy-in for changes to web content, it's not enough to present stakeholders with the proposed finished product. You've got to take these people on a journey with you – and not get their backs up too much by pointing out everything that's wrong with the current content!

Think about it. When you're trying to get sign-off for a draft web page, your draft will differ from a live web page. Unlike a web page, with an offline file you have no sense of:

- where in the navigation this page exists – i.e., the context in which someone might navigate to it
- how a user typically gets there – are people landing on this page from search (and not via the navigation)?
- whether the majority of people are viewing this page on a much smaller screen size.

To get effective input from stakeholders and subject matter specialists, you have to provide them with this context. To do this, I've created what I call a 'content manual'. It's not rocket science – it's basically a document that gives stakeholders that missing context. Based on how common a scenario getting sign-off on new web pages is, I'm surprised I've not seen more examples of it. I see a lot of pixel-perfect design files for new proposed web pages, but this doesn't help a stakeholder understand what's changed and, crucially, why.

The whole point of content design is to use user research to create data-informed design. We should have a better, more transparent way of presenting this back to those who haven't been part of the content design process, allowing them to meaningfully input within set parameters. Figure 4.1 on the next page visualises where I see content manuals sitting in an overall content development and sign-off process.

### *Content manual: template*

**Outline the aim of the document:** Start your content manual by outlining what the aim of the document is. If you'd never heard of a content manual before, it is likely that the stakeholder won't know what it is either.

The aim of the document is three-fold. It should:

- Outline the context in which audiences land on this page:
  - Is it from search, from campaigns or from the navigation?
  - Where does the page live in the site IA; what's the logical hierarchy?
- State what the intended purpose and audience is for the page:
  - What do we know from user research and testing about what these audiences need from it?
  - Define the user needs and the acceptance criteria to meet for the page to be deemed a success.

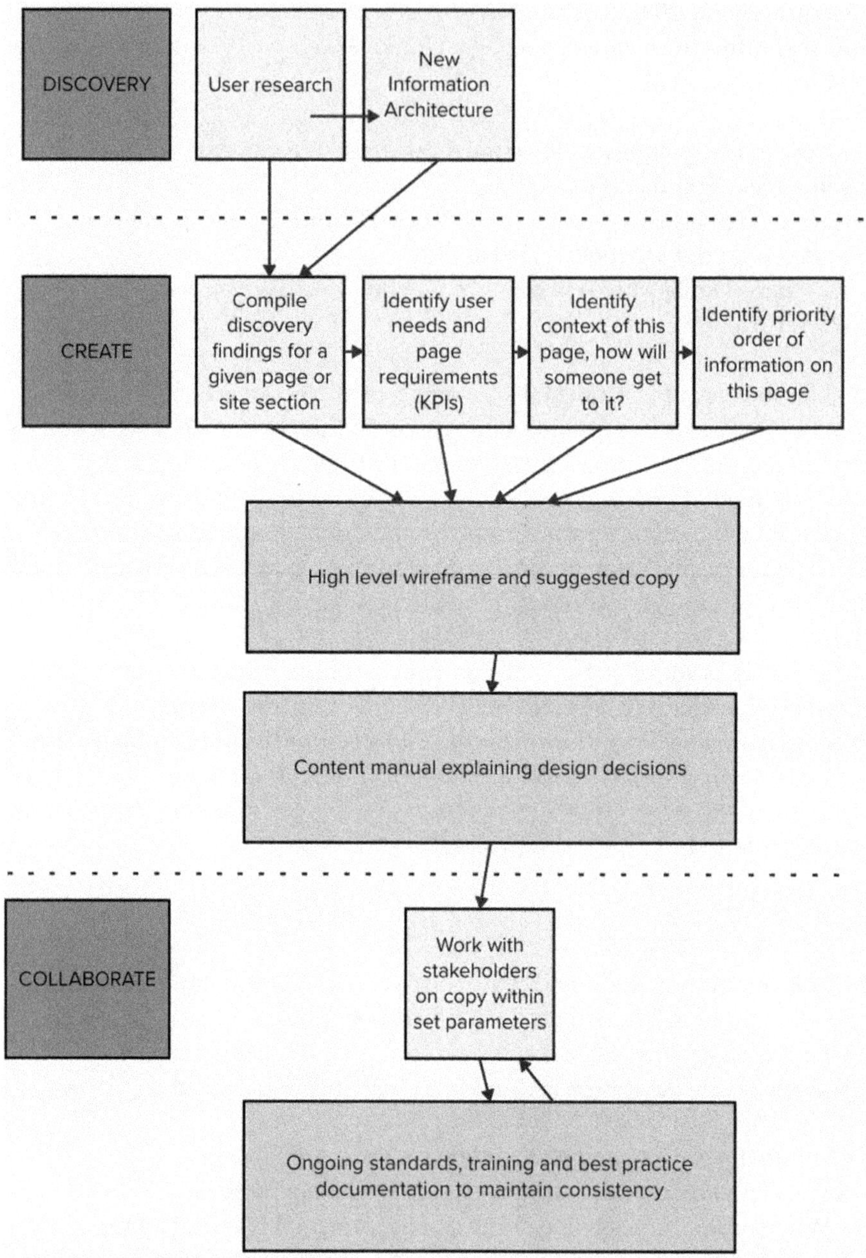


**Figure 4.1** *Process diagram for how a content manual can fit into a content design sign-off process*

- Translate all the above into a suggested design and copy, presenting the information users need in an effective way.

*Example content manual for a 'Plan your visit' page*

Below, I've outlined an example of what I might use as a content manual for a 'Plan your visit' museum page. It provides stakeholders with the conceptual context about what the page needs to do to be a success.

Introduction

**High-level purpose**: This is likely to be the most popular page on the site (after the homepage). It should function like an online storefront to all potential visitors. It should be easy for potential visitors to find the information they need, at the same time as inspiring a broad range of visitors to come to the space.

**Aims**:

- Allow potential new visitors to feel comfortable and inspired to visit the museum.
- Give new visitors the information they need to know about what to expect on their visit.
- Allow returning visitors to check on details that might have changed since their last visit (such as the gallery map).
- Allow users with additional needs to find the information they're looking for.

**Target audience**: All the museum's actual and potential visiting audience.

**Tone**: The tone should be welcoming, clear and inclusive. The purpose of this page is not just to inform but also to engage and inspire confidence in audiences, including new audiences and those with additional needs.

**Requirements**:

- It must be easy for a new user to scan quickly.
- It must be easy for existing users to quickly navigate to details relevant to them.
- Imagery and tone should feel inclusive and inspire confidence.
- Facts should be relayed logically and clearly, leaving no room for misinterpretation.
- Visuals and tone should reflect the warmth of the organisation's ethos and also highlight how visitors can get the most out of their visit (e.g., what they can see).

- It should point to maps and guides that allow new potential visitors to conceptualise the kind of experience they will have and how to plan their trip.

### Visual representation of the modules of the page, rationale and suggested text

This section of the content manual will look different depending on the page you're looking at, how many modules your content management system (CMS) has and what your content design wireframe looks like.

For 'Plan your visit', you might have components for:

- header banner
- opening times
- directions and parking
- access
- what's here
- during your visit.

For each of these, you need to create a subheading in your manual, screenshot what the module looks like and include any suggested text. You should also explain the rationale for the module's placement and content. Here's an example below.

**Module 1 – Heading banner:** Figure 4.2 below demonstrates what this module might look like on this page.

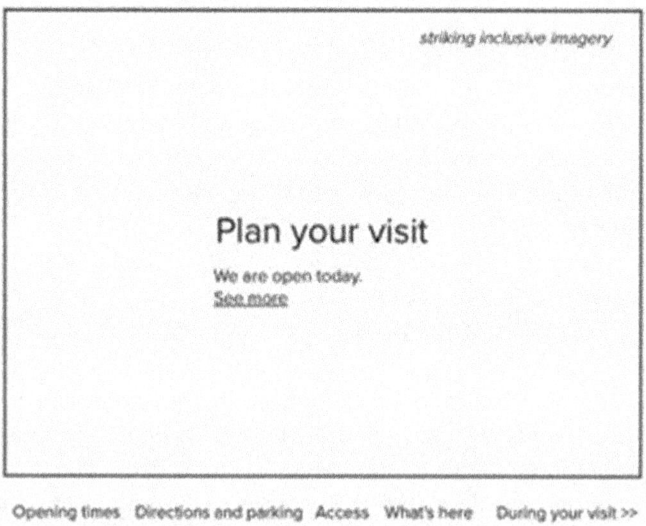


**Figure 4.2** *Lo-fi visual of what the module design looks like*

This is the only module that will be above the fold on all screen sizes. We know from our user testing that the main reason people are on this page is for opening hours. We need to present that information high up to answer that need. We also want to inspire people to feel welcome and included here and we can do that through using inclusive, warm images and language.

I'm less concerned here about what the rationale for each module is, but more the presentation format. You're inviting stakeholders who haven't been part of the process to engage with your content. So, you need a way to present to them what data and insight you have that has led you to the design you're proposing.

**Module 2 – Welcome statement**: As Figure 4.3 below shows, this doesn't need to be complicated.

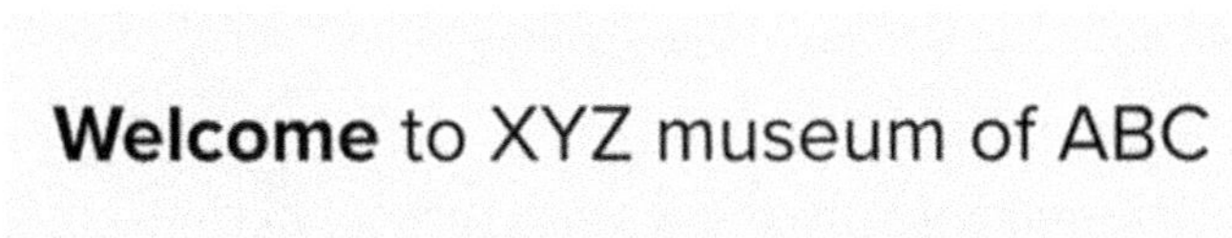


**Figure 4.3** *Second module on page – short welcome statement*

A short welcome should briefly articulate who you are and what you're known for. People may not know this and quite possibly don't know why you're worth visiting. Distil this into a single sentence to keep people reading.

**Module 3 – Opening hours:** See Figure 4.4 below.

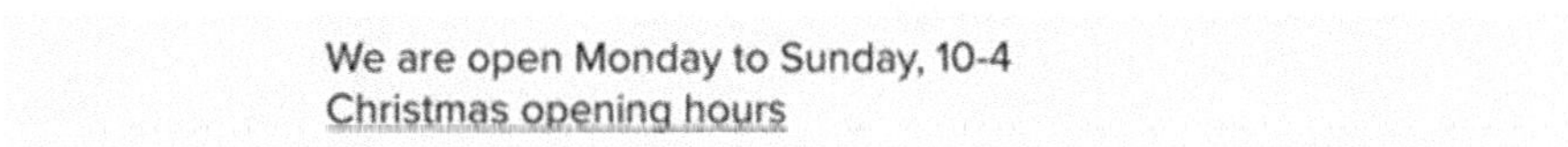


**Figure 4.4** *Third module on page – opening hours*

Most people want to know when you are open on a weekly basis. We found that a small number of international visitors and groups want to plan further in advance around holiday season – this content is provided on a separate page but linked to here.

**Module 4 – Directions and parking:** See Figure 4.5 on the next page.

We know that users take in geographic/spatial information more readily from diagrams than from text. In this image, we're showing where the nearest parking spots are.

The accordions on the right-hand side open and close when clicked and provide more detailed links and itineraries for how to get to the museum depending on method of travel.

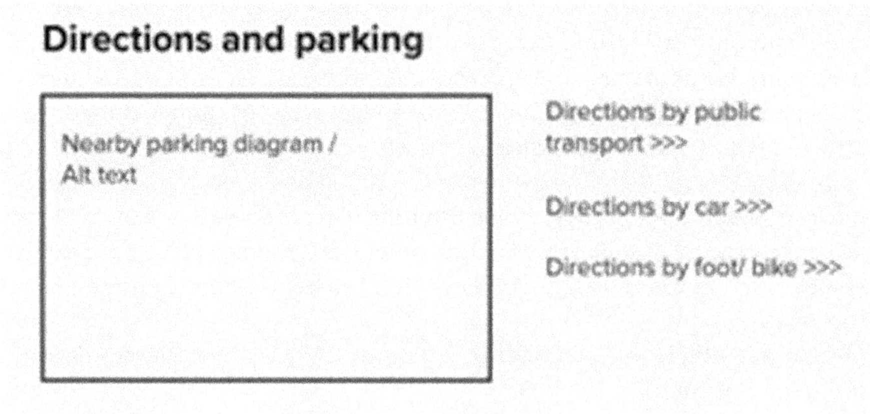


**Figure 4.5** *Fourth module on page – directions and parking*

By using the example of a 'Plan your visit' page, I'm showing you my method of presenting a sign-off document to stakeholders that takes them through discovery and the context of where the page exists on the site and how it will be accessed online. I've found this method useful for engaging stakeholders in the process and for finding ways to collaborate with them usefully and within a set framework. It keeps content design decisions in the digital team but allows inflection points with subject matter experts. This helps create informed content that is within a robust design structure and meets best practice for web content.

## Digital knowledge staff training sessions

The third element of stakeholder management that I've found useful in the context of developing content for a new website is 'digital knowledge' all-staff training sessions. These can be announced early on in the web project and cover topics such as how to use Google Analytics, writing for the web and SEO.

When I've run these training sessions, we've asked all departments to send two members of staff to monthly meetings – one who they consider to be quite knowledgeable on digital skills (and might consider this as part of their continuing professional development (CPD)) and another who is less knowledgeable and possibly a bit more resistant to the change. By having face-to-face time with these staff members, we were able to create a greater shared understanding of the research tools and processes informing the change. This meant that we were able to gain advocates (where we might have had detractors) and could keep an ongoing open line of communication about the project as a whole and how it was evolving.

By the time the website launched, staff across the organisation felt they had more ownership of the final product and an understanding of the skills and knowledge they needed in order to inform new changes to existing pages or create new ones.

## Inclusive web content

Case study 4.1 below gave me goosebumps when I first read it. Since 2020, Museums Galleries Scotland (MGS) has been doing sector-leading work in their commitment to inclusion and anti-racism. Those values have driven how they interact with the sector, but also how they look at, and talk about, their own service and policies. The case study focuses on a new website and how they went about embedding those values in every stage of the redevelopment process.

In digital roles, it's easy to feel quite far removed from the abstract values statements that appear in strategic plans. This case study shows how digital roles can do meaningful work translating strategic commitments digitally and demonstrates how MGS went about doing this on a practical level.

---

### Case study 4.1: Can inclusion drive a website redevelopment?

*Kelly Forbes and the Communications Team, Museums Galleries Scotland (MGS)*

We needed a new website to host and support the next Scotland's Museums and Galleries Strategy 2023–2030 (Museums Galleries Scotland, 2024a), which was due to launch in February 2023. It was important to us that this strategy didn't become a 'document for the shelf'. The ambition was to create a living, breathing, strategy for the full lifetime of its use. The strategy sets out a vision for Scottish museums and galleries to be accessible and inclusive to all. That vision is also a part of our own commitment to be an inclusive, anti-racist organisation (Museums Galleries Scotland, 2024b). So, there were high expectations of any website we built. This case study takes you through our ongoing journey to embed those values into the content, design and structure of our new website.

#### Inclusive design

Several parts of the website design process led to greater inclusion across the site:

- Building from scratch is an efficient way to remove unconscious bias baked into an existing website. If you can't build a new site, you can reduce that barrier by including inclusive prompts throughout your project. We use prompts developed by Nuzhat Uthmani (Museums Galleries Scotland, 2024c). Nuzhat is a teacher and anti-racism educator who provided her expertise on the Empire, Slavery and Scotland's Museums project (Museums Galleries Scotland, 2024d).
- Find a developer who shares your values and will challenge your views. Questions about anti-racism, inclusion, climate and accessibility were part of the tender process. They made sure our chosen developer, Primate (www.primate.co.uk), would be a critical friend, who we could trust and learn from.

- Think about power dynamics in the design of your site. Transactional analysis helped us think about areas of work that, unconsciously, feel paternalistic. Understanding this increased equity by shifting our focus to collaboration and relationships with users, rather than 'speaking as an authority'. It's subtle, but the information architecture on the website groups activity based on this analysis.
- Speak to your users often for feedback, but also speak to people who don't use your site yet. We often stopped to ask, 'who isn't here and why?'. We'd then take action to bring those people into our focus groups and the user stakeholder group.

**Content audit and migration**

We agreed in our first meeting that nothing goes live on the new website until the content meets our commitment to anti-racism, inclusion and sustainability. That decision spawned a complicated content workflow, which involved everyone in the organisation.

We did lots of research on language, inclusive copywriting and website accessibility to seek out best practice. Everyone in the team developed a different area of expertise in writing and copy editing and helped educate others. Each piece of content had three stages of review and approval before it was ready to upload to the website. It was a huge task. The payoff has been twofold. Our website content reflects a greater number of perspectives and experiences and it's easier to read. Plus, involving the entire organisation in content creation has increased the sense of ownership everyone has over the website.

**Inclusive media and educating staff**

While a picture may paint a thousand words, we really don't want that many in alt-text. We use the prompt: 'what can we see in this picture? And what is useful for others to know?'. If there are people in an image, we may describe their life stage, skin tone, hair colour and clothing. But we won't make assumptions about their gender, ethnicity or their relationships to other people in the image. With rich media, no video goes up on the site without captions. We're also working to add transcripts to all our rich media content after feedback from neurodiverse user testers.

We know visual representation is important. It's why our homepage shows a banner of images instead of one hero image. It was a brave choice when the feedback was 'it doesn't look like a homepage'. We've spent time talking to our staff about the importance of representation across the site. We've also created training and guidance on how to maintain high standards of accessibility and inclusion across the site. Our people know it's everyone's responsibility to improve, not simply something for the Communications Team to police. That mindset is important. Making content accessible and inclusive first isn't an imposition, it's another way that we're working to improve things for the whole sector.

**Review, refine, repeat**

The website discovery process was great for finding issues to fix through the new website development. It allowed us to build a dynamic and engaging website with an accessible first approach. But the process isn't over. We're constantly looking for more feedback. New accessibility user testing has provided more insight on where we can improve for users with disabilities.

Reviewing the site content will be an ongoing process too. An annual content review, like the one for content migration, will require our staff to review their content and look for improvements.

Way back in 2021, we set out our mission to 'create a website that embodies the values of our organisation'. The most important thread through all this work is that it mirrors the work we're doing as a whole organisation. Inclusive, sustainable, anti-racist practice is something we're acting on as individuals and as a team. Building the site to be equitable was a collaborative effort, maintaining and improving the site will be too.

## Further reading

If you're about to undertake a major web content project, I'd recommend the following books. They are sector-leading in providing an overview of best practices and thinking in the field.

- *How People Read on the Web* by the Nielsen Norman Group. This book is mentioned above in this chapter and it's the best research I've found. It looks forensically at how people scan web pages, isolates how that's different to how people read print, and outlines what that means for a web content writer. They publish a free summary (Nielsen Norman Group, 1997), but if your institution is happy to pay for the full paid report, there's more detail in there (Nielsen Norman Group, 2024).
- *Content Strategy for the Web* by Kristina Halvorson and Melissa Rach (Halvorson and Rach, 2012). This is a really sensible, step-by-step guide covering a lot of the same ground I've outlined here. It's a good 'how to' manual to have to hand before undertaking your first big web content project. The authors have much larger websites in mind than we typically have in the cultural sector, so you'll need to be sensible about how many of the steps it makes sense for you to follow.
- *Content Design*, 2nd edn, by Sarah Winters (was Richards) and Rachel Edwards (Winters and Edwards, 2024). Sarah was Head of Content at Government Digital Service when they were building the first version of Gov.uk, defining the standards of things like the A–Z style guide and how to employ agile project processes to large web content projects. She created the term 'content design', which has since generated great swathes of employment in the form of 'content designers'. It's a great, pithy read.
- *The Content Strategy Toolkit* by Meghan Casey (Casey, 2015). This book includes around 28 downloadable templates, tools and visualisations taking you through different parts of a web transformation project. As with Halvorson and Rach (2012), it's geared towards much larger web builds, so a lot of the advice and steps in the process you can disregard. It's great as a reference point for specific parts of the process and sense checking your deliverables in a given area.

# Part 3
# Creative and Strategic Content

In Part 2 we covered a lot of ground. We looked at how to build pages that allow users to fulfil their needs on a particular page, be that booking an exhibition ticket or making a donation.

This next part looks more at experiential content, where we're less concerned with visitors completing tasks and more thinking about content that captures their imagination.

In Chapter 5, we explore how to tell stories effectively online. The chapter opens with two case studies: firstly, from writer Anna Faherty, who presents what she learnt in developing online non-fiction stories for the Wellcome Collection; and then a case study from Wellcome itself, looking at how commissioning non-fiction storytelling (including Anna's work) fitted into a wider strategy for the organisation. The final section in this chapter takes a step back to ask what the point of writing online stories is. Editorial, articles, blogs – everyone is creating reams of this type of content. But what purpose is it serving in relation to overarching organisational mission? And how effective is it?

In Chapter 6 we take a step back and look at content strategy more broadly. We use both 'content' and 'strategy' in the sector in very imprecise ways. This chapter opens with an analysis of what is meant by the term and makes the case that most successful 'content strategy' projects are really about audience development. We then explore various research techniques with which you'll want to be familiar in order to enact a content strategy/digital audience development project. These include surveys and focus groups.

The chapter then moves on to look at ways of categorising and visualising audiences; for example, through segmentation and audience development frameworks. We look at different kinds of content strategy, such as social media or paid search strategy and how to enact those. We end with how to assimilate multiple research inputs into a coherent strategy.

Chapter 7 is 'content strategy in action'. Here we consider two case studies from the Tank Museum and Opera North, and look at how these two institutions used a brilliant content strategy to diversify their audiences and generate income.

CHAPTER 5

# Creating Editorial Content

## Telling stories online

One of the most effective ways to make an audience feel something is to tell them a story. Human brains are hard wired for story and storytelling has been linked to a survival mechanism. It enables us to assimilate things outside our direct lived experience. In doing so, we empathise with the actors – the characters – in the story.

Case study 5.1 below provides a guide on how to create a story in the first place, what are the mechanics of storytelling and how does that translate online? When faced with a blank page, you want to have a sense of how to build that page technically (using subheadings and keyword research) but also how to populate that page with a satisfying story around those parameters. This is where Anna's brilliant advice comes in.

Anna Faherty is the author of *Writing Online and Audio Stories* (2024). She is a writer, interpretation developer and trainer who works with cultural and heritage organisations. She's also a lecturer at London College of Communications. She's passionate about developing audience-focused content that delivers desired outcomes.

### Case study 5.1: How stories work and what that means for content creators

*Anna Faherty, writer and Founder of Strategic Content*

When I got a gig writing one of Wellcome Collection's first digital stories a decade ago, I was excited by the contract – for a second. Then I panicked. I had plenty of writing experience, but I realised I knew next to nothing about the mechanics of storytelling.

I'm pretty sure I'm not the only person who's ever struggled with this. Look at numerous 'our story' or 'stories from the collections' web pages and you'll soon see that most online text or audio 'story' content fails to tell a story.

### What even is a story?

To get myself story ready, I buried myself in research, only to keep reading the same mantras: our brains are hard-wired for story; stories help us make sense of the world; stories are memorable; stories are marketable ...

Sadly, none of these clichés helped me make much practical sense of what a story actually is or what stories do, particularly in a non-fiction setting.

Today, after collaborating and writing, teaching and writing, researching and writing, I finally understand that the essence of any story is remarkably simple: all stories introduce us to someone facing some kind of challenge and then show us what happens next.

Readers and listeners are drawn into stories because they want to know how that person overcomes that challenge – whether it's a young Victorian girl who contracted smallpox or how Henry Wellcome found space for his ever-expanding spear collection.

Armed with this understanding of stories, I realised two important things:

1 **Stories about objects don't have the same emotional impact as stories that revolve around people**. If you want to tell an attention-grabbing, emotionally engaging story about a beautiful 18th-century vase, you need to tell a story about someone related to it. That might be the maker of the vase, an owner of it, the conservator who repaired it or someone else entirely.
2 Stories aren't synonymous with comprehensive histories written for Wikipedia. Stories rarely start by telling you when someone was born. Instead, **stories focus on a particular challenge that happened to a particular person at a particular time and place**.

For some cultural content creators, these two points may prompt new ways of kicking-off stories. But even if you have a good opening line, how do you get people to stick around for the rest of the story when they could be consuming listicles and watching TikTok instead?

### The Story Funnel

The Story Funnel can help. Based on narrative theory and empirical research, the Story Funnel is a simplified model of what happens when someone reads or listens to a story. It's a useful tool for understanding how stories work or for constructing and telling stories that keep people with you.

The concept is inspired by the Marketing Funnel, a similar model that illustrates how marketing activities convert a large pool of disinterested strangers into smaller and smaller numbers of engaged purchasers and followers. The Story Funnel, on the other hand, sucks readers or listeners in and pulls them deeper and deeper into the world of the story. It comprises five stages:

1 Attract
2 Involve
3 Transport
4 Transform
5 Act

Let's look at what happens to readers (or listeners) at each stage:

*ATTRACT: readers spot a character in trouble and pay attention*
As social creatures, humans spend an inordinate amount of time monitoring what other people are thinking and doing. When we're online and notice someone like us in trouble, or a stranger facing a challenge that resonates, our natural curiosity puts us on alert. We pause or click through because we want to find out more.

*INVOLVE: readers imagine what's going on and become engaged with the story*
We become involved in a story because we picture scenes within it and build our own interpretation of events. The same process happens when you watch a couple sitting at a table in a restaurant and imagine what's going on with them. You create a feasible backstory by combining the cues you're given with personal knowledge of similar situations. If we identify with the person in the story, we root for them and imagine all the ways they might extricate themselves from trouble – like hoping one of the people at the other table gets away from the obstinate bore they are dining with.

*TRANSPORT: readers become so involved that they leave the real world behind*
When we're fully immersed in a story we detach from real life. We're transported into the environment of the story and want to influence what happens, which is why you might find yourself shouting 'don't go into the cellar!' at a character in a horror film. We travel so deeply into this other world that we suspend disbelief and become vulnerable to influence from within the story.

*TRANSFORM: readers emerge thinking and feeling differently*
Like travelling in real life, travelling into a story opens our minds to alternative ways of thinking and provides new perspectives on the world and ourselves. Numerous research studies show that stories change us. For instance, if you read a story about a holiday destination, you're more likely to view it favourably than if you read a list of facts about it. If a child listens to a story while in hospital, they'll view nursing staff more positively – and even feel less physical pain – than if they played a game instead.

*ACT: readers do something in light of their story experience*
Once you've spent time in a story, you're primed to act afterwards. In comparison with receiving facts about an issue, reading or listening to a story makes you more likely to subscribe to a newsletter, change your behaviour or donate greater sums of money to a story-related cause. It's no wonder literary scholar Jonathan Gottschall describes storytelling as 'witchery' (Gottschall, 2012).

**10 storytelling tips**
You could write a whole book about how to usher readers through each stage of the Story Funnel (as I've done – Faherty, 2024), but the following tips provide quick starting points for writing stories that attract, involve and influence readers and listeners.

1 **Consider your purpose and brand when you choose what story to tell**: People take messages and points of view away from stories. It makes sense for those messages and perspectives to reflect your brand and your organisational goals.
2 **Reflect what's going on in the world and the emotional tone of the moment**: Stories resonate more strongly if they feel familiar – so much so that readers feel more transported into a story about winter when they read it during winter. We also feel

more transported when a story's emotional tone matches our emotional state, which explains why we seek out 'weepie' movies when we feel low.

3 **Choose a likeable character and a challenge that resonates**: When you're telling true-life stories, you can't, of course, concoct the perfect character. You can, however, choose to tell the story from a specific character's perspective – someone your users will identify with. You might even place your user in the story themselves, as these opening questions from a Migration Museum podcast (Migration Museum, n.d.) do: 'How far would you travel to find love? Can you imagine crossing the ocean to marry a total stranger?'

4 **Introduce your character and challenge as soon as possible:** Grab attention by posing the challenge in the first couple of lines, as this National Archives of Australia story (National Archives of Australia, 2023) does: 'On 23 November 1935, American Lincoln Ellsworth flew across the Antarctic to explore and map new territory. But when arduous conditions and insufficient fuel forced his plane to land, he and his pilot were stranded on a remote base with no way to contact the outside world.'

5 **Provide visual and sensory details**: These involve readers and listeners by enabling them to build their own image of where the action takes place and what's going on. Quotes from first-hand sources often do this well, as this line from a pilot who witnessed a British Nuclear Test, featured in an Avro Heritage Museum podcast (Avro Heritage Museum via Spotify, 2022), shows: 'I can still see the skeleton of my fingers through the hole ... when that flash went off'.

6 **Leave gaps**: You might recognise this tip under the more familiar guise of 'show, don't tell', a maxim that enables readers and listeners to create their own interpretation of events. This extract from an Old Operating Theatre Museum's interactive story (Old Operating Theatre, n.d.) shows us just how unsanitary 19th-century surgery practices were, without explicitly telling us so: 'You wipe the knife on your apron and pass it to Furze. He places it back in the velvet-lined box ready for use on the next patient.'

7 **Build suspense**: Transport people into the story world by creating uncertainty about whether the character will overcome their challenge. Once you've sparked initial curiosity, create a momentary information gap, for instance by stepping away from the action to deliver a nugget of backstory. As the story moves on, maintain uncertainty by holding back key information or narrowing the character's options.

8 **Stay real**: Users are more likely to feel transported if they believe the environment, events and emotions within the story to be real.

9 **Resolve the challenge**: Users stick with the story because they want to know what happened — so show them. In true stories, there may not be a neat 'character overcomes challenge' moment, but every story needs a resolving endpoint.

10 **Drive action**: Offer options to share or comment on the story, or set out more impactful calls to action. To exploit the full 'witchery' of stories, be sure to align these with the story content.

It's been ten years since I began my quest to understand how stories work. I couldn't have expected then that I'd write a book on the topic. The writing process filled plenty of gaps in my knowledge, but I hope the end product also fills a gap in practical advice about how to tell short-form nonfiction stories in digital contexts. It's worth remembering that people become involved in stories because they spot another person in trouble. If you can find the trouble and organise the subsequent events to build suspense, you're well on the way to creating an attention-grabbing story with the power to transport, transform and drive action.

Anna's case study tells us about the process of writing stories for a cultural organisation online. Our next case study (see Case study 5.2 below) is from the perspective of the Wellcome Collection itself. Danny Birchall, writing as Digital Content Manager at Wellcome at the time, describes how the institution settled on the approach to content and online storytelling that it did. This piece specifically marks Wellcome's 1,000th Story published on their website. In recalling how the organisation got there, Danny talks about managing editorial content at scale over decades.

You can't get that far thinking about successful examples of web editorial in the sector without referencing Danny Birchall and/or Wellcome's journalistic approach to online storytelling. What's remarkable about this case study is its quiet paean of not reinventing your content formats every six months. Working in digital we're constantly aware of the next big thing. What's refreshing about Wellcome's approach is its commitment to growing a sustainable content format that really speaks to organisational mission. That commitment paves the way for partnerships and growing an audience interested and engaged in storytelling.

## Case study 5.2: Publishing Wellcome Collections' 1,000th Story

*Danny Birchall, then Digital Content Manager, Wellcome Collection*

In late 2022, Wellcome Collection published its 1,000th Stories article, a small but significant milestone for a young museum and library. 'Why the truth is better than a happy ending' (Wellcome Collection website, 2022) by Caroline Butterwick is the kind of story we love to publish: an emerging writer, discussing her complex experiences of mental ill health and disability.

What we do with Stories is a core part of our museum and library, just like our collecting, exhibiting, public programme and book publishing activity. It's a core part of our vision of a world where everyone's experience of health matters.

This is the story behind our 1,000th Story – what we do, how it started and where we go next.

### How we work

I manage a small team at Wellcome Collection who look after the content on wellcomecollection.org (editors Lalita Kaplish, Alice White, Helen Babbs and Vanesha Singh; copyeditor Kate Quarry; and picture editors Ben Gilbert, Steven Pocock and Hannah Brown). As well as maintaining the visitor-focused content on the site, we commission, edit and publish Stories about human health and experience. Each week we publish two to five new stories.

Every Wednesday morning, we meet to commission and schedule new pieces. We look at pitches, talk about new writers and guest editors that we'd like to work with, look for new angles on the history of health, and seek new perspectives rooted in writers' own lived experience of their health, as well as professional expertise.

We then work as editors with the writers to develop their stories, and then with our copyeditor to polish their presentation. Our picture editors find artists and photographers, often with their own lived experience of the articles' subjects (like Ghazal Zargar, who illustrated Furaha Asani's story about social isolation among migrants (Wellcome Collections website, 2023)) to illustrate the stories and give them visual context. We publish standalone articles, guest-edited weeks, six-part serials and webcomics.

### From digital layer to scrolly-wolly

Why tell stories at all? Way back in 2014, as we redeveloped our venue and wrestled with what would become our emblematic new Reading Room, we saw a gap for what we originally (and mistakenly) thought of as a 'digital layer': a digital equivalent to the physical experience, for online visitors.

Some heavy conceptual smackdowns later, and with the help of our friends at design consultancy Clearleft (https://clearleft.com), we came up with 'Digital Stories': chaptered and layered multimedia storytelling experiences. We were influenced by a new mode of storytelling exemplified by *The New York Times'* 'Snow Fall' (Branch, 2012): text-based but interactive; making use of new web presentation technology and often going by 'parallax journalism' or simply 'scrolly-wolly'.

Our two Digital Stories came in six chapters, each exploring their theme (the histories of hypnotism and collecting) deeply, with video, audio and animation. In an era of 'snackable' digital content, they were a six-course meal, to be eaten at a leisurely pace. But they also came online all at once when we launched each one.

Later, when we evaluated what we'd done with the folks at Frankly Green + Webb (www.franklygreenwebb.com), we discovered that people felt they'd had a Wellcome Collection-quality experience, but once they'd had it, there was no reason to return. We'd built an audience for something that we didn't have the resources to reproduce.

### Digital product: less is more

Meanwhile, back at base, we were completely changing the way that we did digital. A new strategy brought together our library and museum and established a new digital engagement department, with in-house platform development teams, meaning our content team and developers sat side-by-side.

In my boss Tom Scott's words, we started to build 'a free and unrestricted digital space where more people than ever can engage, be inspired and challenged to think about what it means to be healthy and human'.

When your ambition's that big, you need to concentrate your firepower. For us, this meant one website, powered by a single platform, with a single design language and a single brand: Wellcome Collection.

We closed the standalone Wellcome Library site and folded its functions into the main platform. This also meant saying farewell to our blogs, where staff and guests had for many years explored the nooks and crannies of our collections and programme. We replaced what had been two separate blogs and turned what had been an old-school 'Explore' section into a new Stories section.

As my colleague Jen Staves wrote, we took 'a journalistic approach to storytelling, creating high-quality, regular content with all the parts stories have ... in formats readers know and recognise' (Staves, 2019).

Through research with readers and looking at our usage data, we built a recognisable schedule. Unlike the original two Digital Stories, users could return often to read new stories. And while they lacked the immersive features of their predecessors, they were part of a stable and robust platform that wasn't in danger of becoming obsolete.

**Fighting the pandemic, fighting racism and ableism**

A lot of things changed in 2020, not only working from homes that rapidly became offices. The police murder of George Floyd sparked a resurgence in the Black Lives Matter movement, that also turned its focus on museums and cultural heritage, most notably by way of a statue of slaver Edward Colston that found itself at the bottom of Bristol harbour in June.

What did this mean for Stories? It accelerated what we had thought of as 'diversity' in the stories that we published into a more urgent need to explore the nature of racism and ableism through the lived stories of those who experience it. We asked how we build resilience in a racist world (Adjoa Parker, 2020, via Wellcome Collection's Stories) and what autistic togetherness during lockdown looked like (Fox, 2020, via Wellcome Collection's Stories).

When Jamie Hale spoke to deaf rapper Signkid about his art and activism, we commissioned a BSL version of the article (Hale, 2020, via Wellcome Collection's Stories). Our commitment to exploring all sides of the climate crisis was reflected in our collaboration with It's Freezing in LA!. We examined the legacy of eugenics in health and medicine.

It also meant thinking about how to better support our writers and artists: for example, adjusting the way that we work with technology for disabled writers and artists. Writing about your personal experiences of racism and ableism can be extremely difficult. We endeavour to give our writers both the emotional space and sensitive editing they need to tell their stories well.

More recently, we've brought together our interest in collecting the works of marginalised artists in a six-part serial about the artist and mental health survivor Audrey Amiss, together with three short films about how we catalogued, conserved and photographed her unique and incredible work.

**Who reads all this anyway?**

As we join the rest of the sector in tumbling off the cliff of our familiar 'Universal' Google Analytics and into the arms of GA4, it's worth reflecting on what we know about our audiences from looking at the data.

Occasionally, Reddit or Hacker News will deliver us a minor viral hit, but the majority of our traffic to new stories comes via social media, either owned channels or through the writers' and artists' own social presence (we ask guest editors and partners to collaborate with us on promotion). Sometimes a social hit takes on a life of its own: Rosie Barnes' photographs of older autistic women (Barnes, 2022, via Wellcome Collection's Stories) became something that people were keen to share, because it reflected their own experiences.

The flipside is that traffic to our long tail or 'evergreen' copy is mostly driven by organic search: some articles (including those on predictably popular subjects such as tattoos, sex and vaccines, but also on subjects that people don't have access to elsewhere, from skin bleaching to Shakespeare's humours) have a long interest-driven afterlife.

What drives the transition might be unpredictable, but there are some lessons we have learned about the values of SEO and microcopy: a cheeky headline could drive traffic on social, but a more accurate (if boring) one could bring a larger audience in the long term.

**In it for the long haul**

Reading back what I've written (and what you are reading, if you've made it this far), it struck me as unusual to be reading (or indeed writing) a story about web content that began nearly ten years ago. Aren't we supposed to move fast and break things?

Stories doesn't stand still: we're always thinking about what new kinds of commissioning and publishing will work: long reads, artist-led stories, and more. We're looking at how we curate our long-tail content and how we might schedule things differently. Meanwhile, as the website develops, we gain features from across the site, like a search that leads people to older stories.

But museums also last a long time and look after things. Perhaps digital content teams can too. When your stories are part of a solid product with a strategy and a clear vision of its audience, you get to keep the wins and build on them. We're in it for the long haul.

In the above case study, Danny analyses not only what he's creating but why, and touches on the kinds of audiences Wellcome Collection wanted to feel were included in their copy. The medium of your content, as well as the message, is just as important when it comes to online content in terms of who you're likely to reach. This is something we look at in more detail next: what is the purpose of long-form content, and – in particular – what role does it play in audience development?

## Analysing the purpose of long-form content

Articles, editorial, blogs, 'news and updates' – every cultural organisation has a section like this on their website. Over time, websites tend to accrue an unwieldy amount of this kind of content. Left unchecked, it's easy for it to lose a coherent shape or purpose.

This section looks at what the point of creating all this content might be – who it's for and what purpose it can serve for your organisation in terms of digital audience development.

In 2016, the Royal Academy (RA) were reviewing the purpose of their online editorial content. As Louise Cohen, the then Head of Content at the RA, set it out in her award-winning content strategy:

- We're amassing a lot of content
- Only a minority of that content is doing well and being widely read
- Content is playing to a core audience but not growing or diversifying that audience.

(Cohen, 2016)

To articulate the new RA content objectives, she framed all their content in terms of how it met their audience objectives of:

1 Grow
2 Deepen
3 Convert
4 Retain.

We'll use this structure to look at different editorial formats and where they sit in terms of growing new audiences and engaging existing audiences.

In Figure 4.6 below, I've created a matrix of the different kinds of content cultural organisations produce. The x-axis represents to what extent content is broadening audiences, as opposed to playing to an organisation's regular audience. The y-axis represents the extent to which that audience is a specialist versus a general public audience. The circles show examples of website content and how they map onto the matrix. In the sections below, we'll look at these different website content types.

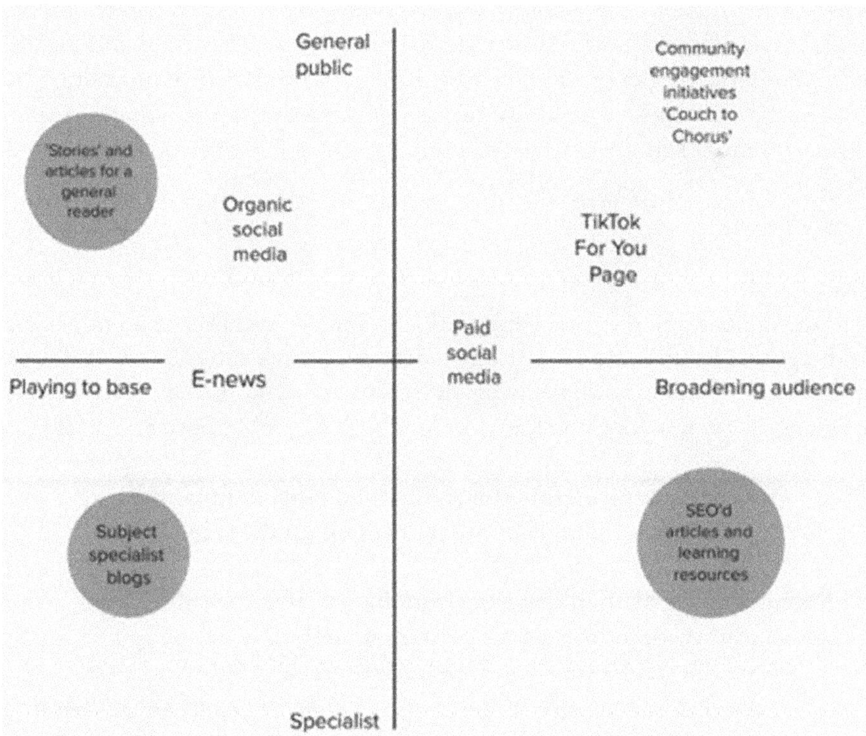


**Figure 4.6** *A matrix of how different content formats affect audience development*

### Engaging existing audiences – specialist

'Digitisation uncovers rare specimens that highlight the diversity of sex in nature' is the title of a 2019 Natural History Museum (NHM) blog (Natural History Museum, 2019). It's an example of a blog post that will engage an existing and specialist audience.

However, they've made sure the content is accessible to a non-specialist by:

- telling readers in the first paragraph what the post is about and what they're going to learn
- starting the second paragraph explaining what the project has involved and why the reader should care
- using pictures to illustrate their points
- having short paragraphs
- explaining technical terms like 'sexual dimorphism'.

Although it's accessible to a general audience, this kind of content is most likely to be of interest to entomologists and hobbyist groups who are already aware of the museum and subscribe to its feeds. That's a deliberate choice on NHM's part – to use their resources here to engage an important and highly engaged specialist group. Having worked in a natural history museum, I'm well aware that they attract a lot of special interest groups, amateurs and hobbyists, and it's important that museums are able to serve and advance the interests of this significant audience.

### Engaging existing audiences – generalist

'Into the hills: digging for Scottish gold' (National Museums Scotland, 2020) is a blog post from National Museums Scotland, written by their Curator of Modern and Contemporary History. From the very start, the piece tells an engaging story, whether you know anything about gold mining or not:

- The opening paragraph puts you right in the heart of the action ('It's February 2020 and I'm in a Landrover roaring up the side of Beinn Chiurn …').
- Striking images taken in real-time from the journey she's describing make the story visceral, personal and immediate.
- By visiting the source ('Scotland's first commercial gold mine'), the curator situates what is essentially a new acquisition story in the context of the landscape where the raw materials came from.

For all its charm and narrative style, this post is not going to bring in a new audience. Most museum blog posts are promoted to a general mailing list and on organic social media. This by default will only reach audiences who have already subscribed to view the museum's updates. It's also unlikely to get many views after it's fallen off the blog homepage – it's beautifully written but it doesn't contain many high ranking keywords to boost its visibility in search.

In the matrix in Figure 4.6 on page 135, I'd place this article (and others like it) in the top left quadrant (the bubble denoted by 'Stories' and 'articles for a general reader'). These are pitched at a general, rather than a specialist audience. Because of the mechanics of how people find content online, they're likely to play to the museum's existing readership rather than a new audience. This is not a problem, so long as you're clear what role this kind of content fulfils. It's definitely still important to tell evocative stories to a general core audience on your mailing list and social media.

None of this is to disparage the work content creators produce, rather it's an acknowledgement that digital content is often expected to be all things to all people – the silver bullet to growing and diversifying new audiences. That's unrealistic for content like this – unless you have a distribution mechanism and/or digital marketing budget that allows you to target your editorial content at audiences who haven't already subscribed to it.

## Engaging new audiences – specialist

One way digital content can move the needle in terms of engaging new audiences is through creating articles around core topics and keywords that are search engine optimised.

Search engine optimisation (SEO) is a complex beast these days and includes a number of factors you won't be able to directly affect (such as how well structured your website code is). We looked at this in Chapter 1. However, where content editors can make a demonstrable dent in the effectiveness of their SEO is in ensuring articles use keywords that someone might enter in Google to find your content.

Shakespedia is an online resource created by the Shakespeare Birthplace Trust (Shakespeare Birthplace Trust, n.d.). It was specifically designed to bring in new traffic from searches related to Shakespeare. Pages like 'William Shakespeare Biography' use terms that have a high volume of average monthly worldwide searches. I'd place this – and other examples like this – in the bottom right of the matrix (denoted by the 'search engine optimised (SEO'd) articles and learning resources bubble' in Figure 4.6). Pages like this still play to a reasonably specialist audience (you're most likely to find it by

Googling a Shakespeare related term) but a broader audience than might otherwise stumble upon the Shakespeare Birthplace Trust's website.

In some ways, this page isn't as editorially clever as the lovely storytelling of 'Digging for Scottish gold'. But it's not trying to be. It's clever in so far as they've looked at the global search queries around Shakespeare and systematically created content around topics that are a good fit with their organisation, have a relatively high search volume, and are relatively low competition. They've then created rigorous, in-depth and expert content on these topics, delivering a great deal of new search traffic and new users (who'd never heard of the Shakespeare Birthplace Trust before) to the website. It still relies on someone entering a specific term into Google, so the new audiences who come across this content are likely to be Shakespeare educators, students and enthusiasts.

## Content as part of a broader ecosystem

When you take a 'blue sky' view of what the point of creating content is and what it does in terms of developing audiences, you need to consider it in the wider ecosystem of different content types.

The majority of editorial web content produced by cultural organisations plays to their existing base (the left hand side of the matrix in Figure 4.6), but can vary in terms of how specialist it is. This is partly to do with how content is promoted. E-mail lists and organic social media, by default, will only reach people who have already heard of you.

There are of course exceptions to this, for example the Museum of English Rural Life's (MERL's) 'absolute unit' (MERL via Twitter, 2018). This tweet was exceptionally good at reaching a millennial audience on Twitter (now X). I'm not sure how realistic it is for most organisation's digital audience growth plans to rely on having a social media manager who can create viral tweets, particularly when the role tends to have a high turnover rate. Plus, using X is far more problematic now than it was in the 'absolute unit' days.

On platforms like Facebook and Instagram, you're essentially working in spite of the algorithms if you manage to create organic viral content, since Meta's business model and algorithm is predicated around you spending ad revenue to reach new audiences. If cultural organisations are serious about cultivating more diverse audiences using online content, organic social is unlikely to be the easiest – or most targeted – way to do it. This isn't to decry the brilliance of creating viral content using organic social media, but rather an acknowledgement that not everyone can do this well and that this approach won't necessarily achieve your audience development goals.

Learning resource content and articles that are well optimised in search can (if done well) be excellent at bringing in new audiences who have a relevant interest in your content. However, it's difficult for cultural organisations to use editorial web content alone to reach more diverse audiences. TikTok's algorithm and 'For You' page are currently relatively sympathetic to this. Aside from that, digital initiatives that are embedded in community participation and filling a social need for a particular demographic (e.g. Opera North's 'From Couch to Chorus', which we feature as a case study in Chapter 7) are much more likely to affect systemic change among an audience you're not currently reaching than a well written blog/tweet/article.

Above all, cultural organisations should be clear and upfront about what they're trying to do and include those objectives in every internal conversation about online editorial. Strategy is all about making decisions and if you try to do everything, you risk doing nothing at all.

CHAPTER 6

# Content Strategy

There are so many different definitions and understandings of what 'content strategy' is. First of all, we're going to unpack how the term is used and different examples of it. Then we'll arrive at a fixed definition for the purposes of this book.

Next, we'll look at the component parts typically needed for creating a robust content strategy. This includes audience research, segmentation and benchmarking (or competitor analysis), as well as how to get the most out of your analytics.

Finally, we'll cover what you need to think about to knit all these insights together into a strategic plan and vision.

## What is content strategy?

One of the tricky things about being a content strategist is that people have wildly different understandings of what content strategy is. This is partly because there's a certain amount of woolliness around how we use the words 'content' and 'strategy'.

### What is content?

One of the biggest misconceptions I come across is that content is 'just words'. If you strip out every bit of wording from a museum website, the importance of words becomes quite apparent, as we can see in Figure 6.1 on the next page.

However, content isn't necessarily just words. It might be 'pictures, diagrams, charts, links, calendars, a series of questions and answers, videos, addresses, maps, calculators, spreadsheets, printable documents, and many more besides' (Winters, 2017, 2).

Almost every GLAM or heritage institution is already creating some kind of content around temporary events, shows and/or exhibitions. The numbers creating content around the evergreen and unique reasons to visit an

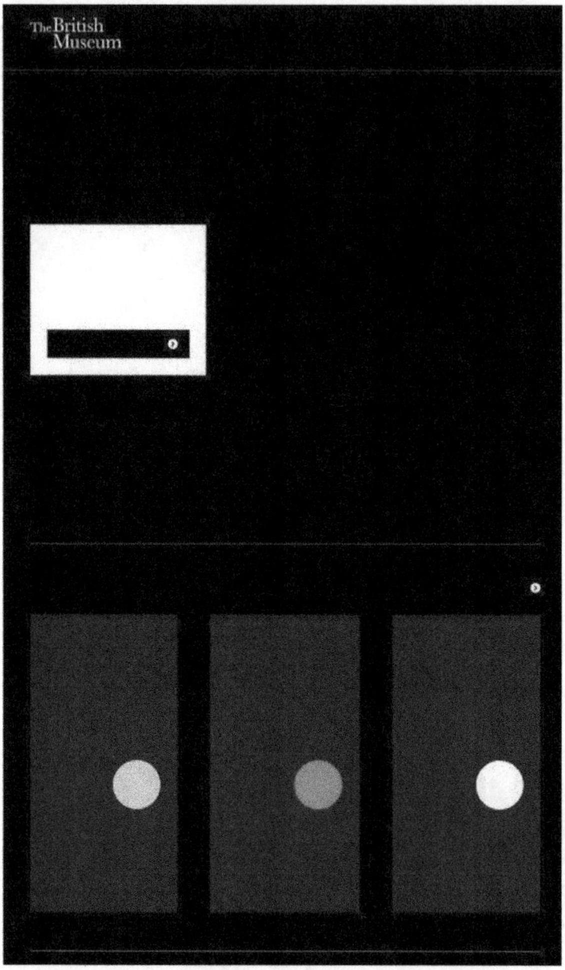


**Figure 6.1** *The British Museum homepage with all written content removed*

institution are much more limited. It's even rarer, if those pages exist, for them to use SEO principles to effectively tell Google what is significant and particular to the institution about those unique reasons (be that a key collections piece, a local story or the knowledge of your experts).

It's easy for an institution to think how it was performing last year is the competition. But in the eyes of a cultural institution's audience, Netflix is your competition – what have you got that's more interesting than a few hours on the sofa with a film or series? Does your website and social media articulate that? And is it the same group of people reading that content as were five years ago?

## What is strategy?

Richard Rumelt, author of *Good Strategy, Bad Strategy*, defines strategy as:

> A cohesive response to a challenge. A real strategy is neither a document nor a forecast but rather an overall approach based on a diagnosis of a challenge. The most important element of a strategy is a coherent viewpoint about the forces at work, not a plan. A good strategy is a coherent mix of policy and action designed to surmount a high-stakes challenge.
>
> (Rumelt, 2008, 35)

One of the important differences between the 'strategic plans' of most GLAM organisations and a 'strategy' (as defined by Rumelt) is that a strategy must look at what's *not* working. It must be clear-eyed and objective about the ways in which the organisation is not keeping step with a changing landscape and identify drivers to change that trajectory. Our sector is good at creating documents that essentially say, 'here are some things we're all working towards and thinking about right now' or 'here are some wonderful things we did with your funding and support, thank you', rather than present an actual strategy.

Strategies also have positive elements, for example, identifying the unique strengths of an organisation and the opportunities that a particular moment or set of circumstances afford. However, a strategy must also be outward looking; it must understand the landscape in which the organisation operates and the forces at play.

For an arts organisation's digital content strategy, one of the challenging forces at play is likely to be around attention. We create content in a busy and competitive environment and cutting through the noise is increasingly difficult, particularly without a distinctive online approach. A digital strategy can't simply be an internally facing document that just compares itself this year with itself last year. That's not going to cut through the noise.

## Different definitions of content strategy

It is easy to talk about a content strategy like it's a recognised format, but it's not. One of the knottiest difficulties around content strategy is that there are lots of different definitions. Kristina Halvorson was the earliest figure to dominate the field and her book *Content Strategy for the Web* (Halvorson and Rach, 2012) is still widely referenced. She states that content strategy:

- defines how you're going to use content to meet your business (or project) goals and satisfy your users' needs

- guides decisions about content throughout its lifecycle, from discovery to deletion
- sets benchmarks against which to measure the success of your content.

> In summary: Content strategy guides your plans for the creation, delivery, and governance of content.
>
> (Halvorson and Rach, 2012, 28)

This last sentence in the quote above was picked up by Wikipedia and, in 2022, it was the most likely answer you got if you Googled 'what is content strategy?' (Wikipedia entry on content strategy from 2022). However, this is not a definition. A strategy might focus on how to win a battle, or it might focus on how to dominate in search for a new brand of cereal. What it focuses on does not tell us what strategy is.

In 2024, Wikipedia's definition changed to:

> Content strategy guides the planning, development, and management of content. It is a recognized field in user experience design, and it also draws from adjacent disciplines such as information architecture, content management, business analysis, digital marketing, and technical communication.
>
> (Wikipedia entry on 'Content Strategy')

Again, this tells you what content strategy does, but not what it is. I also think this definition could equally apply to content design. As I see it, both Kristina Halvorson's *Content Strategy for the Web* and Sarah Winters' *Content Design* books describe similar processes that are different from what the sector means by 'content strategy'.

I'll unpack this more below, but in simple terms, I think it's useful to define content strategy as a strategy where effective content is used to meet the organisational challenge.

## What the sector means when it says 'content strategy'

In my capacity as a senior content strategist in the cultural sector, I work on a wide range of projects called 'content strategy'. Here are some example 'briefs':

- We've got funding for a new website, help us design a strategy and implementation plan for our content to make it as good as possible.
- We want to work out how to use digital to meet our business aims more effectively around, for example, income generation, expanding

audiences, fundraising and converting our existing audience into deeper levels of engagement.

- We want to work out how to use digital to meet our philanthropic aims around more effectively, for example, supporting marginalised audiences in the community and delivering our learning projects, or working collaboratively with audience groups we know we haven't reached historically, or realising our founding vision in formats appropriate for a post-2020 audience.
- We tried a bunch of stuff online in 2020, now we've also got to run a museum again. What should we do to optimise both (with no increase in net resource)?
- We spend loads of time and effort on digital tasks, but we're not sure if we're spending our energies in the most effective ways. Help!

What's interesting here is that there is a slight difference between what Kristina Halvorson, Sarah Winters and the broader content discipline mean when they talk about 'content strategy', and how the cultural sector often uses the term.

Both Kristina Halvorson's and Sarah Winters' backgrounds are in websites. Kristina works largely with large corporate websites in the private sector and higher education. Sarah's work is derived from her creation of www.gov.uk and is informed by user needs in a web public service context where users need to get the right information quickly and efficiently. These are slightly different from the user needs and questions cultural organisations are asking when they talk about 'content strategy'. Sometimes, cultural organisations do have a specific project that purely wants to work out how best to make their website content, or part of it, more effective. But often the questions are broader and it is less certain that the best strategy for them will be purely website content related. A solution is likely to also encapsulate social media, in-gallery digital, e-mail and so on. Often, the most effective solution in these scenarios will be smarter website content in conjunction with other online platforms and organisational change.

## Final words on what content strategy is

If we follow Richard Rumelt (2008) on strategy – 'a policy and action designed to surmount a high-stakes challenge' – content strategy is using digital content as a means to surmount that challenge. This may seem confusing. If strategy is working out the means to the end, doesn't it pre-empt things to stick 'content' in front of it? And why is content strategy such a large and growing field if it's a contradiction in terms?

The reason content strategy as a discipline has taken off is that it's very likely that better digital content will help answer wider organisational challenges. When we talk about content strategy, particularly in the cultural sector, we're often talking about audience development by stealth. 'Content strategy' is used as a means to solve more difficult questions, such as:

- How can I make my institution more relevant to a wider group of people?
- How can I make sure we're visibly in-step with digital trends in our online comms?
- How can we engage a younger demographic?
- How can we use digital to capture wider interest?
- Are we doing enough to reach non-traditional audiences?

Examples of how content strategy is used as an audience development case study in the sector might include:

- 'We could see we weren't recruiting millennials so we got really good at X/Twitter' (a strategy that worked well from c2016–2020 – today we might swap out X for TikTok).
- 'People couldn't come and see us perform during COVID, therefore let's create a platform so that those audiences – and audiences we wouldn't normally reach – can engage with us digitally'.
- 'Our segmentation model shows us we over-index on X, Y and Z, but underrepresent A, B and C'. Identifying how best to grow, reach and engage A, B and C will likely involve content strategy.

For most museums today, a good content strategy will define policies and actions to redefine the role digital can play in audience development.

I've presented a definition of 'content strategy' as a mix of policy and action designed to surmount a high stakes challenge using digital content. Understanding the digital competitive landscape you are operating in is critical to developing good strategy. In the cultural sector, we really use content strategy to talk about conducting audience development using digital means. In the next section, we'll look at the techniques you can use to find out more about your audiences and gain a clear-eyed situational analysis of the strengths and weaknesses of your organisation in relation to its audiences.

## Who are you currently talking to online?

The first prerequisite to doing effective audience development is to have a clear-eyed understanding of who you're talking to. It's unlikely that your physical audience (as in the people who turn up at your door) are exactly the same as your digital audience. For example, physical visitors are likely to be:

- repeat visitors
- people who live close to your site
- people who've been recommended to visit.

Online visitors may include people who have visited in person, but also:

- those interested in the topics of your collections
- those stumbling across your content on social media.

To get anywhere with audience development, you need to understand who you're talking to digitally and to what extent that's different from your physical audience.

## Demographic surveys

The most effective tool we have to get data on audiences is surveys. Generally, when we communicate, we know who we're talking to and how to pitch what we're trying to say. But online we devolve the distribution of our content to the mysterious discovery mechanisms of the internet. It can be difficult to create content for an online audience when you have a hard time conceptualising who they are and what's relevant about your institution to them.

When I worked at a museum I remember helping out with the in-gallery audience surveys. Each year we'd spend hours collecting hundreds of survey responses from visitors. The survey questions asked about things like what level of job the visitor had, their sexual orientation and whether they had a disability.

And it wasn't just us. All Arts Council's National Portfolio Organisations are required to do this. But what struck me at the time was that the data we needed to collect about our digital audiences, compared to our in-person audiences, was very thin. We're communicating daily with thousands of global and diverse audiences via the Internet. But there's no requirement to find out more about them in the same way as our in-person audiences.

Which seems to me an oversight. Especially as collecting online survey data is much less labour intensive, once you know how to do it.

In this section, I'm going to look at how cultural organisations might go about surveying their online audiences. In Chapter 4, we discussed usability surveys and how they can be used in the context of doing research into how well your website is performing. Here, we're going to look at a different kind of survey: demographic surveys. The purpose of these is to get more detail about who is currently using your website or digital services and social media, what their motivation for being there is, and how satisfied they are with what they see.

These types of surveys can be useful for gaining qualitative data. However, due to the amount of data you're collecting you're likely to get smaller uptake than for usability surveys (which are quicker to fill out).

It's possible to extract some demographic information about your website visitors from analytics packages like GA4, or on social media platforms from demographic insights. But none of these tools will give you granular demographic detail or tell you *why* respondents are on your site or social platform.

Because demographic surveys are longer than usability surveys, there's more potential for this type of survey to become overly complex. But this creates a greater barrier to participation. Below are some best practices for creating these longer online surveys.

## Best practice in long surveys

### *Only ask questions that will give you data you'll actually use*

Work out in advance what you're actually trying to find out from these surveys. You could ask every question under the sun, but try and limit it to information you are going to use within the context of what you're trying to achieve right now.

### *Include a privacy policy*

This is a legal requirement in a post-GDPR world. You must let people know why you are collecting this data, what you're intending to do with it, how you're storing it and how long you're keeping it for. Aside from the legal remit, this also helps encourage your respondents' sense of trust in your organisation.

### *Use free text fields sparingly*

Avoid using a text field when you could answer the question in the same way with radio buttons or checkboxes for multiple choice. Some survey packages will let you add a list of radio buttons and then an 'other' field, where users can choose to qualify what that 'other' is. All of this makes it easier and faster for the respondent to complete the survey, as well as for you to analyse the data.

*Use an incentive to complete*

This is an example of offering a survey 'incentive':

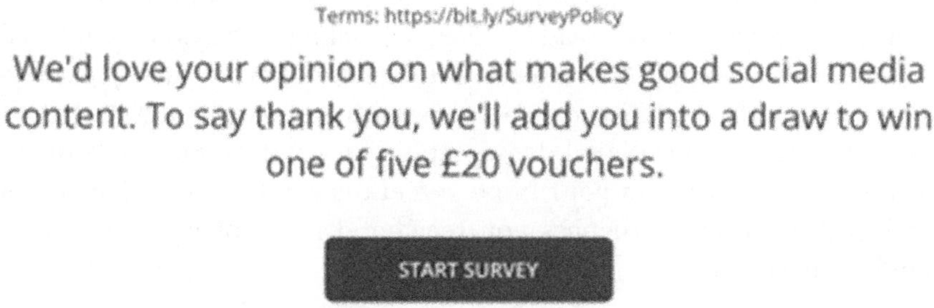


**Figure 6.2** *A survey incentive message*

I wouldn't normally incentivise usability surveys as they only take about 30 seconds to complete. But it's good practice to incentivise a demographic survey as these take much longer and we are getting much more detailed information from participants. This can allow you to get away with a much longer survey as respondents are incentivised to see it out to the end (they need to get to the end to enter their details to be in with a chance of winning).

*Include how long it will take to complete the survey and a progress bar*

We are all busy people. While we might like to be entered into a draw for £200, we might not like it enough to spend 20 minutes on it. But we might be happy to spend five minutes.

Say upfront at the start of your survey how long it takes to complete. Test this by filling it out yourself and/or get a friend or colleague who hasn't written the survey to time themselves.

Even if you put at the start how long it will take, not everyone will read it. It's useful to also give people a progress bar to see how far through the questions they are. This responds to Nielsen Norman Group's usability heuristic 'visibility of system status', which states that 'communicating the current state allows users to feel in control of the system, take appropriate actions to reach their goal, and ultimately trust the brand' (Harley, 2018). You can improve the usability of your surveys by allowing users to see how far along they are in the process of completing the survey.

*Make sure your survey is accessible*

Don't forget to test your survey questions on mobile. It's likely that around 50% of your website traffic will be from a mobile device and this will be much higher on social. Not every survey package renders well on mobile, so it's worth scoping that out before you spend time building the questions in it.

Your survey should be accessible to audiences with additional needs, including those using screen readers. Usually, making surveys accessible will just involve a few simple CSS tweaks. But again, not every survey package will let you modify the CSS code, so this is worth checking at the start.

Once you've got your digital demographic survey data you can compare your online audience with your in-person audience. This will give you an overall picture of the audiences you reach and help answer some of the following questions:

- Are there significant differences between who you're talking to online and in person?
- What do these two different audiences want from your organisation?
- Are there groups you speak to on both channels?
- Identify who you're *not* talking to online – is this a problem? If so, what might a future-facing content strategy look like to solve that?

## Focus groups and qualitative interviews

Survey data is all well and good, particularly for giving you a big picture view of what's going on with your audiences. It's less useful for really drilling down and understanding *why* those patterns are there. For example, survey data can show you that:

- you're not reaching local audiences, but it can't tell you why
- people rate your website poorly, but it can't identify the specific barriers they're facing
- all your current audiences are really happy with your offer, but not how underrepresented audiences feel about it.

Usability testing (see Chapter 4) does what it says on the tin – it's great for understanding the usability of your website. However, it's not going to tell you how to target audiences who would never end up on your website in the first place. To find this out, you need to know more about those audiences: what culture they consume; to what extent they're influenced in their cultural planning by what they see online; and if they're influenced by online media and, if so, on which particular platforms. This is where focus groups and qualitative interviews come in. For example, you can ask participants to screen share and then look together at your organisation's website and social media to get their thoughts on particular aspects (this can be particularly interesting among groups who don't currently engage with you).

For focus groups and qualitative interviews, as with usability tests, it's best to recruit five participants of the same audience type. More than five and typically you start getting the same answers back; under five and it's difficult to spot patterns. For example, if an attraction wants to know how local audiences respond to their social media, I would seek to recruit five audience members from within the local area and ideally try to have an equal split of genders and ages. I'd also look to recruit a mix of those who are familiar with the organisation and those who are not.

For large audience research projects, where I'm interviewing upwards of ten individuals, I find it useful to store interview insights in a coded spreadsheet. Directly after an interview, it's easy to think that you'll remember all the key insights from the study when you come to write up. However, I find that a few months after I've done the interview, I'm rather foggy on it. So, I've now got into the discipline of working out at the start what key research questions the interviews are trying to answer and then coding the findings from the studies as I go. For example, if I'm running a large study to find out about the relative strengths and weaknesses of a digital product and to assess the potential of different platforms/services/content strands for specific audience types, I might create a spreadsheet similar to the example in Table 6.1 below.

**Table 6.1** *Coding spreadsheet*

| Source | Insight | Audience development aim | SWOT | Audience type |
|---|---|---|---|---|
| EDI interview 2 (access EDI) | Interviewee 2 thought the provision for those with additional needs was brilliant; particularly what's listed in what's on, but she thought it was a misstep not to advertise this more prominently on the access page itself. | Engage | T | EDI |
| EDI interview 3 (socio-economic EDI) | There can be a class barrier beyond cost. People in low economically deprived places feeling like this place is not for them. There's an opportunity for Visitor Experience to develop more local specific tours and welcome. | Engage | O | Locals |
| International visitor interview 1 | Visitors were more likely to follow attractions that were local to them than places they'd visited abroad. Is this a general trend? Does our social play more to a domestic audience? | Engage | T | International |

The spreadsheet can then help me compile all my findings relating to the central research question (around how to develop audiences, the strengths and weaknesses of current digital provision, and how that differs by audience type). When I come to consolidate my findings from the research, I can sort columns by the different parameters relevant to the research questions and quickly pool insights from multiple sources (internal and external interviews, desk research and data analysis).

## Personas and segmentation

There is a great quote anecdotally attributed to statistician George Box: 'all models are wrong, but some are useful.' This seems a good place to start when thinking about audience segmentation, personas and marketing funnels. All of these help you generalise patterns of audience behaviour in a way that is intuitive and a useful reference point for future activity within your organisation.

Let's think first about the reality of all the different users that in some way interact with a single cultural institution. It's a big messy soup of infinitely complicated variables. Any one person is unique and fantastically intricate, from a biological, cultural and psychographic perspective. So, how do we get from this messy soup of extremely complicated individuals to a useful model of who we are and aren't attracting?

To build helpful models – that is, helpful simplifications of the (extremely complicated) reality – we need to know what the significant variables are. How can we 'type' people in a way that matters? In Table 6.2 opposite, I've set out the different models I've seen used in the sector and in what scenarios they are useful.

In Table 6.2, the first three models in the first column are 'simple' models. These are followed by two more complex or proprietary models – Audience Spectrum and Culture Segments. These are all explained in the following sections.

### Paddlers, swimmers and divers

*What is it?*

This is a system for categorising different types of users depending on the level of information they need at any one time.

- **Paddlers** want concise information. In the context of a website homepage, this might be a high level overview of who you are and what differentiates you from other cultural institutions in the area. Paddlers don't typically spend a lot of time on a web page.

**Table 6.2** *Segmentation models comparison*

| Name | Good for... | Less useful for... |
|---|---|---|
| **Paddlers/Swimmers/ Divers** | ☑ Writing for web training (using different amounts of detail in different parts of the site)<br>☑ Also used in in-gallery interpretation | - Marketing (doesn't tap into motivation)<br>- Audience development (no clue why users are engaged) |
| **Browsers/Followers/ Searchers/Researchers** | ☑ Mapping types to different web sections<br>☑ As above for writing for web training | As above |
| **Falk** | ☑ Building out personas<br>☑ Having one system for digital and physical visits | As above |
| **Audience Spectrum** | ☑ NPOs<br>☑ Local authority orgs<br>☑ Audience development – mapping reach<br>☑ Targeted marketing by culture | - Writing for web<br>- Describing user needs for different website sections |
| **Culture Segments** | ☑ Targeted marketing<br>☑ Unconscious bias checking<br>☑ Audience development<br>☑ E-mail, membership campaigns | - Harder for teams to implement alone<br>- Writing for web<br>- Organic social |

- **Swimmers** are a bit more motivated than paddlers to start with, but don't try their patience. They may want to know specific details or spend a small amount of time finding out more about something of interest.
- **Divers** want details. There's typically a misconception in the sector that people don't read long articles. Divers do. And – good news – Google likes 'in-depth' articles, ideally 1,500 words or more. Longer articles cover a topic in detail and have clear section headings so divers can quickly understand what's being covered and skip to any particular areas of interest.

### *Why is it useful for digital content teams?*

I find this three-part system a simple way of getting across the idea of 'progressive disclosure' in the context of writing for the web. Not everyone needs to know everything all at once. Online you have the option to nestle more detailed information beneath higher level pages.

Paddlers/swimmers/divers is a good segmentation model for writing for web training, particularly the point around using a different amount of detail in different parts of the site. For example, on a landing page you will want to include a concise overview of the child pages. This will help paddlers get a sense of what's in this section and whether it's interesting. It'll also help more motivated users like swimmers and divers get where they want to more quickly. In contrast, on detail pages you want to begin with a high level summary and then use subheadings throughout the piece. The piece itself can then go into detail. This allows less motivated users to get a sense of what's there and gives divers the detail they want.

This system is also used in in-gallery interpretation, for example, in the V&A's 'Ten Point Guide to Writing Gallery Text at the V&A' (V&A Museum, 2018). It may therefore already be familiar to curators.

The system is less useful for:

- marketing – as it doesn't tap into audiences' motivations
- audience development – as it doesn't give an idea as to *why* users are more/less engaged in your digital content.

### Browsers, followers, searchers and researchers

#### *What is it?*

This model is similar to swimmers, divers and paddlers, but contains more of a sense of the capacity in which a user might interact with you. It's a model developed by Morris Hargreaves MacIntyre (2005).

#### *Why is it useful for digital content teams?*

This model conveys more of the reasons why someone might be engaging with your content. For example, if they're a 'researcher', they're likely to be on your website in a professional capacity, whereas a 'searcher' may be more of a hobbyist.

I use this system when I'm trying to articulate at a high level who a page is for or the different kinds of users a page may be for and how to accommodate their needs. I've also used this segmentation model for categorising more detailed persona types. For example, Figure 6.3 opposite shows a typical 'audience index' I might create for a web project. Under browsers, followers, searchers and researchers, I've grouped more specific 'types' (represented in light grey and dark grey spots for current and potential audience types). In this example, I've plotted all types on a spectrum of motivation (along the horizontal axis) and familiarity with the organisation (along the vertical axis). I've then plotted individual visitor types depending on where they sit against these two parameters. These include new visitors, regular visitors, teachers, members, staff and peer curators.

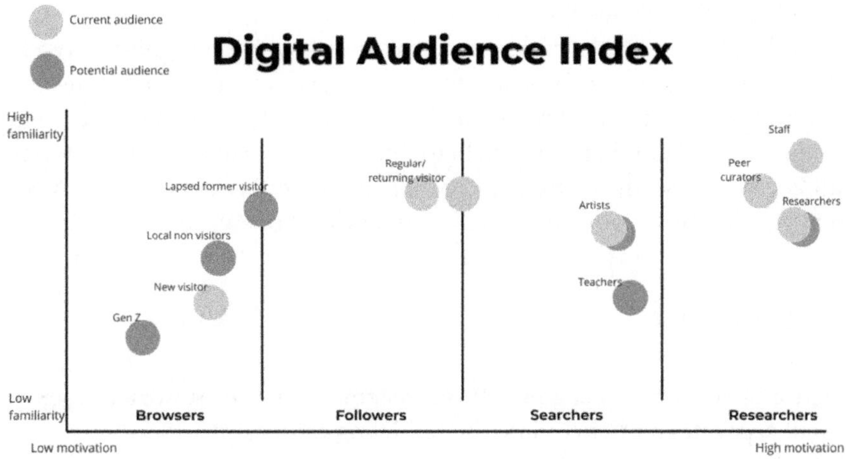


**Figure 6.3** *A digital audience index showing how a segmentation system can help group individual personas of more distinct types (e.g. 'members')*

## Falk

*What is it?*

In *Identity and the Museum Visitor Experience* (2009), John Falk presented five museum 'types':

1 **Explorers**: Visitors who are curiosity-driven with a generic interest in the content of the museum. They expect to find something that will grab their attention and fuel their curiosity and learning.
2 **Facilitators**: Visitors who are socially motivated. Their visit is primarily focused on enabling the learning and experience of others in their accompanying social group.
3 **Professionals/hobbyists:** Visitors who feel a close tie between the museum content and their professional or hobbyist passions. Their visits are typically motivated by a desire to satisfy a specific content-related objective.
4 **Experience seekers:** Visitors who are motivated to visit because they perceive the museum as an important destination. Their satisfaction primarily derives from the mere fact of having been there and done that.
5 **Rechargers:** Visitors who are primarily seeking a contemplative, spiritual and/or restorative experience. They see the museum as a refuge from the work-a-day world or as a confirmation of their religious/spiritual beliefs (Falk, 2012).

*Why is it useful for digital content teams?*

I find the Falkian model the best system in terms of having recognisable types. We can recognise in ourselves when, for example, we've landed on a museum website in the capacity of a 'professional', but then started looking at a current exhibition a friend or relative would like (shifting roles to the 'facilitator' type).

Falk's system also allows for the fact that you can fall under different types both in your lifetime and even within the context of one visit.

## Audience Spectrum

*What is it?*

Audience Spectrum is a segmentation system from The Audience Agency (2025). It separates audiences into the following categories:

- metroculturals
- commuterland culturebuffs
- experience seekers
- dormitory dependables
- trips and treats
- home and heritage
- up our street
- frontline families
- kaleidoscope creativity
- supported communities.

Until 2023, Audience Spectrum was the de facto segmentation product for local authority cultural organisations and those reliant on National Portfolio Organisation (NPO) funding.

*What is it used for?*

One of the key differences between this and other systems is that it is mapped against the population. This makes it much better for audience development as you can see not just who you're talking to, but how that maps against the population as a whole.

If you're a local authority institution, you can use their Audience Finder tool to compare how your audience breakdown compares with the segmentation in your local area. So, if you're mainly attracting affluent 'metroculturals' from London, but your local population is mainly working class 'frontline families', then you can see you have some work to do if you have a mandate to engage your local audience.

Most NPO organisations in the UK will also have used Audience Spectrum in their in-gallery surveys of audiences. Running a similar survey online is a great way of doing a comparison of the extent to which your online and in-person audiences overlap.

I'd use Audience Spectrum for digital audience development if I was already using it for in-gallery audiences, and to analyse the types of audience (particularly socio-economic and geographic) I'm reaching.

*Why is it useful for digital content teams?*

Again, I wouldn't find this segmentation tool helpful in every scenario. If I was trying to think about areas of the website and how to make them more user friendly, it wouldn't be terribly instructive for me to rewrite the collections page for a 'trips and treats' type (particularly if none of that type of audience is finding its way to that page anyway). As with Culture Segments (see below), in the context of web copy, it's also difficult to think what does writing for 'home and heritage' and 'trips and treats' actually mean?

Audience Spectrum is a useful way to type users socio-economically and geographically. It's useful for thinking about the equity of your services and how accessible they are across different class brackets in the UK. It's less useful for international audiences or for thinking about user needs on different parts of a cultural website.

### Culture Segments

*What is it?*

Culture Segments is a psychographic profiling tool from the consultancy Morris Hargreaves McIntyre (MHM). It categorises potential visitors into eight types based on their motivation to engage with culture. The types are:

1. Enrichment
2. Entertainment
3. Expression
4. Perspective
5. Stimulation
6. Affirmation
7. Release
8. Essence

They also have a handy quiz on their website so that you can 'type' yourself (www.mhminsight.com/culture-segments/survey).

### *What is it used for?*

Culture Segments is designed to map the 'types' who are and aren't motivated to come to your venue, which makes it a useful tool for identifying unconscious bias. In many of MHM's case studies, they find that cultural organisations tend to be good at attracting segments similar to themselves. This kind of profiling, done at an organisation-wide level, can help you be more deliberate about the segments you're communicating effectively with.

### *Why is it useful for digital content teams?*

Culture Segments is useful for planning digital campaigns messaging, for example, e-mail, membership and marketing campaigns that are attempting to motivate a particular activity or action.

It's worth noting that it's difficult to identify Culture Segments in the abstract and this system will be difficult to implement in a digital context if your organisation as a whole is not already using it. It's also a proprietary tool and you would be in breach of copyright if you tried to identify the Culture Segments of your audience without commissioning MHM to do the work.

As with Audience Spectrum, Culture Segments is less useful in the context of writing informational web pages.

## In summary

- **Paddlers/swimmers/divers** is a simple way of dividing up audiences by how much motivation and familiarity they have with the topics you cover.
- **Browsers/followers/searchers/researchers** is a system that allows you to separate audiences into different groups depending on the capacity in which they interact with you.
- **Falk** unites recognisable user types (e.g., 'facilitator' as parent) with the typical scenarios in which you might interact with a cultural institution. It allows for the fact that we will engage with museums and cultural institutions in a different capacity even over the course of one visit. You can see how this can work nicely in a user story that we might use for web planning.
- **Audience Agency's Audience Spectrum** is a way of visualising the socio-economic profile of your local audiences and what that means in terms of their receptivity to different kinds of culture. It's UK-specific but interesting to get a sense of who you are and aren't talking to in a local area.

- **MHM's Culture Segments** is a way of profiling audiences by their attitude to culture. It's more useful for psychological profiling in the context of a desired behaviour change and audience development than for creating web page copy.

Ultimately, there's no silver bullet – just infinitely complicated reality. What model works for you depends on what you want to use it for. You're going to want to have a small number of archetypes (for which you could use one of these structures). This archetype can then help you organise more detailed pen portraits/personas that sit beneath (see Figure 6.3 on page 155). How much detail and which types you work up will vary depending on what you're using a segmentation system for.

## Case study 6.1: Having a good e-mail strategy in place

*Alicia Eames, Head of Relationship Marketing, Royal Academy of Arts*

One of the key differences between social media/website content and e-mail platforms is that with e-mail, you control the distribution. This also means it's possible for you to segment your e-mail list in ways that are significant to you and your content (or audience development) strategy.

'We have separate "preference" based newsletters for groups like families, teachers and those interested in our architecture programme,' Alicia Eames, Head of Relationship Marketing at the Royal Academy of Arts, tells me.

'We also segment based on booking history. We've built a Sketch Club segment for those who have booked onto one of our Saturday Sketch Club events, who get sent specific sketch book content alongside tailored event reminders. These newsletters achieve extremely high engagement rates compared to our broader averages, which tallies with some recent data insight showing how this audience segment behaves quite differently from other event bookers. Sketch Club bookers are a very specific, returning audience – almost a community in itself – who book (and engage with Sketch Club content) again and again.

'We sometimes send segment-specific exhibition newsletters depending on whether an individual has (i) bought tickets, (ii) attended the exhibition, or (iii) hasn't yet converted. Differences across these are in the messaging and product inclusions (less in the "digital content" due to the resource we have in the team) but the approach allows us to frame the same piece of content in a different way depending on the booking behaviour of each reader. In our first test of this approach, for the Marina Abramović exhibition, we saw a small but significant uplift in engagement among bookers who had already attended (compared to our benchmark averages), and a more extreme jump in engagement within the "booked but not yet attended" group. Beyond providing more tailored and relevant comms, the approach was extremely successful for the shop range, which we upweighted to those who had already booked or attended. It resulted in a 400% increase in shop revenue directly from e-mail compared to similar exhibition e-mail campaigns.

Our latest experiment has been adding introductory content to a new two-stage, automated pre-visit journey. The first stage of this is a pre-visit e-mail sent seven days ahead of a visit, which uses conditional blocks to serve different content based on the exhibition each recipient is coming to see. The idea is that we can use content to enrich the booker's visit before they even step through the doors and extend their experience through what they receive before and after their visit on site. It's early days for this approach but we've already seen the introductory content (our "Start Here" articles) perform well compared to other pieces of content – in particular, they have a longer "life-span" and see more consistent traffic across the run of an exhibition compared to other content, which may see engagement decline after a one-off feature on social or e-mail.'

Alicia tells me more about how the Royal Academy increased the engagement rate of their e-mail database through a 'content-first' approach in lockdown: 'during lockdown we created a newsletter approach called "your art escape" – a weekly newsletter filled with content to keep you entertained.'

She continues: 'it resulted in extreme spikes in traffic to the website – the highest ever recorded at the time. For the first time, the e-mail/CRM team and the digital content team were collaborating closely on a joined-up schedule of content released primarily through e-mail. This worked so well as it responded to an audience need at the time and also worked for the RA strategically.

'Sometimes light-hearted, sometimes in-depth or longer-form, our content fitted what people were looking for plus allowed us to create a regular heartbeat of comms that felt authentic and relevant to our brand – all at a time when we knew we needed to keep our audience engaged or risk losing them long term.'

Alicia explains where they're at now, post-COVID-19; 'Nobody wants marketing messages shoved down their throat with every newsletter you open (unless it's a discount code!).

We mix our approach now to make sure content is still front and centre, providing a way in to learn more about our exhibitions or events – with a convenient book now button/conversion point always within sight.

We're still seeing spikes in engagement around light-hearted content, for example, quizzes, and have also seen subtle differences in the content audience segments respond to. Our members respond well to curator or expert-led pieces, while our public (and younger) audiences favour the short-form/quiz content.

The main take away from this post-Covid era has been that content is still key for audience engagement and, ultimately, conversion. It's a crucial part of a successful CRM strategy as it's what keeps your audience coming back for more. While engagement can sometimes be seen as a less direct KPI, without it we wouldn't be able to hit the ambitious revenue targets the organisation holds us to.'

## Digital audience development frameworks and funnels

So far, we've talked about ways of categorising users. There are also ways of framing and talking about what you want to do with different audience types.

We've already referenced the Royal Academy's four-part digital audience development framework for their audiences:

- grow
- engage
- convert
- retain (Cohen, 2016).

This is similar to marketing funnel frameworks like Awareness, Consideration and Conversion. In all these models, you can intuit how digital audience development aims to move audiences along a funnel to engage more with your organisation.

You are likely to have different audiences at different points in the funnel. For example, the Royal Academy knew they had a solid base of well-off, ageing members, but were weaker on younger millennial audiences. So their 'grow' strategy focused on young, digitally savvy millennials, while their 'retain' strategy was focused on their existing base and membership.

More commercial outfits often reference 'RFM' or 'RFV', which stands for Recency, Frequency, Monetary Value. It describes a way of tracking users by metrics around how much they visit your site, how frequently they visit and how much they spend. The upward or downward trends of these metrics are often seen as a good indicator of how well the organisation is forecast to do financially. This can also be applied to editorial. The Financial Times (FT) Strategies Head of Insight has talked about how they used an RFV model to evaluate the success of their paywalled content:

> We used to be a majority print business, [it was around] ... 70, 80% of our revenue. It's now the reverse in terms of digital. And we also used to be a predominantly ad-based business, again, similar numbers, but we now [have] far more subscriptions as a source of our primary revenue.
>
> (Montagu, 2023)

The FT needed to create a monetised digital strategy in order to survive commercially in a global environment where people are buying fewer print newspapers. The strategy paid off and now the majority of their revenue comes from their digital content.

Once you have conducted your research about who you are and aren't reaching, it's the job of the digital strategist to knit together the most significant opportunities for you to develop your audiences digitally, based on an understanding of the digital landscape, your audience base and the likelihood of converting other new audience types.

One of the significant ways you can get a sense of the opportunities for your organisation in a competitive online environment is to conduct keyword research using search intelligence tools. We'll look at this next.

## Competitor analysis: search

To enact a successful digital content strategy, we need to be clear on the competitive digital landscape in which those audiences and your organisation operate. Particularly online, there is a lot of competition for users' attention, and not just attention from within the cultural sector.

It's not enough to design a solution that meets the needs as expressed by your audiences. Particularly if you're trying to grow your audience, that solution also has to be better than the existing alternatives – and often quite a lot better in order to unseat existing patterns of behaviour.

Your audience will undoubtedly be visiting more websites and social media than just yours, so it makes sense for you to understand the competitive landscape in which your audience sees your content. Importantly, it stops you being complacent. It's also part and parcel of how great content evolves, building on innovations that have gone before. In meme and trend-based content, it's important to be aware of contextual relevance that is building upon certain stock phrases or images in order to be able to understand where your organisation has a relevant hook (and to recognise that in a timely manner).

To support the above, it makes sense to conduct a competitor review, or at the very least look at what similar organisations are doing. There's no set way to conduct a competitor review and how you go about it will depend on what kind of content you're evaluating. We'll look first at comparing the performance of different websites and then look at social media comparison data.

To compare your institution's website with others, you need to have some comparative data to hand, otherwise it's just comparing your opinion of which site is more successful and not based on performance data. There are free and paid ways of getting that performance data. The paid tools get you much more detail, but you can make some progress for free. For example, as a quick (and free) exercise, try Googling the terms you'd hope your organisation would rank in search for and see whether it does.

## Free tools

You can find out for free what queries people enter to land on your site using Google Search Console. Google Search Console is a free product that is separate from GA4, but does a similar job, particular to your search data. Typically, the majority of the most popular keywords will be 'branded'. For example, if you're the Museum of Pies, the top terms people enter into Google to land on your site might be:

- 'Museum of Pies'
- 'pie museum'
- 'museum pies'.

You get the picture. These would all count as 'branded' search terms. (Although the last one is ambiguous, it could be people being lazy and typing 'museum pies' when they mean 'museum of pies'. Of course, it could also be people searching for any museum that happens to serve pies.)

In Google Search Console, you'll find terms that don't directly correlate with your organisation name. For the Museum of Pies, search terms might include 'gala pies', 'pie pastry recipe' or 'victorian pie recipe videos'. These are known as 'unbranded' search terms. Unbranded search terms are interesting as they give you a sense of the pages and topics that are most effective at drawing a new audience in from search.

Your top unbranded search terms might surprise you. They might not reflect what you would consider to be the highlights of the collection. For example, the Museum of Pies might have written a blog on ancient Roman pies, but this isn't an area of strength in the collection. However, let's imagine there's a viral TikTok #RomanPieRecipe trend. The museum might then find that the search term 'Roman pies' was generating quite a lot of traffic to this blog post.

In this situation, the museum might be pleased to have content that ushers in a new audience of TikTokers. However, let's say the Museum considers the most important item in its collection to be original Victorian pie recipes. The museum might then want to know who is dominating in search for these terms, as well as any other terms it would consider themselves to be the authority on. The simplest way to find this out is to Google the terms you'd hope to rank highly for and see where you appear in search results listings.

Things to note:

- Some work computers have Microsoft Edge or Bing as default search browsers. However, these aren't used by most people. Google Chrome has 65% of the total market share for internet browsers (averaged across all devices) (Oberlo, 2024). For the moment, it's the dominant search engine, so, it makes sense to check how you're ranking on Google.
- It's best to use an incognito version of Google to conduct your searches. Otherwise, the results will be biased by what you have searched for previously. (Google's good at personalising search, but, in this case, you're interested in what a new user would find for any given term.)

While you're doing this, it's useful to look at what 'people also ask' queries appear and which websites Google is pointing to for those results. This helps give you a sense of popular subtopics for a given query. It also allows you to reflect on whether your museum has expertise that could improve upon what's already on the internet.

### Paid tools

Paid tools give you more data. In particular, they give you data to indicate *why* a particular site is ranking higher than another. If the Museum of Pies is being outranked for 'gala pie' content on Pie Delivery UK's blog, paid tools can tell them:

- the volume of search traffic for their site and the competitor site
- the volume of search traffic for that particular page on each site
- the number of external sites on the internet linking to your site and the competitor site
- the volume of paid search traffic going to your site and the competitor site.

All this allows you to build up a picture of where you are strong and weak in terms of search visibility.

Let's imagine that the Museum of Pies has a blog with lots of individual articles. Not all of these articles have useful keywords in the title. The Museum has realised that Pie Delivery UK's blog is often appearing before their blog in Google's search results. One key difference between the two is that Pie Delivery UK's blog has distinct 'categories', for example, they have a 'Victorian pie recipe' landing page. This page contains a short paragraph about the distinctive features of Victorian pies and then links to lots of individual articles containing Victorian pie recipes.

The Museum of Pies has similar content. Gallingly, it also owns the original written recipes for a lot of these pies. However, their blog simply presents individual article titles like:

- Eel pie anyone?
- The origins of gala pie
- Victorian mincemeat – what's changed?

These are all mixed in with blog posts on other topics related to pies. These titles all sound interesting to their existing audience who already visit the blog, but they're not as effective as Pie Delivery UK's approach for new users. For example:

- Pie Delivery UK are using high traffic category pages on their blog. This helps make it clear what topics they cover. It also gives a sense of the information architecture of the articles. Google, and new users, instantly know which articles are 'victorian pies' versus 'roman pies' or 'modern pies'.

- These category terms are generally more widely searched than specific article titles. By not having category pages, the Museum of Pies is missing out on more entry level and widely searched terms.

This is not a rogue example. Typically GLAMs create lots of individual online articles, but have little prominence in search. Often these articles have built up over time: an initial editorial portal was launched with 20–30 articles (often called 'Discover', 'Explore' or 'Stories') and a set of filters was set up to sort content, but by default, content is ordered by published date. Over time, this editorial section mushrooms to contain hundreds of articles, but the default sort order and filters haven't changed much. This makes it increasingly difficult for both a human and Google to get a sense of what this section contains.

In SEO terms, the trick that's being missed is around creating landing pages in your editorial that ensure you rank for topic 'hubs' that are related to high volume searches on topics you have authority on. These effectively act as honeypots for search queries and give your articles a clear thematic structure for website browsers.

Here's an example of the difference. Typically, a GLAM website editorial section will have:

- a landing page that orders articles chronologically from the most recently published and a set of filters that allow you to display articles by a small number of themes
- series of articles.

In this case, you've done the hard work of defining what your categories of content are: these exist in the filters. However, these filters aren't search friendly. When a user applies a filter (which happens around 5% of the time: it is not a common user behaviour), the page reloads but without changing the page title. There is very little search benefit to using a filtering system to categorise your content as Google can't pick up keywords in a filter in the same way that it can in page titles, headings and subheadings.

## How to make your editorial search friendly

Search opportunities exist in the overlap between three things:

1 terms people are searching for (to get this you will need search volume data)

2 low competition in search listings
3 topics your institution covers and that you have expertise in.

You already have a good idea of what topics your institution covers (point 3 above), but most GLAMs have a relatively poor idea of 1 and 2: what terms people are more or less likely to search for within those topics and how great the competition is in search results listings for any given term.

Part of the reason for this lack of knowledge is that to get this data you need access to a paid search platform that will give you search volume and competition data for specific terms. Tools like Google Trends give you the relative global search traffic between up to five terms, but it won't give you the raw number of global searches. This makes it useful for making incremental edits to existing page titles, but doesn't give you granular enough data to re-architect your content under a new SEO strategy.

Google Ads Keyword Planner provides more granular data on the number of global searches for different terms, but it is still limited. For example, it will tell you if search terms have:

- under 1K monthly searches
- between 100 and 1K monthly searches
- between 10k and 100K
- between 100k and 1M.

These categories are really broad. A lot of museum search opportunities are going to exist in the between 10k and 100k monthly searches band (see Figure 6.4 below), but there is obviously a lot of variation in how useful these terms are depending on where in the bracket a museum falls.

| Keyword ↑ | Avg. monthly searches | Three month change | YoY change | Competition |
|---|---|---|---|---|
| black death | 10K – 100K | 0% | 0% | Low |
| great plague | 100 – 1K | -90% | -90% | Low |
| queen victoria | 100K – 1M | -90% | 0% | Low |
| slavery | 10K – 100K | 0% | 0% | Low |

**Figure 6.4** *Example of search analysis for terms in Google Ads Keyword Planner*

There are a number of paid search platforms on the market that provide competitive intelligence such as search volume, which can be very handy for keyword research, and build up a picture of what the most searched for topics are that relate to your strengths.

Let's assume at this point that you've conducted an analysis on a number of different topics within your collection. You've identified the relative search volume of different areas and the current competition. You now have a good idea of where the opportunities are for you to rank highly in search and how to reorganise your existing editorial around higher level topic pages that are honeypots to capture high ranking search queries. What next?

You probably at this point have a large and heavily annotated spreadsheet that makes more and more sense to you, and less and less sense to anyone else. It's time to switch gears and put your content design hat on and start thinking about how clusters of frequently searched for topics could form distinct category landing pages. So, your page structure might look like:

1 Editorial landing page introducing a series of 'themes' to stories.
2 Theme landing page: on this you might include a short paragraph hitting significant keywords related to the topic and then list individual articles.

In this user journey, Google has much more contextual information about the categories of content you have. In the lottery of what people are searching for online, adding more keywords to higher level topic pages (as above) makes it much more likely that your content will be returned in search for a given query.

This is similar to the scenario we outlined in Chapter 3 about the difference between a 'Search the Collections' page versus an 'Explore the Collections' section that presents users with a series of gateway 'theme' pages to structure exploration of thousands of individual collection records. In both cases, those thematic landing pages are doing the heavy lifting in terms of making visible the categories of content that you cover.

## Final takeaways

- Creating overarching **category pages** for key themes that run through your collections is more useful (in terms of search) than having a string of individual article pages.
- Use **search volume** and **competition data** to understand where the interest is and what opportunities exist within topics you can talk authoritatively on.
- **Search analysis** may well yield format inspiration as well as topic inspiration – we've observed countless long tail queries around a given topic plus timelines, quizzes, games, maps and family trees. This content is more difficult to produce so tends to be lower competition (but frequently searched for).

Of course, not all digital user journeys start from Google and end on a website. A great deal of web content is discovered and consumed within social media platforms. Next, we'll look at how to conduct a competitive social media analysis.

## Competitor analysis: social media

In Chapter 2, we looked at the various social media platforms, how they work and the opportunities they present cultural organisations. In this section, we'll look at how you might use social media competitor data to benchmark yourselves against other organisations. This is useful to get a sense of your unique strengths and weaknesses relative to peer institutions.

Within the context of a digital team, it's useful to have agreed 'touchpoints' of accounts whose tone or approach you think is a good fit with your own. It can also help give you inspiration based on things you think are working well or that have collaboration potential. If you're conducting a social media competitor review as part of an audience development plan, it can be useful to look at accounts that are succeeding in attracting the type of audience you would like to appeal to and analyse how they have gone about doing that.

There are various components of a competitor review:

- analysing your own performance
- choosing the competitors themselves
- picking competitive metrics
- showcasing overarching examples, themes and trends from your comparative analysis.

### Analysing your own performance

I typically begin a competitor review with an overview. The overview compares the organisation's different social channels using criteria such as:

- number of followers
- follower growth
- audience demography
- volume of posts this month
- engagement rate this month
- most popular post this month
- most popular post of all time.

In analysing a cultural organisation's social media, my aims are to establish:

- what we can tell from social media demographics about who is accessing the account's content (and how much does this differ from platform to platform and to in-person audiences)
- the kinds of content that are performing well
- the relative strengths of particular social accounts in terms of follower numbers, reach and links to the website
- the performance of any digital advertising campaigns running
- the relative velocity in growth of the different accounts (particularly looking at how this differs during periods of staff turnover and pre- and post-COVID-19 pandemic)
- the degree of variation in top performing content between the accounts over the last couple of years.

I've provided an example in Table 6.3 below. Here, we see Twitter/X has the most followers, but the least growth and least engagement. This is typical of what I see when I conduct social media competitor reviews in the sector. Similarly, Instagram has the lowest followers of the set but the most engagement.

The overview in Table 6.3 provides a quick at-a-glance view of the relative strengths and weaknesses of one organisation's channels and what kinds of demographic groups they are talking to on each.

**Table 6.3** *Social media competitor review*

| **Platform** | **Followers (or Facebook page 'likes')** | **Growth (last 12 months)** | **Demographic notes** | **Volume of posts and engagement this month**<br><br>**Relative to top posts for engagement** |
|---|---|---|---|---|
| Facebook | 50k | 1.2% increase | 80% female, local | 30 posts<br>3% engagement rate |
| Twitter/X | 140k | 0.2% increase | n/a | 50 posts<br>0.5% engagement rate<br>Top post example |
| Instagram | 20k | 8% increase | 80% female, national | 12 posts / 20 stories<br>5% engagement rate<br>Top post example |

### Picking the competitors themselves

Picking competitors for your review tends to be more art than science. Very often you'll be aware of other content creators you'd like to emulate on a given platform, but it's rare that they will be strong on all the channels you're active on. We generally compare 9 to 12 accounts across web and social platforms and this allows you to get a sense of your strengths and weaknesses across the whole social media landscape relative to this set. It can be useful to look at institutions with a similar footfall of physical visitors to yourselves.

You can compare different accounts on different channels but it's also useful to get a sense of how creators are repurposing or cross-linking between their social accounts and digital products. It also shows how relatively few content creators are strong or even maintaining content on every channel. In the sector, we often try to be active on every platform but with a relatively small return. By having a higher degree of focus and an understanding of a smaller number of platforms, we can be more deliberate about what we're trying to achieve with them and for whom.

It's often useful to look at institutions outside the sector, as well as individual content creators (particularly on platforms like YouTube and Instagram), who may have more licence to speak with a distinctive voice and focus on creating a loyal audience.

### Picking competitive metrics

One of the significant differences between web and social media is the visibility of social media data. It's very easy – and tempting – to compare organisations by follower numbers or the number of likes on any given post. But these metrics are problematic. For one, we know that people are seeing increasingly less from pages they 'follow' and much more from algorithmically picked content that appears on their feed based on their interests and content they've engaged with previously. While the number of likes on any given post might be an alluring and visible metric, it's not necessarily reflective of what's going on on a page. It's difficult to 'engineer' a viral post – so comparing yourself to a very visible single example from another institution may be misleading (and a little disheartening).

Some of the more illuminating metrics are difficult to get comparative data from competitors on. For example, if you're auditing your own social media data, you might want to look at things like:

- engagement rate – the number of interactions a post has had divided by the reach

- average reach per post – if you're putting out 12 posts a week and have a total reach of 120K, each post is getting (on average) 10K impressions. That would be a seemingly healthier account than one that posts 42 times a week with a total reach of 42K (where each post here only gets 1K impressions). Since time is at a premium in cultural sector social media departments, the reach per post metric can be a good shorthand of how effective time spent on the platform was.

However, you won't be able to see the engagement rate of other organisations' social media posts. Although you can see visible engagements (things like likes, comments and shares), you can't see things like link clicks, profile visits and bookmarks. Also – crucially – you can't see the reach of a social media account you don't have social analytics access for.

Some paid tools will do a lot of the data collection for you and produce graphs comparing your performance to others for publicly available data. This allows you to compare your follower growth, volume of posts and the volume of public engagements. Some tools also attempt to create an estimated engagement rate based on the number of followers and the volume of public engagements, but this is inaccurate.

These tools also often seem to fail to separate paid from organic social content. Typically, the most 'liked' social content on a platform like Instagram in a competitor review will be exhibition-related content. It seems likely that this content has been boosted by ad spend, but the social intelligence tools don't seem to be able to pick this up reliably.

All that being said, these tools are much faster than collecting competitive social data manually. You can produce useful insights about how well your institution's channels are performing in terms of:

- how the rate of growth of your different channels compares to your competitors (and how much of this is down to paid spend)
- the volume of content posted and how your institution compares – channel by channel – with competitors
- the volume of visible public engagements on each of your accounts and how that compares to the average of your competitors
- particularly popular formats or examples – per channel – from across your competitor set and what's working about them.

All this helps your understanding of where you are strong and weak in a competitive digital landscape and the direction of that change, for example, whether you are keeping pace or resting on legacy high follower numbers.

In terms of your audience development aims, you can look at who you're talking to on social media and undertake a survey to get more granular information about who's currently there (for more on this, see Chapter 6 – demographic surveys). From there, you can conduct a gap analysis between who you are currently reaching and who you want to be reaching. Social media, particularly paid social media, is likely to be one of the most effective ways to reach new target audiences. As part of that gap analysis, ask if paid spend is being spent where you are most likely to develop target audiences.

In the course of this review, it's likely that you'll get ideas and spot patterns that may be relevant to your own social media content creation. It's important to capture those thoughts and ideas and make that part of the qualitative/thematic section of your social media competitor review. These observations can be the starting point for wider internal discussions and fleshing out new ideas and themes in your own content development.

Ultimately, you can have all this data, but content is an art as much as a science. Really brilliant iconoclastic digital content – particularly social media content – won't necessarily have been heavily planned and strategised to reach a certain audience. Sometimes, magic just happens where you post the right thing at the right time and the internet aligns to make a moment. It can be pretty heady when that happens.

## Using data to create a strategy

So far in this chapter, we've looked at some of the different research tasks you can use to inform your strategy, including user research, segmentation and competitor analysis. The next stage is bringing all that data together and making a strategy out of it.

One of the most useful tools for getting a clear-eyed sense of the forces at work is a SWOT analysis (see example in Table 6.4 below). SWOT stands for strengths, weaknesses, opportunities and threats. It is designed to map out the competitive advantages and disadvantages you have, but it is also forward

**Table 6.4** *SWOT analysis*

| Research input | Insight | SWOT |
|---|---|---|
| Website data analysis | We have very low levels of international traffic | W |
| Demographic analysis | We're reaching very few audiences under 30 | T |
| Audience interviews | Audiences who find our content really like it ... | S |
| Website data analysis | ... but overall numbers are low | T |
| Staff interview | Our guided tour content would make great social content and our welcome team are great on camera | O |

looking, seeking to identify the direction things are going in and what aspects of future change represent opportunities and threats for the organisation.

Typically, as I'm collecting my data (from interviews, data analysis, competitor reviews, business documentation), I 'code' all insights in a spreadsheet according to SWOT (see Table 6.4).

In this way, over the course of the research phase of my project, I compile hundreds of insights from different sources that I've coded as an organisational strength, weakness, opportunity or threat. I tend to distinguish a 'strength' from an 'opportunity' based on whether the future of that thing is a given or not. For example, in Table 6.4. I've coded 'putting tour content on social media' as an opportunity as it's not something the organisation is doing currently (but it would likely be successful). I wouldn't class that as a strength as it's not something that has been realised yet. Similarly, a 'threat' is different from a 'weakness' in that it's something that could become a more significant problem in the future, like reaching few under-30s. This is a future-orientated problem as it suggests the demographic is ageing out.

However interesting I find an insight at the time, I can be sure that two months down the line I've either forgotten it or it's become less pertinent to me than something I heard more recently. Coding insights like this helps me retrieve the important insights relating to situational analysis.

When I've finished the research inputs of my strategy, it's useful to review all the insights by strengths, weaknesses, opportunities and threats and determine:

- what are the overarching strengths and weaknesses, generally as an organisation and particularly as regards digital content and the focus of the strategy?
- what are the opportunities and threats, factoring in the wider forces at play in the digital landscape and society?

A good strategy is the golden thread that connects your unique strengths and weaknesses with the changing factors at play in the wider landscape; identifying the most significant opportunities and/or mitigating against the most pressing threats. If you have lots of SWOT factors, it can be difficult to isolate the golden thread that runs through them that will help you seize an opportunity at the same time as capitalising on a strength and mitigating a threat.

In these situations, it can be helpful to overlay a TOWS (threats, opportunities, weaknesses and strengths) matrix to give your SWOT analysis some focus and direction. A TOWS matrix helps 'develop strategic options by looking at the relationships between the factors identified in your SWOT analysis' (Lister, 2023, 87).

It's easiest to make sense of the TOWS matrix through a worked example. Table 6.5 shows an example TOWS matrix using the SWOT variables in Table 6.4:

**Table 6.5** *An example TOWS matrix*

| | **Strengths**<br>Audiences who find our content really like it | **Weaknesses**<br>We have very low levels of international traffic |
|---|---|---|
| **Opportunities**<br>Our guided tour content would make great social content and our welcome team are great on camera | Make our content more visible online and so accessible to a wider audience | Start broadcasting our in-gallery tours online and experiment with livestreaming on platforms like TikTok and Instagram that have a wide international reach |
| **Threats**<br>We're reaching very few audiences under 30 | Test the content we do create with an audience under 30 – do they like it when they do come across it? | Think about proactively raising awareness among young people across the world using social media |

Unfortunately, a TOWS matrix will not do all the hard work for you. It's up to you to assess which are the most pertinent SWOT factors and build one single coherent response to your situational analysis. A TOWS matrix will help you present the pertinent factors from your situational analysis that are at play in the strategy direction you've identified.

Most sector action plans contain a myriad of strategies for different audiences and in different ways. A good strategy needs to be more single minded than that, and, ideally, represent one central direction that can be actioned across the wider organisation.

There's a whole different topic on how you go about implementing strategic change and creating collective buy-in. Sometimes this is more complicated than fixing on the right strategy itself. Suffice to say it can help to bring people along the journey with you, and involve key stakeholders in significant parts of the research. For example, if you can sense there is some resistance to change from internal managers, but the data you're getting from the public is that change is necessary, invite those stakeholders to usability testing sessions.

Part of the art here is understanding what data will be persuasive to whom, and what insight will unblock current barriers to change. There are also ways to workshop a SWOT and feel like you're collectively arriving at a single strategic direction and vision. Whether you're writing a strategy to inform your work or fixing on a strategy for an entire team or organisation, being able to quickly retrieve pertinent data that give you a clear-eyed assessment of where you sit in a competitive landscape, is key.

In the next chapter, we'll look at two case studies: Opera North's 'From Couch to Chorus' and the Tank Museum's success on YouTube. These are both great examples of content strategy (as we've defined it in this book) in action. They both use digital content as a means to develop audiences and respond to a challenge at the time.

# CHAPTER 7

# Content Strategy in Action

In Part 3 of this book, we've looked at how creating digital content can be strategic. I've argued that the content strategies that matter in the sector today are the ones that affect audience development.

In this chapter, we look at two case studies of content strategy in action that do exactly that: Opera North's 'From Couch to Chorus' and The Tank Museum's success on YouTube. Both of these diversified audiences (albeit with very different groups) and were able to drive commercial income, while extending access to those without financial means.

## Diversifying audiences and driving commercial income

Opera North's 'From Couch to Chorus' is a case study of how successfully targeted digital content can successfully contribute to diversifying audiences and generating income. This is my favourite case study of an online content or service that:

- reached and engaged new audiences
- made sense in terms of the organisational aims and expertise
- made money (£140k!)
- provided a tangible wellbeing benefit to more vulnerable audiences and/or those with additional needs.

### Case study 7.1: 'From Couch to Chorus' – Opera North's ever-evolving online singing project

*Marie Lemaire, Digital Education Manager, Opera North*

In 2015, I joined the Education team at Opera North, initially managing the Youth Company. Six years later, I took on the new role of Digital Education Manager, creating innovative digital education projects and content and bridging the gap between Opera North's Communication, Marketing and Development teams and Education. This has been such a fantastic opportunity for me to develop digital skills and combine my interest in communications with my passion for music and education.

**About 'From Couch to Chorus'**

When the COVID-19 pandemic hit in 2020, Opera North's immediate priorities were:

- to stay connected to audiences, supporters and participants
- to keep making music
- to focus on how to replace lost income.

'From Couch to Chorus' was a unique virtual choir: a five-week series of online workshops where participants learned to sing opera choruses via Zoom. Open to singers of all ages and abilities, each edition culminated in a live-streamed interactive concert featuring the Chorus of Opera North. The project was set up as 'Pay As You Feel' to ensure that price did not represent a barrier and that everyone could take part.

During lockdown, Opera North delivered three editions in Summer 2020, Christmas 2020 (The Festive Edition) and Spring 2021 (Sing into Spring). Since then, the project has kept evolving and two more hybrid 'Sing into Spring' editions took place in 2022 and 2023, with in-person side-by-side rehearsal and performance with the Chorus of Opera North.

> During the live rehearsal and performance, I was surrounded by buzz, excitement, gorgeous melody, powerful bass and soprano voices, laughter, smiles, humour, and an incredible feeling of cohesion between the many, including the Zoom participants from around the world.
>
> (Sing into Spring 2023 participant)

**The impact of 'From Couch to Chorus'**

*Income generation*

The income generation strategy of this digital project delivered significant income to the organisation at a time when we were unable to achieve our regular, reliable means of ticket income.

Taking Gift Aid into account, 'From Couch to Chorus' generated over £140,000 income in the last three years. With a total of 6,550 donations, an average donation amount of £18 and 50% of people donating being new donors, it certainly played a key part in Opera North's lockdown activity. Since in-person activities resumed, numbers of participants and donations have significantly dropped, but the project has continued to bring in new audiences and raise Opera North's profile.

*Widening audiences*

Over the last three years, 'From Couch to Chorus' has reached a considerable number of people who had not engaged with Opera North before, as we can see in Table 7.1 opposite. Even though participants' demographic aligned with traditional opera audiences (majority of women over the age of 50 from a white background), men and women ages 21 to 90 from all over the UK, Europe, the United States, Australia, Japan and India, who wouldn't normally be able to attend an Opera North performance or workshop, joined.

'From Couch to Chorus' has thus been great at cultivating a new, engaged audience. The percentage of participants new to Opera North has remained significant throughout the project with an average of 42%.

> Loving the energy of this Couch to Chorus; it's my first time and I'm hooked!
>
> (Sing into Spring 2023 participant)

**Table 7.1** *Participant numbers for 'From Couch to Chorus'*

| Edition | Number of participants | % of participants new to Opera North |
|---|---|---|
| First Edition (2020) | 2,197 | 60% |
| Festive Edition (2020) | 1,977 | 46% |
| Sing into Spring (2021) | 2,329 | 43% |
| Sing into Spring (2022) | 879 | 29% |
| Sing into Spring (2023) | 652 | 31% |
| AVERAGE | 1,607 | 42% |

It is interesting – see Table 7.2 below – to notice a rise in participants who consider themselves as disabled or with long-term health issues in the last two editions and to see the very high percentage of participants interested in taking part in more editions in the future.

**Table 7.2** *% of participants with a disability and % that would like to participate again*

| Edition | % identify as disabled/ long-term condition | % would like to take part again |
|---|---|---|
| First Edition (2020) | 11% | NO DATA |
| Festive Edition (2020) | 10% | NO DATA |
| Sing into Spring (2021) | 7% | 89% |
| Sing into Spring (2022) | 25% | 92% |
| Sing into Spring (2023) | 22% | 98% |
| AVERAGE | 15% | 93% |

As it develops, 'From Couch to Chorus' seems to become more and more significant for those taking part who can't physically come to performances or engage in participative activities in person. Data also clearly shows an appetite for more online editions going forward.

> Great to be able to engage with this. Have had to give up choir as have an immuno-compromised OH so need to avoid crowded face-to-face activities due to infection risk.
> (Sing into Spring 2023 participant)

*Creating a sense of wellbeing and encouraging people to learn something new*
From the start, we envisaged 'From Couch to Chorus' as a way to improve people's physical and mental health and wellbeing, to encourage people to learn new skills and to build a sense of community.

The post-event surveys confirmed that the main impact on participants seems to have been an increased sense of wellbeing and learning something new, as we can see in Table 7.3 on the next page.

**Table 7.3** *% of participants for whom 'From Couch to Chorus' increased their wellbeing and % who learned something new*

| Edition | % reporting increased sense of wellbeing | % learned something new |
|---|---|---|
| First Edition (2020) | 88% | No data |
| Festive Edition (2020) | 90% | No data |
| Sing into Spring (2021) | 89% | 80% |
| Sing into Spring (2022) | 71% | 83% |
| Sing into Spring (2023) | 73% | 88% |
| AVERAGE | 82% | 84% |

Individual feedback from participants supports this too:

> I've absolutely loved this course, it's contributed to my physical and mental wellbeing, and it's been the best start for my week!
>
> (First Edition 2020 participant)

> I was a bit scared to try anything new, but definitely would now!
>
> (Sing into Spring 2023 participant)

> I loved having an opportunity to discover singing opera and [it] has ignited an interest in doing more.
>
> (Sing into Spring 2023 participant)

**Raising profile and brand awareness**

In 2022, Opera North won the first Digital Culture Award for income generation with 'From Couch to Chorus', raising its profile on a national level (Digital Culture Network, 2022). The project has been important in terms of brand awareness and the post-event surveys indicated that participants felt much closer to Opera North as a company and were much more likely to book with us in future (see Table 7.4 below).

**Table 7.4** *% of participants likely to book tickets for an Opera North event*

| Edition | % likely to book tickets for a future event |
|---|---|
| First Edition (2020) | 88% |
| Festive Edition (2020) | 88% |
| Sing into Spring (2021) | 83% |
| Sing into Spring (2022) | 83% |
| Sing into Spring (2023) | 92% |
| AVERAGE | 87% |

> Absolutely loving the workshops. I've only ever sung at football matches and don't think I will be starring on the stage any time soon, but really enjoying the experience. [...] I've also never been to an opera but now have every intention once we are able to get out again. Thank you for opening a whole new world up to me.
>
> (Sing into Spring 2021 participant)

Opera North has made me realise I actually enjoy operas!

(Sing into Spring 2023 participant)

**Going forward**

Even though we see a clear appetite for future editions of 'From Couch to Chorus', there are certainly questions and challenges to address going forward.

*How to fit 'From Couch to Chorus' around other Opera North activity?*

'From Couch to Chorus' was created during lockdown, at a time when less was happening in terms of production, participative work or marketing activities and we needed to find different ways to engage audiences and support their wellbeing and creativity at home. Now that shows are back on stage (and the focus of our marketing team is on selling those shows) and our extensive participative programme is back and running, we need to think of ways to keep adapting the project without compromising the quality of the offer.

*How to diversify audiences in terms of age and ethnicity?*

Engaging with younger and more diverse audiences will be one of the main challenges of 'From Couch to Chorus' going forward. This might be done through the choice of repertoire or by focusing on the wellbeing benefits of taking part.

*How to keep catering for our core audience?*

Despite the changes we want to make, we will need to still cater for our core audience, who have been enjoying 'From Couch to Chorus' in its current form for the last three years.

---

I think 'From Couch to Chorus' is a fantastic example of content strategy. The pandemic threatened Opera North's operating costs as people could not visit them as before. At the same time, they could see that people were struggling with self-isolating and they used the community benefits of singing to create a virtual choir. This was a new product offering for new times. But, since the pandemic, Opera North have also evolved who this programme most suits and where it goes next.

This next case study is another excellent demonstration of content strategy, but with a different approach. The Tank Museum is based in Bovington, Dorset. It attracts a fairly stable base of families within a reasonable drive time of the attraction. However, they knew the interest in tanks was much wider than the numbers they could get through their physical doors on the south coast of England. Their online content serves international tank fans, allowing them to reach and cultivate globally distributed audiences, united by their love of tanks.

Over the last couple of years, The Tank Museum has hit the headlines for its meteoric success as an online content creator. In 2023 the Museum hit half a million YouTube subscribers (that's more than the Met Museum in New York). Not only that, but it's managed to build a global community of enthusiastic tank fans who are willing to pay for the Museum's content.

## Case study 7.2: The creator economy – a big opportunity for museums

*Nik Wyness, Head of Marketing and Engagement, The Tank Museum*

The Tank Museum experience offers a proven strategy that delivers an increase in charitable benefit, reach, the creation of a loyal community and a significant increase in revenue.

### Museums house the best stories in history – so why are so many reluctant to share them online?

The Tank Museum experience shows that there is much to be gained for institutions wholeheartedly extending their scope online. In 2023 we hit 500,000 subscribers and 100 million views on our YouTube channel (www.youtube.com/@thetankmuseum), reaching a global audience with our mission to 'tell the story of the tank and the people that served in them'. We're more complete in the fulfilment of our charitable objects as a result, but we're also more effective than ever at raising funds from those beneficiaries.

In 2022, The Tank Museum generated over 25% of its total turnover online from non-visitors. We did this by adopting identical strategies that have allowed entrepreneurial YouTubers to make a comfortable living from content creation. We've been pioneering a content strategy that values distinct online programming, distributed on free online platforms, to build an audience that has grown into an engaged community of 'fans'.

We're now realising the value of this investment.

### YouTube and the creator economy

My 8-year-old watches hours of videos starring Nathan Johnson Graham – aka 'Unspeakable' (www.youtube.com/@Unspeakable). He watches this American YouTuber, who has amassed 14 million subscribers, playing Minecraft or engaging in silly stunts. Not my cup of tea, but I'm not the target audience. On the other hand, he loves it.

He is now the proud owner of an Unspeakable hoodie and baseball cap, purchased from Unspeakable's online store (www.unspeakable.com). He's a fan. And this is a great example of how the creator economy works.

The 'creator economy' is the term that classifies the commercial activity that has grown up around the content creation industry. Nathan Johnson Graham made over $28 million in 2021. He'll have made this through a combination of advertising revenue, sponsorships, endorsement deals, licensing and merchandise sales. You've probably never heard of him, but he is one of many independent content creators earning their living from the content they produce and the niche audiences they have developed.

Such creators offer modern audiences greater relevance, accessibility, relatability and authenticity than their mass media counterparts. In exchange, audiences are willing to invest to support the output of the creators and the values they embody.

At the other end of the social value scale, the *Guardian Online* remains free to access thanks to 1.5 million supporters in 180 countries who wish to support its independent journalistic values. This shows that engaged online communities will financially support the creators who offer purpose and value in their output – even if they can get it for free.

It is by learning from the emerging creator economy that The Tank Museum has been able to benefit financially from its own niche online community.

### Making quality content

To grow a community, creators must invest in the creation and distribution of quality content that serves a niche enough audience to earn their affection, loyalty and trust.

Unsurprisingly, our online community is composed of those with an interest in the history of armoured warfare. This is a very niche interest, but the internet is a big ocean and there are plenty of fish.

My three key rules for defining quality content are:

1 **Usefulness**: it must satisfy a need among the audience. You must give them something they want and value. We offer stories that inspire and facts that add to their knowledge in a style that works for them.
2 **Authority**: as a museum we must be a thought leader in our specific subject area – and the accuracy of what we are saying is essential. But to be authoritative online, you must be respected and interesting at the same time.
3 **Consistency**: being consistent with your audiences' expectations, consistent with your topic, and delivering on a consistent basis.

Creating for your niche means specifically not creating content to appeal to other audiences. This also means creating what they actually like and not what your stakeholders think they ought to like.

### Building niche communities

The museum industry has a noble obsession with trying to reach audiences other than the ones they already have. But overlooking your base is the single reason why I think most museums are failing to build a coherent and loyal community online.

The lesson here is that if you are successfully reaching your niche, your online audience will not be entirely representative of your visitor base. Because of the way algorithms work, this is something we must get comfortable working with.

The Tank Museum's YouTube audience is very different to our museum visitor profile. It's 98% male, compared with around 55% of visitors. 60% are under 44 – much younger than our average museum visitor. 30% of our viewers are from the US with just 21% based in the UK. Museum visitors are 90% UK, with less than 2% being from the US.

While these hardcore tank enthusiasts make up 99.9% of our online audience, they are only about 20% of our actual visitors in any given year. There are only so many people that will visit us in Dorset, but there are tank enthusiasts all over the world.

### Messaging to monetisation

Our online content and messaging is underpinned by our mission and values: positioning ourselves as the charity that communicates, preserves and conserves this specific history for future generations. So we've been developing a group of people who have an emotional attachment with The Tank Museum because our mission is one they wish to watch succeed.

They're basically fans. Through them, we're now raising significant funds through:

- **advertising revenue**: the more viewers you have the more you earn on YouTube
- **online memberships, tips and micro donations**: by asking for viewer support on platforms such as Patreon (www.patreon.com/tankmuseum) and YouTube Memberships (www.youtube.com/intl/en_uk/join)
- **brand sponsorships**: working with corporate sponsors who wish to reach our niche audience

- **e-commerce**: our e-commerce (https://tankmuseumshop.org) has increased from £120,000 in 2019 to £1.4 million in 2022 – and it's still growing, with subject-specific books, models and brand merchandise being our biggest sellers.

As a registered charity, the importance of this new revenue stream is impossible to overstate. It's a modern form of fundraising. It's not philanthropic and it's not transactional – it's somewhere in between.

The resulting relationship between The Tank Museum and our online community is very different to any other group of stakeholders and has more in common with the supporters of a football club than those of a traditional museum or gallery. They are geographically diverse, tend to be younger and male, they are unlikely to be among the social elites nor to consider themselves 'patrons of the arts'. There are many of them and they don't have to visit the ground to support the team. Yet their contribution is now significant to the sustainability of The Tank Museum – and it's only going to increase.

**Conclusion**

The Tank Museum experience in the creator economy offers a proven strategy that delivers an increase in charitable benefit, increased reach, the creation of a loyal community and a significant increase in revenue. This is why I believe that the museum sector is uniquely placed to take advantage of the creator economy, satisfying a real demand from online audiences for rich, authoritative content.

As the museum sector is full of content-rich, storytelling organisations, it's not like they are unequipped to do it. So, why don't they?

## Principles of effective monetisation

The above case studies tell a similar story in terms of how digital products have successfully generated income. We can see that live and interactive video, particularly with a community aspect, is something that audiences are willing to pay for online. I could have included examples here like the V&A Academy (www.vam.ac.uk/info/academy), live online educational workshops that have also accrued a willing paying audience beyond the pandemic.

Although it's lovely to laud the successes of monetising digital content that also brings in new audiences, it's worth noting that this is not the reality for the majority of cultural sector organisations. For the majority, there is a lot of mileage to be had in simply getting the basics right when it comes to monetising digital.

What do we mean by getting the basics right?

- understanding and making use of targeted paid ads
- having a customer relationship management (CRM) strategy
- making contextual donation asks throughout the site.

I'll talk more about each of these next.

## Understanding and making use of targeted paid ads

Some practitioners don't want to give more money to Meta and Google. I empathise. However, targeted advertising is an effective way to reach new audiences. A great many of your audiences are on these platforms and choosing to consume content and ads. By default, the majority of ads will be for for-profit companies and services. By creating targeted ads for your museum you help redress the balance of ads on these platforms.

Understanding how these ad platforms work is also helpful as it lets you see how it's possible to target and segment specific audiences. That can be very useful when planning how to grow new audiences and, particularly, how to make those new target audiences aware of programmes, content and services that have been created for them. (See Chapter 2 for more about how these ads work.)

## Having a CRM strategy

Many small cultural organisations do not have a system that allows them to e-mail segments of their database effectively; for example, to e-mail just their members or only their non-members, or to e-mail frequent visitors versus those who have just completed their first visit. For many in the sector, it's rare to have a customer data platform that allows them to send the right targeted marketing to people. This is an incredibly valuable tool when it's set up right. It's not surprising that, if museums put out the same membership and donation messages to everyone with no level of targeting, they will not get a very high rate of return.

Part of the objection to this can be that museums feel targeting audiences is a 'black hat' technique used by the likes of Facebook and not what the cultural sector does. But this is a false assumption; sending the same e-mail messages to all audiences is more likely to provide those people with a worse experience overall. People expect more personalised experiences that speak to their preferences. For more detail on e-mail strategy, see Case study 6.1.

## Making contextual donation asks online

Let's think about online donation for a moment. If you've ever made an online donation, think about what it was for and how you came across it. In most cases, people make online donations based on specific prompts. They might donate after having been prompted by a targeted e-mail or by an online pop-up with a message that is contextual to what they are doing at the time.

In 2022, Wikipedia launched a donation message in the form of a series of informational messages to all Wikipedia readers. This appeared above whatever they were reading on the Wikipedia site at the time and they had to scroll beneath it to access the content. The message informed them simply and straightforwardly about the gap in funding that the organisation needed to plug to remain independent. The message used compelling statistics like:

- 'This is the 1st time we've interrupted your reading recently'
- 'If everyone reading this donated $2.75, we could keep Wikipedia thriving for years'
- 'Wikipedia is sustained by the donations of only 2% of our readers'. (Wikipedia, 2024a)

The message is well contextualised. It appears as people are on Wikipedia using the resource that has a funding shortfall. It references a specific (and small) amount – less than the cost of a cup of coffee – and how many would need to make that donation to plug the gap. This plays on individual readers' sense of the utility they get from Wikipedia, but also its value to society at large. Although the placement (across every page of the site) is bold, it emphasises that the organisation does not take making an ask lightly.

Let's return to museums. Frankly Green + Webb's *Insights for Change (2021)* survey findings (Scottish Heritage Social Media Group, 2022) show that while 28% of cultural audiences have made a donation to a museum or heritage venue, 43% have never seen a request for a donation online. They conclude that 'your audience is more willing to make a donation to your charity if you show them a way to donate'.

### *Why aren't people seeing donation messages?*

I've yet to meet anyone who spontaneously decides to donate to a museum with no prior prompt or context. 'A donate button — no matter the size, color, or position — has never compelled someone to donate on its own' writes Mark Root-Wiley in 'The Nonprofit WordPress Guide', 'Donate buttons just need to be easy to find once you've convinced someone to make a donation' (Nonprofitwp.org, n.d.).

### *How do you convince someone to donate?*

By asking the right person at the right time in the right way. People come in all shapes and sizes. Some of your audience will be much more receptive to donating than others; for example, previous donors, friends and repeat visitors. If you've got a contacts database with this information in it, you can avoid mass e-mailing everyone and target messages to your top supporters within your database.

Almost everyone coming to your website will be there for something other than making a spontaneous donation. But many of those will be willing to donate as an upsell to an additional service or product that they want from you. In this case, reducing the friction of making that donation is key. People might be happy to add a donation onto an existing ticket purchase, particularly if that option is presented to them as an add-on while they've already got their card details out and are anticipating making a payment.

The donation ask itself is also important. Even with a perfectly optimised form, if the fundraising message makes no sense or isn't compelling, it's unlikely to generate any funds. People need to know why to donate, why it matters, why now and how much is effective.

During COVID-19, Tyne and Wear Museums and Archives released a donation e-mail campaign message to those on their events mailing list. This explained their need for additional support during COVID-19 but also why their existence as an organisation matters. They positioned themselves as keepers of the history of the North East. This cause translated well across the digital divide – local people felt it was important that their history was recorded and protected, even at a time when they could no longer interact with physical museum objects.

This illustrates the difference between describing what you do and why you do it. Alongside the conversation of optimising platforms and targeting, the simple art of crafting a well written narrative of what your organisation mission is and why your organisation does what it does remains important.

## Content strategy in action: in summary

The case studies in this chapter – 'From Couch to Chorus' and The Tank Museum – illustrate the potential of monetising online content. What is significant about them is that they create the possibility for digital to be a destination in its own right, as opposed to being purely an accessory of the physical visit.

By default, the sector still thinks about everything through the lens of physical audiences. When it thinks about diversifying audiences, the established idea is to programme more diverse exhibitions to attract a wider range of audiences. This feels short-sighted to me. It seems unlikely that an exhibition planned years in advance and costing around £25 is going to diversify your audiences beyond the profile who normally come through your doors.

And are those audiences still going to be around and in the same numbers in 10 or 20 years' time? The numbers you can get through the physical doors of your museum are always going to be more limited than who you can reach virtually.

Museums matter. They are among the few public institutions still trusted to explore complex, nuanced ideas around identity, belonging, history and the future. But their continued relevance depends on their ability to engage audiences where they are, and increasingly, that's online. Relying solely on traditional programming, often planned years in advance, will not be enough. Audiences are shifting, both demographically and in terms of how they engage with content. If the sector doesn't adapt, it risks losing connection with the very communities it aims to serve.

It's time for the sector to reconsider how digital is seen within audience development. At present, digital is often treated as a support function – used to promote physical events or enhance in-gallery experiences – rather than being seen as a creative, strategic tool in its own right. Today digital should be central to how we build and connect with audiences, particularly those who are currently underserved or disengaged.

Institutions like the Tank Museum and Opera North provide a compelling model. They have developed a parallel digital offer that not only reaches a global audience of tank and opera enthusiasts but also generates income and deepens engagement. This proves that museums and performing arts organisations can deliver meaningful experiences digitally, beyond the walls of the physical site. But such models are still the exception, not the norm.

Museums need dual marketing funnels: one for in-person audiences and one for digital (see Figure 7.1). These must work in tandem but also stand independently, each with clear objectives, resources and creative direction.

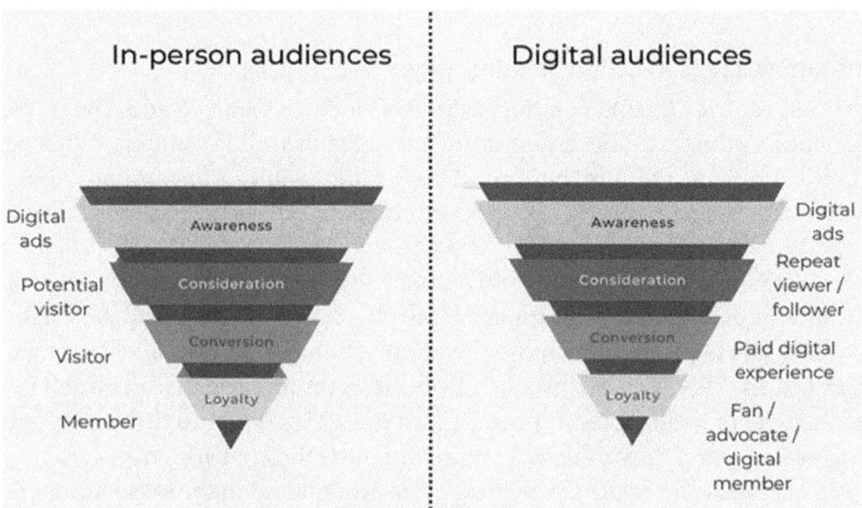


**Figure 7.1** *Parallel marketing funnels for digital and physical audiences*

We need to consider digital products not simply as advertising for the physical experiences but as a destination, a product, in their own right. Digital content can and should bolster the physical audience profile, but it's not only that.

CHAPTER 8

# Conclusion: Why Does All This Matter Anyway?

We've reached the end. Congratulations! Hopefully, I have given you some useful 'how tos', ideas and structures to help you with tasks that come into your in-tray.

In Part 1, we looked at the discoverability of digital platforms and how to make people aware of your digital content. Part 2 considered how to optimise the user experience once people land on your digital channels. Finally, Part 3 took us into the land of creative content and strategy and I made the case that content strategy in the sector is part of audience development. These days, you can't do one without the other.

This is not a book that's about digital leadership. That's really the topic of a whole other book (watch this space). But if I were to leave you with a brief teaser it would be: digital strategy in the sector feels hard because we're not used to evidencing how digital impacts audiences.

Overarching museum strategies tend to think about audience development happening offline and in the gallery. Digital is seen as a means of promoting that. However, digital needs to be seen as part of audience development, not just an online announcement board. It is a means to create new ways to digest, nerd-out and benevolently tribalise the subjects we're passionate about.

## Why does any of this ultimately matter?

If we look at most online content we passively receive in our feeds from social media, we're constantly being sold stuff. This isn't what the internet was originally about. In a time of divided, partisan politics and culture 'wars', there's surely a space to celebrate, to embrace the human condition, with less content telling us that buying stuff is the answer and more that encourages us to empathise with common hopes, fears, genius and vulnerability.

Museums are not the authority online. In an analogue world, heritage institutions have a lot of kudos as they look after big collections and historic monuments that have stood the test of time over thousands of years. But online, they're small fry. Kim Kardashian > Stonehenge on Instagram. What that means is we can't afford to be complacent and rest on our offline reputation.

It's not enough for heritage organisations to simply follow trends, to simply consume digital culture. Heritage organisations that want to be at the forefront of digital culture need to think creatively about how they can be a part of a media landscape that is currently running on without them. How can they creatively and meaningfully engage with technologists and digital creators to tell human stories across time and place? How can they redefine what storytelling about our cultural heritage looks like in a multiverse world? Perhaps this will land us in a place where we see a few less Kim Kardashian selfies in our feeds!

# Appendix: Planning a Digital Career in the Cultural Sector

From 2016 to 2020, I held seven different full-time jobs. I applied and interviewed for four more. That sounds like a lot, but it was necessary – partly because a lot of the roles I occupied in that period were short-term ones (there are more short-term arts digital jobs than permanent ones) and because my partner is in academia (where permanent jobs are even more elusive). In 2019, my partner got his first permanent job – 257 miles from where we had been living since 2014, facing us with a horrendous commute from Oxford to Newcastle. Well, at least it wasn't Beirut (which was one of the alternatives).

It seems that we're not alone. As a millennial couple working in the arts and academia, getting a permanent job for both parties in the same city is hard. So, it feels like a good time to spread some karma and share the knowledge I've picked up along the way through my own experience of carving out a career in the cultural sector.

I'm going to focus on six things:

1 Finding the job you want.
2 How to use LinkedIn.
3 Doing a good application.
4 Doing a good remote interview.
5 Working out if you in fact want this job more than the job you've got.
6 Thinking about working 'with' museums (i.e., in agencies and consultancies) rather than purely jobs 'in' museums.

## 1. Finding the job you want

To find a job you want you're going to need some fixed parameters. What do you care most about?

- location
- sector (probably 'cultural' if you're reading this)
- discipline
- pay grade
- permanent/fixed term.

I'm normally looking at all five, but location and discipline are key for me. In the sector, the best job vacancy sites I've found are:

- The Guardian Jobs (https://jobs.theguardian.com/jobs/arts-and-heritage)
- Leicester Museum Job Board (https://le.ac.uk/museum-studies/jobs)
- National Museum Directors' Council (NMDC) job listings (www.nationalmuseums.org.uk/jobs)

The Guardian Jobs site has an excellent job alert filter so you can search for jobs in a certain location and with a keyword that denotes your area of expertise (in my case 'digital') and get an e-mail as soon as anything comes up.

Larger organisations (like Tate, National Museums Scotland and National Galleries Scotland) have their own job alerts that you can set up from within their website. The Museum Computer Group discussion list posts lots of jobs in MuseTech but there's no ability to search or filter by location from a listing (Museums Computer Group, 2024). I found LinkedIn pretty good for UK government, tech, commerce and agency jobs, but it didn't seem to aggregate museum jobs properly.

## Looking for a job in a specific or new location

When my partner got a permanent academic job in Newcastle, I knew no one professionally north of about Leeds and had no idea who the cultural employers were. I used Mark Fisher's *Britain's Best Museums and Galleries* (Fisher, 2004) to get an overview of what collections-based institutions exist and quickly discovered that the North East has got about 10% of the coverage of London. This gave me some names so that I could start bookmarking vacancy pages.

I also discovered that some national organisations, like Historic England, National Trust, National Lottery Heritage Fund and Arts Council have regional offices (including in the North East), so I added them to my list. Even so, the North East does have much less cultural funding (Barker, 2020) than the rest of the country. It became clear that 'museums within a commute of Newcastle' was going to afford me more options than Newcastle itself at a similar salary to what I had been getting down South.

### Finding out more about the role before applying

Once you've found a job you're interested in, don't be scared to contact people ahead of time to chat through the role. You might not be able to speak to them directly, or you might get HR instead, but any additional information can only be useful. LinkedIn, which I'll talk about next, can be helpful for finding out more about the team you'd be working with for a given job and this will help you stand out, if you were to put an application in.

## 2. How to use LinkedIn

LinkedIn is, I think, a little maligned. Yes, there are some quite dorky posters on there, but there are on every platform. Of all the social media platforms, I think LinkedIn has stayed the most consistent over the years and it has a point to it. I feel like time invested in LinkedIn is likely to deliver returns to you personally, if you know what you're doing, in a way that I can't say I've found to the same extent on other platforms (particularly since Mr Musk took over X).

### Find out more about the people working in digital in a specific team

If you search for the organisation you're interested in on LinkedIn, you can then navigate to the 'people' tab. From there, you can search for keywords like 'digital' and view the team you would be working with.

Note, by default, LinkedIn will tell someone if you've viewed their profile. I don't mind this and am pleasantly surprised if like-minded folk have a look at mine in return, but it's worth knowing that that is how the platform works (and how to change your settings if you want to avoid that happening).

### For profile building

One type of post that has been doing the rounds recently is getting AI to 'roast' your LinkedIn profile (https://roast.monica.im). Bot-analysis aside, LinkedIn is a great visual way to present your CV and things you've worked on. It has some neat features like the ability to assign 'skills' you've acquired to particular jobs (see Figure A.1 on the next page).

In the Figure A.1, the bolded text 'Content Strategy, Audience Development, etc.' show some of the skills listed against my One Further role. All this helps if you want to appear in LinkedIn's search tools as qualified for a particular job and gives anyone looking a quick summary of what your strengths are.

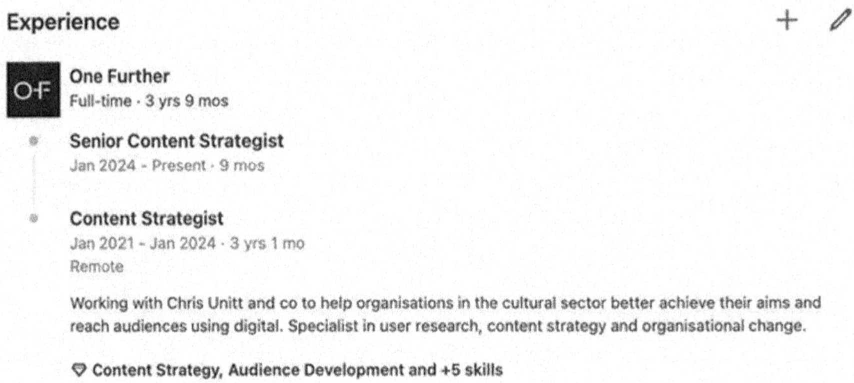


**Figure A.1** *Skills on LinkedIn*

## For networking

LinkedIn allows you to write a short message to people you don't know. I've found this invaluable. It's less of a 'cold call' than an e-mail out of the blue (which might get blocked if you're e-mailing from a Gmail anyway), as the recipient can look at your profile for some context on who you are and what you do. If I want to know more about a specific topic, I can use LinkedIn to find someone in the sector who looks like they do and reach out to them to ask for advice. It's an example of a decent internet tool for connecting people based on their skills and knowledge. The more you do it, the more 'connections in common' you'll have, all of which helps with social validation.

People like being seen as sources of inspiration, so there's absolutely no harm reaching out to more senior people in the sector asking for advice and being up front about wanting to work on their team. Worst case, you won't hear back, but best case, you get some great advice and forge a connection that helps you in your next career move.

## For getting public endorsements

One feature of LinkedIn that I don't see widely used in the sector is the public endorsement and recommendation feature (see in Figure A.2 opposite). On your profile, you'll have a 'recommendations' block. Some kind souls might give you a recommendation unasked, but this is rare. You can 'request a recommendation' from colleagues and peers who are also on LinkedIn (you can even do reciprocal recommendations, you scratch my back, etc.). However, it's best to ask them offline/outside of LinkedIn first!

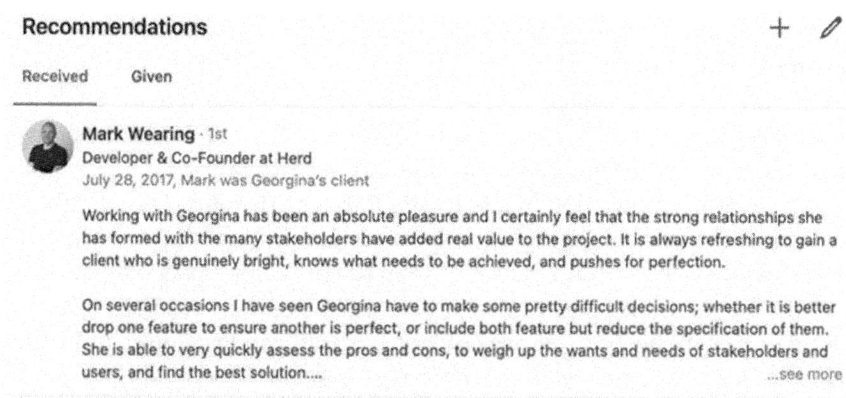


**Figure A.2** *LinkedIn's recommendations feature*

I've found this very useful for being able to cite things like soft skills on job applications. I can link to a publicly available testimonial from someone who has said I am smart, capable or good at handling complex interdependencies (or whatever it is the job description is asking me to evidence).

### For publishing your expertise

LinkedIn has its own publication tools (LinkedIn Pulse) that work in a similar way to other article publishing platforms like Medium. I've found it more useful to publish content via Substack but then promote those articles via LinkedIn. Substack is an e-mail newsletter platform that generates URLs for each mailout you send. That means that e-mail content is easily shareable and searchable online, as well as distributed to your mailing list. Having a newsletter or publishing platform also gives you a reason to contact experts or people you'd like to connect with to ask if they'd like to write a guest post for your newsletter.

## 3. Doing a good application

I've come to learn that there's a bit of a knack to writing job applications for big museums and cultural institutions. Here are some key points to note:

- understand that each point in a job description will be scored against your application, typically: (0) not met; (1) partially met; (2) fully met
- the above point means you have to give equal weight to seemingly vapid or innocuous criteria like 'ability to use Microsoft Office' and/or 'ability to work in a team' (LinkedIn recommendations can be a great way to cite

how you can evidence things like soft skills/team working/ability to handle multiple tasks at once)
- essentially, you want to be able to make it almost impossible for them not to invite you to interview because you've evidenced 2–5 bullet points that show how you fully meet each individual criteria point
- don't get your application in late – even if the job deadline is midnight on a Sunday and no human is going to read it until Monday morning, automated systems won't include you in the download pack that gets sent to the recruiting panel. Also, if you are one of those humans doing the recruitment and you've already got 175 applications, you're unlikely to be looking for a reason to make that list 176.

## 4. Doing a good interview

### Pacing yourself for the number of questions

Ask how many questions you've got at the start of the interview. In most cases, each response to a question you give will be scored individually and summed at the end. If you don't leave yourself enough time for the later questions, you risk losing points. By asking at the start how long you've got and how many questions there are, you can do some quick mental maths and work out approximately how long you should be speaking for each.

### Prepping in advance

Re-read your job application before the interview. The interview will be scored by a similar rubric to your application and you'll already have given tons of examples about how you're a good applicant in that. You may think you're being repetitive by citing the same examples at interview, but – from my experience being on the panel – the interviewers have seen so many applications that exactly what you said in yours will not be at the forefront of their brains. And even if it was, you need to use the examples from it in order to be scored highly for those questions. By mugging up on the application shortly before the interview, you'll have revised your arguments for why you fit the bill.

Prepare typical questions. The most likely questions to come up are (in my experience):

- why do you want the job?
- why do you think you'd be a good fit for the job?

Note, if you get asked why you want it, it's good to also articulate why you'd be good at it as this is likely to be what recruiters are more interested in! I also always prepare 'describe a difficult situation in your career and how you resolved it' as I've found that one a tricky one to think of on my feet (and it often makes sense to have a different example depending on the organisation/role you're interviewing for).

When you're giving examples to questions, be specific about what YOU did and what the outcome was. I often hear candidates say, 'we did this … we did that'. The organisation is not considering hiring your team, just you – so you need to be crystal clear about what you specifically did and what your individual role was. The panel are also likely to want to hear about your thinking, so set the situational context, explain how this answers their question, explain your thinking at overcoming whatever challenge you faced and what you specifically did to address it, and what the impact was.

In digital content roles, we have the benefit of lots of data, so interviewers are keen to hear about the demonstrable impact of initiatives you led; for example, did your SEO strategy lead to a 200% increase in views? Did your social media generate more engagement than the organisation had ever seen on those platforms before? It's useful to have specific numbers and evidence points to hand to quantify the impact of your work and experience.

Think of some questions for them. Getting a new job will change your life and you should have some questions about what it's going to be like!

Make sure you state at the end that you really, really want the role. Don't leave them in any doubt!

## Zoom interviews

Interviews are weird at the best of times. Interviewing in your living room over Zoom/Teams is, for most people, even weirder. Here are a couple of things I learnt from being on the other side of the recruitment process:

1 Test your tech in advance, there's nothing to put you (and the interview panel) off-kilter like not having enough bandwidth.
2 If you have a presentation to deliver online, it will sound more dynamic if you can ad lib some of it and not simply read off a script.
3 It's a bit odd having a conversation with someone whose eyes are looking to the side of yours. Most people are used to that in a conference call situation and that's how 90% of our online meetings work. But in interviews, it is a bit different. Try to look directly into the webcam, occasionally looking back at people's faces on your screen to take in their non-verbal reactions.

### 5. Working out if you actually want the job

Applying for a job, and being in the position of accepting it, can feel quite different. I know when I was offered my first job in the museum sector – at the Ashmolean – I very nearly didn't take it as I was only three months into a job at a tech start-up and felt I had unfinished business. However, it is one of the best career moves I've ever made. The human brain is pretty bad at weighing up different arguments for and against a decision and coming up with a balanced view of that will – long term – be best. It's easy to be swayed by things that feel lower effort in the short term, will cause less difficult conversations and are more certain, but those aren't good principles to base a job move on.

My decision-making has been greatly aided by creating a weighted matrix of pros and cons. I'll sum up the pros and cons of both the existing job and the proposed new job to help guide my thinking on my priorities and what I actually care about in my work. Doing these weightings will also force me to reassess how important certain things are (e.g., how much do I value permanency compared to salary). When I start summing up the pros and cons, I also begin to get a 'gut feel' about which one I want to come out on top. In terms of accurately appraising your current job, it's easy to overweight short-term frustrations, but there will be unknown frustrations in your future work!

In terms of your overall weighting, and a final appraisal of what makes sense in terms of your long-term goals, think about what you want to achieve in the long view of your time in work. In making my own career decisions, I've had to sit down and do some thinking about why I get out of bed every morning and what 'calling' do I want to make my work respond to. For me, it's using digital tech to help public-facing, cultural organisations achieve their aims and reach audiences.

### 6. Working with, rather than strictly 'for', the cultural sector

When I was working for a museum, I was on an interview panel for a job with 640 applicants. By the time we got to interview, everyone was really, really good. It felt like it shouldn't be this hard for qualified, hardworking candidates to get a job. The statistical odds of that job were 1:640 (0.15%). That – combined with how few relevant museum vacancies I saw coming up in 2020 – made me think a bit more broadly than job options that purely involved working directly for a museum.

I had a slightly rocky career transition at the start of 2021. I was headhunted and then offered a job as Senior Digital Project Manager at an agency called the Roundhouse. It didn't set my world on fire, but it was permanent, I reckoned I'd learn a lot, and in the post-COVID-19 job market I felt I couldn't logically justify turning it down. Three days before I was due to start, they called me to say they no longer had the funds to pay me and so had terminated my contract before it had started. I found myself unexpectedly unemployed. It was incredibly sobering how little protection you have in a situation like that.

Fortunately, I landed on my feet with a job as Content Strategist at One Further. The whole process of occupying (however briefly) three jobs within the space of 12 months clarified a few things for me. Firstly, that remote working works well for me as it means I can work for big cultural clients but do so from Newcastle, where the cost of living is more affordable than anywhere else I've ever lived (and also/mainly because it's where my partner lives). Secondly, the cultural sector is important to me and it felt like a welcome return when I ended up working with One Further, rather than for an agency with far fewer cultural sector clients.

I've been hugely fortunate to work in some fantastic museums, but I definitely don't think it's the only way to get cultural sector experience or tick that box of wanting to work with like-minded people. I've spoken about this at the Fair Museum Jobs Careers Summit – the private sector is in some ways better at training, progression and digital skills (and you're unlikely to be up against 640 other candidates for the same role), so I think there are benefits in oscillating between the private and public sector.

And on that note, whatever your 'calling', I wish you good luck!

# References


ACMI (2024) 'About Us', www.acmi.net.au/about.

Adjoa Parker, L. (2020) 'Building Resilience in a Racist World', 17 March, https://wellcomecollection.org/articles/XmipCBIAACAAfBOd.

Ashmolean Museum (2022) 'Welcome', https://web.archive.org/web/20220920003415/https://www.ashmolean.org.

Assetpreneurs (2022) 'YouTube Shorts', www.youtube.com/shorts/L4H6t3VaDeM.

Attitude is Everything (2016) 'Access Starts Online', https://attitudeiseverything.org.uk/industry/welcoming-disabled-audiences/access-starts-online.

Audience Agency (2025) 'What We Do', https://theaudienceagency.org/en/what-we-do/audience-spectrum.

Avro Heritage Museum via Spotify (2022) 'Flying the EE Canberra into Nuclear Mushroom Clouds', https://open.spotify.com/episode/4yZRuVFy4J3cVDJTi74M92.

Barker, D. (2020) https://x.com/danbarker/status/1315965814349221889.

Barnes, R. (2022) '"No You're Not" – A Portrait of Autistic Women', *Wellcome Collection,* 8 February, https://wellcomecollection.org/articles/Yd8L-hAAAIAWFxqa.

Branch, J. (2012) 'Snow Fall', *The New York Times,* www.nytimes.com/projects/2012/snow-fall/index.html.

British Museum via LinkedIn (2024) 'The British Museum', *LinkedIn,* www.linkedin.com/company/the-british-museum.

Brooke, G. (2019) 'Getting Sign Off From Academics', *Content Design London Blog,* 11 January, https://contentdesign.london/blog/getting-sign-off-from-academics.

Brooke, G. (2023a) 'Cultural Content – Benchmarking Online Collections', *Cultural Content,* 16 November, https://substack.com/@culturalcontent/p-138887764.

Brooke, G. (2023b) 'YouTube, TikTok, Threads', *Cultural Content,* 2 November, https://culturalcontent.substack.com/p/cultural-content-youtube-tiktok-threads [since taken down, a screenshot of the post appears in this newsletter].

Buffer.com (2024) '20+ Top Social Media Sites and Platforms to Grow Your Brand in 2025', 10 May, https://buffer.com/library/social-media-sites.

Burn-Murdock, J. (2024) https://x.com/jburnmurdoch/status/1838194949847654712.

Casey, M. (2015) *Content Strategy Toolkit*, New Riders.

Clayton, A. (2023) 'Threads App Usage Plummets Despite Initial Promise as a Refuse from Twitter', *The Guardian*, 14 August, www.theguardian.com/technology/2023/aug/14/threads-app-slump-daily-active-users-twitter-competition.

Cohen, L. (2016) 'GLAMi Nomination: Digital Content Strategy', *MW17: Museums and the Web 2017*, https://mw17.mwconf.org/glami/digital-content-strategy/index.html.

Content Design London (2022) 'Homepage', https://web.archive.org/web/20220111123139/https://contentdesign.london.

Cooper Hewitt (2019) 'Camera in a Box', www.cooperhewitt.org/2019/10/28/camera-in-a-box.

Cultural Content (2023) 'Benchmarking Online Collections Performance', *Cultural Content*, https://substack.com/@culturalcontent/p-138887764.

Cultural Content (2024) 'Cultural Content – Guest Post Monterey Bay Aquarium', *Cultural Content*, https://culturalcontent.substack.com/p/cultural-content-guest-post-monterey.

Digital Culture Network (2022) 'Digital Culture Award Winner Case Study: Opera North', *Digital Culture Network*, https://digitalculturenetwork.org.uk/knowledge/digital-culture-award-winner-case-study-opera-north.

Faherty, A. (2024) *Writing Online and Audio Stories*, Routledge.

Falk, J. (2009) *Identity and the Museum Visitor Experience*, Routledge.

Falk, J. (2012) *The Museum Experience Revisited*, Routledge.

Farah, H. (2023) 'Meta Launches Web Version of Flagging Threads App', *The Guardian*, 22 August, www.theguardian.com/technology/2023/aug/22/meta-launches-web-version-of-flagging-threads-app.

Fisher, M. (2004) *Britain's Best Museums and Galleries*, Allen Lane.

Forbes (2024) 'Top Website Statistics Today', www.forbes.com/advisor/business/software/website-statistics.

Fox, K. (2020) 'Autistic Togetherness During Lockdown', *Wellcome Collection*, 1 July, https://wellcomecollection.org/articles/XuNqyRIAACIArun9.

Freedomscientific.com (n.d.) 'Using the JAWS Find Command', www.freedomscientific.com/SurfsUp/JAWS_Find.htm.

Fruitmarket.co.uk (2022) 'Daniel Silver: Looking', www.fruitmarket.co.uk/daniel-silver-looking.

Google (n.d.) '[GA4] Customize Report Navigation', https://support.google.com/analytics/answer/10460557.

Google (2023) www.google.com/search?q=flying+scotsman.

Gottschall, J. (2012) *The Storytelling Animal: How Stories Make Us Human*, Mariner Books.

Gov.uk (2019) 'Sample Accessibility Statement', www.gov.uk/government/publications/sample-accessibility-statement.

Gov.uk (2024) 'Style Guide', www.gov.uk/guidance/style-guide/a-to-z.

Hale, J. (2020) 'Giving Shape to Sound', *Wellcome Collection*. https://wellcomecollection.org/articles/XzqMThEAACEA5LhA.

Halvorson, R. and Rach, M. (2012) *Content Strategy for the Web*, 2nd edn, New Riders.

Hammer Museum (2024) 'About Us', https://hammer.ucla.edu/about-us.

Harley, A. (2018) 'Visibility of System Status (Usability Heuristic #1)', *NN/g*. www.nngroup.com/articles/visibility-system-status.

Hepworthwakefield.org (2022) 'The Hepworth Wakefield', https://web.archive.org/web/20221031135103/https://hepworthwakefield.org.

ICOM (2022) 'Museum Definition', *ICOM Museums*, https://icom.museum/en/resources/standards-guidelines/museum-definition.

Internet Live Stats (2024) 'Total Number of Websites', www.internetlivestats.com/total-number-of-websites.

Jewish Museum New York (2024) https://web.archive.org/web/20240426115354/https://thejewishmuseum.org.

Kahneman, D. (2011) *Thinking Fast and Slow*, Penguin.

LaPope, L. (2024) 'The Content Audit Toolkit', https://lapope.com/toolkits/get-the-content-audit-toolkit.

Lebow, S. (2022) 'Facebook Still Generates Most of Meta's Ad Revenues, as Instagram Drives Growth', *EMARKETER*, www.emarketer.com/content/facebook-still-generates-most-meta-ad-revenues-instagram-drives-growth.

Lister, C. (2023) *Marketing Strategy for Museums*, Routledge.

McGillivray, M. (2021) 'Google Sheets, Creator Directory', https://docs.google.com/spreadsheets/d/11dupPJsrJTp0xqdANXrZoN1VWzlxU-AvKCw3Pbcm1T8/edit#gid=0.

Mercado, A. (2025) 'Key Threads Statistics 2025: Unveiling Users, Demographics and Growth vs Rivals', *Skillademia*, www.skillademia.com/statistics/threads-statistics.

MERL (2021) 'The History of the Servants' Ball', https://merl.reading.ac.uk/blog/2021/12/history-servants-ball.

MERL via Twitter (2018) https://x.com/themerl/status/983341970318938112?lang=en-GB.

Meta (2024) 'Widely Viewed Content Report: What People See on Facebook', https://transparency.fb.com/en-gb/data/widely-viewed-content-report.

metmuseum.org (2021) 'Before Yesterday We Could Fly', The Metropolitan Museum of Art, www.metmuseum.org/exhibitions/afrofuturist-period-room.

Migration Museum (n.d.) 'Departures Podcast Episode 2 – Maidens' Voyage', www.migrationmuseum.org/output/audio/departures-podcast-episode-2-maidens-voyage.

MoMA (2024) 'About Us', www.moma.org/about.

Montagu, G. (2023) 'Digital Works Podcast: George Montagu', *Ash Mann's Substack*. https://ashmann.substack.com/p/digital-works-podcast-george-montagu.

Morris Hargreaves McIntyre (2005) *Never Mind the Width, Feel the Quality*, www.culturehive.co.uk/wp-content/uploads/2013/04/Never-mind-the-width.pdf.

Museums Computer Group (2024) 'Join the MCG Community Discussion List', https://museumscomputergroup.org.uk/join/mcg-community-discussion-list.

Museums Galleries Scotland (2024a) 'Scotland's Museums and Galleries Strategy', www.museumsgalleriesscotland.org.uk/strategy-hub.

Museums Galleries Scotland (2024b) 'How We Work', www.museumsgalleriesscotland.org.uk/about-mgs/how-we-work.

Museums Galleries Scotland (2024c) 'Focus On: Inclusion', www.museumsgalleriesscotland.org.uk/blog-article/focus-on-inclusion/#inclusion-at-your-museum-or-gallery.

Museums Galleries Scotland (2024d) 'Empire, Slavery and Scotland's Museums', www.museumsgalleriesscotland.org.uk/project/empire-slavery-scotlands-museums.

National Archives of Australia (2023) 'Rescue in the Antarctic', www.naa.gov.au/blog/rescue-antarctic.

National Museums Scotland (2020) 'Into the Hills: Digging for Scottish Gold', https://blog.nms.ac.uk/2020/05/14/into-the-hills-digging-for-scottish-gold.

Natural History Museum (2019) 'Digitisation Uncovers Rare Specimens That Highlight the Diversity of Sex in Nature', https://naturalhistorymuseum.blog/2019/10/25/digitisation-uncovers-rare-specimens-that-highlight-the-diversity-of-sex-in-nature-digital-collections-programme.

Newton, C. (2023) 'How the Attacks in Israel are Changing Threads', *Platformer*, www.platformer.news/how-the-attacks-in-israel-are-changing.

Nielsen Norman Group (1997) 'How Users Read the Web', *Nielsen Norman Group*, www.nngroup.com/articles/how-users-read-on-the-web.

Nielsen Norman Group (2024) 'How People Read Online: The Eyetracking Evidence', *Nielsen Norman Group*, www.nngroup.com/reports/how-people-read-web-eyetracking-evidence.

Nielsen, J. (2000) 'Why You Only Need to Test With 5 Users', *Nielsen Norman Group*, www.nngroup.com/articles/why-you-only-need-to-test-with-5-users.

Norfolk Museums (n.d.) 'Mission and Vision', www.museums.norfolk.gov.uk/article/30751/Mission-and-vision.

Nonprofitwp.org (n.d.) 'On Small Donate Buttons & Contextual Requests for Support', https://nonprofitwp.org/blog/on-small-donate-buttons-contextual-requests-for-support.

Oberlo (2024) 'Browser Market Share in November 2024', www.oberlo.com/statistics/browser-market-share.

Old Operating Theatre (n.d.) 'The Old Operating Theatre', https://old-op-theatre.itch.io/the-old-operating-theatre.

One Further (2022) 'The Cultural Content Report 2022', www.onefurther.com/blog/cultural-content-survey-2022.

One Further (2023) 'Discovering Online Collections', www.onefurther.com/discovering-online-collections.

One Further (2024) 'Google Ad Grants', www.onefurther.com/services/ad-grants.

Peace Museum (n.d.) 'The Team', www.peacemuseum.org.uk/the-team.

Peace Museum (2024) 'Digital Collections', www.peacemuseum.org.uk/digital-collections.

Phan, T. (2021) 'A Netflix User Will Browse the App for 90 Seconds and Leave if They Find Nothing', x.com/TrungTPhan/status/1445768087832182796.

Ritschel, C. (2021) 'Red Flag Meme: What is Twitter Deal-breaker Trend and What Does it Mean?', *Independent*, October 14. www.independent.co.uk/life-style/red-flag-meme-trend-meaning-twitter-b1938487.html.

Royal Museums Greenwich (n.d.) 'Who was the First Woman in Space?', www.rmg.co.uk/stories/topics/who-was-first-woman-space.

Rumelt, R. (2008) 'Strategy in a "Structural Break"', *McKinsey & Company*, www.mckinsey.com/capabilities/strategy-and-corporate-finance/our-insights/strategy-in-a-structural-break.

Rumelt, R. (2011) *Good Strategy, Bad Strategy*, Profile Books.

Scottish Heritage Social Media Group (2022) 'Creating Convincing Social Media Content', https://scottishheritagesocialmediagroup.com/2021/02/16/creating-convincing-social-media-content.

Search Engine Journal (2024) 'The Top Ten Social Media Sites & Platforms', www.searchenginejournal.com/social-media/social-media-platforms.

Shakespeare Birthplace Trust (n.d.) 'William Shakespeare Biography', www.shakespeare.org.uk/explore-shakespeare/shakespedia/william-shakespeare/william-shakespeare-biography.

Sir John Soane's Museum (2022) 'About Us', https://web.archive.org/web/20221129164618/https://www.soane.org/about.

Siteefy (2024) 'How Many Websites Are There in the World?', https://siteefy.com/how-many-websites-are-there.

Smart Insights (2024) 'Search Engine Marketing Statistics 2024', www.smartinsights.com/search-engine-marketing/search-engine-statistics.

Social Shepherd (2024) '25 Essential TikTok Statistics You Need to Know in 2025', https://thesocialshepherd.com/blog/tiktok-statistics.

Statista (2023) 'Number of Smartphones Sold to End Users Worldwide From 2007 to 2023', www.statista.com/statistics/263437/global-smartphone-sales-to-end-users-since-2007.

Statista (2025) 'Most Popular Social Networks Worldwide as of February 2025, by Number of Monthly Active Users', www.statista.com/statistics/272014/global-social-networks-ranked-by-number-of-users.

Staves, J. (2019) 'The Story Behind Stories and Our Journalistic Approach to Digital Content', *Medium*, https://stacks.wellcomecollection.org/the-story-behind-stories-and-our-journalistic-approach-to-digital-content-ad196b8665ab.

Supercool (2020) 'How To: Write Good Alt Text', https://supercooldesign.co.uk/blog/how-to-write-good-alt-text.

Taneja, H. (2019) 'The Era of "Move Fast and Break Things" is Over', https://hbr.org/2019/01/the-era-of-move-fast-and-break-things-is-over.

Tech Crunch (2021) 'TikTok Just Gave Itself Permission to Collect Biometric Data on US Users, Including "Faceprints and Voiceprints"', https://techcrunch.com/2021/06/03/tiktok-just-gave-itself-permission-to-collect-biometric-data-on-u-s-users-including-faceprints-and-voiceprints.

The Art Newspaper (2021) 'Immerse Yourself in V&A's New Digital Platform of 1.2 Million Objects', www.theartnewspaper.com/2021/02/09/immerse-yourself-in-vandas-new-digital-platform-of-12-million-objects.

The Guardian (2024) 'Why the Guardian is No Longer Posting on X', www.theguardian.com/media/2024/nov/13/why-the-guardian-is-no-longer-posting-on-x.

The Jewish Museum (2022) 'New York: 1962–1964'. https://thejewishmuseum.org/index.php/exhibitions/new-york-1962-1964.

Threads (2023) www.threads.net/@nationalgallery/post/C6gLAzdNgQo.

Threads (2024) www.threads.net/@nationalgallery/post/C6tPe7vtTb-.

TikTok (2020) 'Legal', https://web.archive.org/web/20200426000353/ https://www.tiktok.com/legal/privacy-policy?lang [2020 version of the page].

Twitter (2021a) https://twitter.com/TrungTPhan/status/1445768087832182796?lang=en.

Twitter (2021b) https://x.com/fair_jobs/status/1348946165685956608.

Twitter (2023a) https://twitter.com/jack/status/1676018291918372864.

Twitter (2023b) https://twitter.com/dominos/status/1634277015963553801.

Unlimited (2018) 'Demystifying Access: Resource for the Performing Arts', https://weareunlimited.org.uk/resource/demystifying-access-a-resource-pack-for-the-performing-arts.

V&A Museum (2018) 'Writing Gallery Text at the V&A – A Ten Point Guide', www.vam.ac.uk/blog/wp-content/uploads/VA_Gallery-Text-Writing-Guidelines_online_Web.pdf.

V&A Museum via LinkedIn (2024) 'Victoria and Albert Museum', *LinkedIn*, www.linkedin.com/company/victoria-and-albert-museum.

VocalEyes (2022) 'Heritage Access 2022', https://vocaleyes.co.uk/research/heritage-access-2022.

Webarchive (2022) 'Exhibitions', *Tate*, https://web.archive.org/web/20220308054637/http://www.tate.org.uk.

Wellcome Collection (2022) 'Why the Truth is Better Than a Happy Ending', https://wellcomecollection.org/articles/Y0ViZhEAAA__2G1u.

Wellcome Collection (2023) 'Social Isolation and the Search for Sanctuary', https://wellcomecollection.org/articles/YzG4jBEAAM-ggCfp.

Wellcome Collection (2024) 'About Us', https://wellcomecollection.org/pages/Wuw2MSIAACtd3Stq.

Whitney Museum of American Art (2022) 'Welcome to The Whitney', https://web.archive.org/web/20220919035731/https://whitney.org.

Wikipedia (2024a) 'Wiki Asking for Donations', https://imgur.com/gallery/wiki-asking-donations-FAJphVZ. Referencing Reddit, 'What's Going on With Wikipedia Asking for Donations and Suggesting They May Lose Their Independence?', www.reddit.com/r/OutOfTheLoop/comments/wr1uyf/whats_going_on_with_wikipedia_asking_for.

Wikipedia (2024b) 'Facebook–Cambridge Analytica Data Scandal', https://en.wikipedia.org/wiki/Facebook%E2%80%93Cambridge_Analytica_data_scandal.

Wikipedia (2024c) 'Wikipedia: Contributing to Wikipedia', https://en.wikipedia.org/wiki/Wikipedia:Contributing_to_Wikipedia.

Wikipedia entry on 'Content Strategy', as visible here: https://web.archive.org/web/20220313183609/https://en.wikipedia.org/wiki/Content_strategy.

Winesmith, K. and Anderson, S. (2020) *The Digital Future of Museums: Conversations and Provocations*, 1st edn, Routledge.

Winters, S. (2016) 'The History of Content Design in the UK Government', *Content Design London Blog*, 27 August, https://contentdesign.london/blog/history-of-content-design-in-the-uk-government.

Winters, S. (2017) *Content Design*, 1st edn, Content Design London.

Winters, S. and Edwards, R. (2024) *Content Design*, 2nd edn, Content Design London.

York Museums Trust (n.d.) 'The Impact of Curator Battle', www.yorkmuseumstrust.org.uk/blog/the-impact-of-curator-battle.

York Museums Trust (2024) Homepage, https://web.archive.org/web/20240203041308/https://www.yorkmuseumstrust.org.uk.

YouTube (2023) www.youtube.com/watch?v=oxzuAmE2DcA [now a private video].

# Index